∧ subscript (H₂0)

✌ apostrophe

∨ superscript (a²)

⊙ colon

⸮ semicolon

❖/❞ quotation marks

❨/❩ parentheses

[/] brackets

⊥/M em dash� the usual kind

⊥/N en dash (from⸗to dash)

= hyphen

○   ✗ broken letter; dirty letter or space

○   ∂ inverted letter

○   (wf) wrong font

=\\ align horizontally

||\\ align vertically

][ ] center horizontally [

⊔⊓ center vertically

○ eq equal ⌄space⌄throughout⌄line

○ / used to indicate the end of

each marginal mark

⊥/2 → ½

If two *identical* changes fall together within the same line, don't repeat the change; instead draw an extra stroke. If more than three identical changes fall together, draw one stroke and follow it with the number of times it is to appear (put that number within a circle).

3// After reading pages 1ȼ3 and 1ȼ5, do Exercises   (lc)/(6×)

A, B, C, D, E, and F.

computer-assisted symbols

X∧{24} → x²⁴

X_{24} → x₂₄

Copyediting

Copyediting:
A Practical Guide
Second Edition

KAREN JUDD

Crisp Publications, Inc. / Los Altos, California

Second Edition

Printed in the United States of America

Library of Congress Cataloging in Publication Data

Judd, Karen, 1943—
    Copyediting, a practical guide.

    Bibliography: p.
    Includes index.
    1. Copy-reading.   I. Title.
PN162.J8   070.4′15′02375   81-17184
ISBN 0-931961-94-7   AACR2

Contents

Preface

What? Another style book? Not quite. There are many excellent style books around. They tell you how to spell the names of musical notes and whether to capitalize "president of the United States." What they don't tell you is how to transpose two terms, what to do with artwork, and how to handle permissions; in other words, they don't tell you *how* to copyedit. It's not enough to know that you must use proper grammar and substitute sparkling words for dull ones; you have to know how to deal *physically* with a manuscript.

I wrote this book as an answer to the hundreds of people who have asked me over the years, "Where can I learn to copyedit?" Up till now the answer has been, "You can't." Sure, there are night and summer courses at many colleges, but they concentrate mostly on the Maxwell Perkins tearing-apart-and-rewriting-into-brilliant-prose kind of editing. Although many course teachers are copyeditors themselves, they rarely bring the publisher's point of view to their work. I represent the publisher, and, after all, it's the publisher you have to please. Whether you're currently a teacher, a student, a typist, or even someone who would just like to work at home, you can learn copyediting from this book.

What is likely to make me succeed where others have failed—or haven't tried? Well, I've been a managing editor for over fifteen years, and I taught copyediting for eight. I've corrected hundreds (at *least!*) of copyediting tests, so I've seen what aspects of copyediting cause problems to new copyeditors—and experienced ones. I've been a copyeditor myself, both in-house, working on engineering magazines and college textbooks in subjects from French to labor relations, and freelance, handling everything from mystery novels to cross-country skiing to multiple regression analysis.

If you've had some copyediting experience already, you will find that this book reiterates the rules you already have learned, but in a succinct format that I hope will make them easy to remember. If you're new to copyediting, you can use the book as a learning tool and supplement your education with some of the style manuals listed in the bibliography. If you're an author, you can use it as a guide to editing your own material before sending it to a potential—or signed—publisher; if you're lucky, perhaps your manuscript is stored on disks, and you can make changes neatly and consistently with no hassle.

Copyediting is a challenging and interesting occupation. If you'd like some extra spending money, consider freelance copyediting in addition to your full-time job. If you have children who need you at home, you may want a full-time freelance copyediting career. Don't expect to get work right away from all kinds of publishers; you need to get some experience first on simple projects. But with patience your services will soon be in demand.

So get out your pencils (better not use pen until you've got some experience) and start learning this rewarding business!

KAREN JUDD
San Francisco

Acknowledgments

It is with tremendous gratitude that I acknowledge the contributions of the dozens of people who helped me with this project, which is the result of the 1980 Cass Canfield Sabbatical, granted to me by Harper & Row, Publishers. First my thanks go to the sabbatical committee: Win Knowlton, Brooks Thomas, and Mike Bessie; and to Chet Logan and Ann Peller, who administered the award. I also wish to thank my first publisher, Bill Kaufmann, for his faith in the manuscript, and a terrific word processor, Lavon Dixon, for faithfully recording as manuscript every character of my second draft.

Then, too, there are the people who took the time to respond to my questionnaire: Carol I. Beal, Lee Berton, Marjorie M. Bitker, Rhoda Blecker, Elsa Branden, Donald F. Brophy, John Charnay, Glenn Clairmonte, Edward Cone, John N. Drayton, Florence G. Edelstein, Patricia Fastiggi, Amanda Clark Frost, Alice S. Goehring, J. Ezra Goldstein, Rick Harmon, Sara Held, Arthur Hettich, Frederick S. Holley, Patricia Jenkins, Lisa Kaplan, Bruce Kinnaird, Nancy H. Knight, Irwin Landau, Abby Levine, Gary Mcdonald, Lane Palmer, Margot S. Raphael, John Roach, Trumbull Rogers, Ernest L. Rothschild, Paul M. Schrock, Julie Segedy, Neal Shine, Allan M.

Siegal, Jeffrey C. Smith, Nancy Steele, Geoff Stevenson, Jane Vandenburgh, and Robert E. Whitlock. Their suggestions appear throughout.

Many people graciously agreed to meet with me in 1980 to discuss their expertise and to provide me with invaluable advice on style points: John F. Baker, Alison Bell, Leta Bostelman, Barbara Campo, Charlotte Carter, Barbara Coffey, Virginia Croft, Barbara Dill, James Fox, Lisa French, Philip Friedman, Eleanor Jacovina, Molly Jordan, Barbara Kellogg, F. Andrew Leslie, Cyrus Rogers, Nina Rusinow Rosenstein, Dolores Simon, Joy Simpkins, and Christine Valentine.

Several friends gave me suggestions and encouragement during the various stages of the first edition; I'd like to acknowledge once again the contributions of Eve Strock, Stan Werner, Laura Argento, Richard Lucas, Ted Ricks, Janet Greenblatt, Clifford Strock, and Carol Pritchard-Martinez. My original copyeditor, J. M. B. Edwards, made many helpful suggestions.

After the first edition was published, I received many very kind letters; a big thank-you to the people whose suggestions and questions occasioned additions or changes to this edition, particularly Eleanor Dugan, Elizabeth Hoffmann, Thomas McDade, Margaret Ricci, Florence Trefethen, Margaret Vota, Taryn Waltke, and students in John Bergez's copyediting class at the University of California Extension. Sue Swenson, with whom I proofread many an index 20 years ago, contributed long-forgotten information about pair proofreading for this edition.

Finally, an extra-special thank-you to the copyeditor of my second edition, Janet Greenblatt. With all the changes made to the manuscript of the first edition, plus the additional suggestions from readers, I thought Janet would be bored doing the copyediting of the second edition! How foolish I was! She checked to see that I had followed my own comma rules (I hadn't), asked whether *two* should have been "2" (it should have), and queried all the things I couldn't imagine anyone not understanding but that on second reading maybe weren't all that clear. Janet proved why copyeditors will always be needed—even by the author of a copyediting book.

My grateful appreciation to all of you.

K. J.

C H A P T E R **1**

What Is Copyediting?

It doesn't even appear in *Webster's;* "copy editor" is there, but "copyediting" is not. The *Subject Guide to Books in Print* lists only "Copyreading" and "Editing." I—and many others before me—have made "copyediting" one word, even though *Webster's* says that "copy editor" is two. With "proofreading" indisputably one word, it seems appropriate that "copyediting" should be also. And "copyeditor." As we shall see, a copyeditor does not edit copy; a copyeditor *copyedits* copy.*

But what *is* copyediting?

According to the thirteenth edition of *The Chicago Manual of Style* (which used to be called *A Manual of Style,* published by the University of Chicago Press and fondly nicknamed the *Chicago Manual*), copyediting (one word) "requires close attention to every detail in a manuscript, a thorough knowledge of what to look for and of the style to be followed, and the ability to make quick, logical, and defensible decisions." My favorite part of this definition is "what to look for." All the grammar rules you learned in school, all the information

---

The Random House Dictionary of the English Language, second edition, says that "copyeditor" is one word.

you have at your fingertips, are useless unless you know *when* to look up something, *when* something seems questionable, *when* something was treated differently 200 pages earlier.

Words into Type is another authority in the world of style. It says that the copyeditor "must be familiar not only with the techniques for preparing manuscripts. . .and with the conventions of book makeup. . ., but also with the details of copy-editing style, typographical style, grammar, and the use of words."

In preparing to write the first edition of this book, I sent questionnaires to managing editors and copyeditors around the country. Among the questions I asked was, "What is your definition of copyediting?" Here are some of the responses I got.

From newspaper publishers:

> Reading copy to correct all errors—of commission or omission, from technical to cosmic.

> It's a creative job that should improve the quality of copy between writer and reader.

From magazine publishers:

> Doing no less than is necessary to guarantee that the writer's copy meets the publication's standards—but no more, either.

> Making sure [manuscript] says what it intends.

> Copyediting is that part of the editorial process that eliminates discrepancies in facts and inconsistencies in spelling, abbreviations, capitalization, and so forth. Copyediting also involves grammar, syntax, punctuation, the relation of captions to artwork, and the logical progression of ideas. Copyediting should produce a well-written, consistently styled, error-free article.

From a book publisher:

> Copyediting is the glorious opportunity to be present at the creation. The hardest thing to learn is when to leave something alone. The unforgivable sin of copyediting is to take something that is right, change it, and make it wrong. A copyeditor must always be on guard against unwarranted interference.

From copyeditors:

> Copyediting is facilitating clarity and understanding—in the author's own style.

> Copyediting takes the form of creating a finished manuscript that raises no questions in the minds of other people who have to handle it during production.

And my favorite:

> I let authors get away with a lot if it's clear, and I see my job as making my work invisible.

Fortunately, experienced copyeditors and publishers generally agree on what a copyeditor's responsibilities are. And all these definitions are fine, in general terms. To be able to pin down a copyeditor's specific responsibilities, however, we must see how a copyeditor fits into the publishing process. With so many people called "editor," how can we distinguish copyeditors from the rest?

We can begin by looking at the publishing industry in general and then at the process of publishing. We'll look at a fairly recent phenomenon, desktop publishing, and where the copyeditor fits into the formula. Finally, we'll see what those other people called "editor" do and how a copyeditor's job differs.

THE PUBLISHING INDUSTRY

Every item intended for reading should be copyedited: books, magazines, newspapers, reports, even (or maybe especially!) advertising copy and the little booklets that come with new appliances. Let's review the major areas now; publishers of specialized material (and their idiosyncrasies) will be covered in Chapter 11.

Books

According to the Association of American Publishers, there are over 12,000 book publishers in the United States and Canada; even in the non–English-speaking world, hundreds more book publishers hire English-speaking employees. *Trade* book publishers publish fiction, nonfiction, children's books, drama, and poetry—books of general interest. Then there are the *mass-market* book publishers, those who hit the newsstands and supermarkets and bookstores with millions of copies of paperback bestsellers. *Educational* publishers market their books in elementary and high schools, colleges, and professional schools. Dictionaries, encyclopedias, and other reference books constitute an important branch of publishing. People publish datebooks, cartoon books, and just about anything else you can think of. Corporations often publish employee handbooks; your church or temple may publish inspirational pamphlets; bus companies and airlines put out tourbooks; banks offer booklets describing their services. How many other "book" publishers can you think of?

Because of the seasonal nature of their work, larger book publishers use freelance copyeditors almost exclusively, and many smaller ones use a combination of staff and freelance copyeditors. Most corporations and small publishers hire copyeditors to work in-house. But whether you want a full-time staff or freelance job or just occasional freelance work in addition to your staff job or other responsibilities, you have literally thousands of book publishing companies to choose from.

Magazines

When you go to a newsstand or drugstore, you are faced with a selection of about 250 magazines; my local bookstore has over 400. There are newsweeklies; magazines for brides; magazines that discuss dance, home repair, and running; magazines for every kind of computer buff; even magazines for game enthusiasts. Once a year or on a twenty-fifth anniversary, the publisher of a long-lost magazine may issue a retrospective. But as vast as that choice may seem, keep in mind the thousands of other English-language magazines that you never see. An engineering publisher, for example, may publish forty different engineering journals. A business publisher may put out twenty professional magazines. Everything needn't be *Newsweek* or *TV Guide*; all magazines need copyeditors, and often the more technical ones provide better training than the so-called glamour ones. (I got my training at an engineering publisher.) Usually magazines hire staff copyeditors only, unless they also publish books, in which case they may have limited need for freelance copyeditors.

Newspapers

Can you think of a single town, however small, in the United States or Canada that doesn't have its own newspaper? Some of these papers are published only once a week and have more gossip than news, but all of them—especially those weeklies—need copyeditors and often don't have them. Copyeditors on newspapers in large cities are the most highly paid of all copyeditors—about $800–$1000 a week after 5 years' experience. No freelancers are ever used on major papers, but you could certainly offer your services to a small-town weekly for a little money but lots of recognition and good experience if you want freelance work. Many of our favorite columnists and TV news anchors got their start on small-town newspapers. Don't dismiss this important opportunity!

Newspapers also hire staff rewrite editors. If you feel happier writing—and we will see shortly how writing and copyediting are two quite different activities—you may wish to consider rewriting as a career. But in any case it will pay you to study copyediting.

Corporate Publications

That notice in your utilities bill about how to save money on electricity; the booklet describing how to complete the new, simpler tax form; a Pan Am timetable; a press release from Lockheed; almost everything that appears in print could benefit from copyediting. I'd like to tell you that you'll be able to convince anyone to hire you, either freelance or full-time, but realistically we both have to assume that that won't happen. But do keep in mind that every major corporation has its publishing division. Sometimes it's called corporate communications, sometimes the publications department, and sometimes something completely different. But it always exists. Check with the switchboard operator to get the exact name. Ask who is in charge of publications, and then explain what you mean if the operator doesn't understand. Corporations put out all sorts of brochures, annual reports, house organs, and manuals. Most use staff copyeditors, but it's worth a try to contact them—particularly the smaller ones— for freelance work if that's what interests you.

Corporate publication divisions have staff jobs other than copyediting. The most popular of these is technical writing. You do not have to be an expert in data processing to work in a computer corporation, nor a geneticist to work in a genetics research lab. Writing skills are essential (remember, they're different from copyediting skills), and you must be able to assimilate information from pamphlets and reports provided by the corporation. Technical writers normally have the job of making difficult technical information more accessible to the general public.

THE PRODUCTION PROCESS

So that you can see where copyediting fits into the general scheme of things, let's look now at the steps involved in turning a manuscript into a published work. This discussion will be in very general terms so that all kinds of publishing can be included. Later we'll look at specific levels of editing for each kind of publishing.

The flowchart in Figure 1.1 lays out the basic production process in ideal terms. Bear in mind that almost any stage can be cut out, depending on how refined you want the final product to be. Thus you *could* make thousands of photocopies of the manuscript and call the final product a book or magazine or report (at a minimum of 3 cents per page, however, photocopying is not a very attractive method of printing). I've even seen a book made directly from original student papers, including the errors, the cross-throughs, and the grading professor's comments. But if you want a slightly better product, you'll typeset the manuscript first, then print it instead of photocopying it. If you want something even better, you'll edit the manuscript before typesetting. And so on down the line. Each step refines the process a little further, but only the writing and reproduction stages are actually necessary.

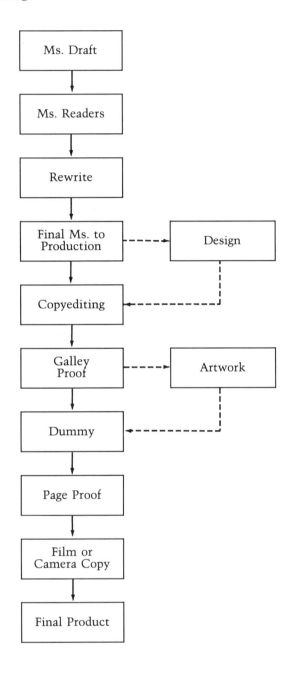

Figure 1.1. The production process. The dummying process refers to the layout of galleys to resemble the final pages. To make up pages, the compositor follows the dummy.

The first person involved in the production process is the author. The author may be a staff member charged with writing the corporation's annual report, a congresswoman reading a speech before the House of Representatives, or a person sitting at a typewriter in Barbados banging out the Great American Novel. The author is the person responsible for the idea; the author's written idea is called *copy* or *manuscript* or *typescript.*

At some point the copy goes through a review process. A novel often goes to an agent, who decides whether to try to sell it to a publisher. A textbook gets reviewed by one or a dozen expert readers in a particular academic field. An annual report at least passes under the nose of the company president. Usually these reviewers make suggestions for improving the copy, and the author revises accordingly.

The review process may be repeated now, or else the material is accepted for production: The company knows it's going to publish the material, but may not be certain that it's in final form. So it goes to an editor, or sometimes several editors. Each has a specific job to do; each refines the material in some way.

After the editing process, the manuscript is returned to the author for approval, and then it goes to a *compositor* (also called a *typesetter*). (There may be another or a different step here, which I will discuss in the next section.) The manuscript that has been set into type (or, more recently, keyed onto disk) is called *proof;* usually the first typeset stage is galley proof. Galley proof is usually a photocopy of a galley; a galley is a strip of paper showing all the type as it's going to appear in its final form, but without footnotes and art in position. (Galley proof can also be rekeyed manuscript printed onto computer paper in computer type.) The galley proof goes to the author or a proofreader (or both) for reading character for character against the original manuscript (a character is any letter, number, or symbol). The compositor makes whatever corrections are needed and repositions galleys (either on a computer screen or by using the actual, physical galleys) into pages of the exact size of the finished work, adding footnotes, art, and anything else that will complete the page. Pages are reproofread—or at least the parts that needed correction are—before the compositor provides repro copy or film for the printer. (Repro is high-quality proof that can be photographed to make film for offset printing, the most common printing process. To describe the printing process further would require another book! For more information about printing, see the bibliography.) The printer, remember, may be nothing more than an office copy machine, in which case the "repro" is simply the cleanest piece of copy you can provide. Using the repro or film, the printer makes plates and prints one or more copies of the finished product from the plates.

Well, that's what happens during production. Before we look at those editorial jobs, let's spend a bit of time looking at desktop publishing, which is a specific subset of the publishing process.

Desktop Publishing

Like a lot of people before me, I have fallen in love with computers. If I had been able, I would have taken the compositor's disks from the first edition of this book, converted them to either Macintosh or IBM, and written the entire second edition on the screen, using the first edition as a jumping-off point. But I was not planning to make *that* many changes in tearsheet (tearsheet is a pasted-down printed page from a previous edition or another book), and the cost of converting compositor disks turned out to be more than I was willing to pay.

I would not have thought that I could take so readily to working on a screen. Until the computer age dawned for me, I always wrote my memos longhand and gave them to my assistant to type, or I typed them myself from the handwritten versions. I've written two lengthy procedures manuals longhand; I didn't even draft them on the typewriter. I never thought I'd be able to compose on a screen because I couldn't at a typewriter. But the difference is that when you work on a screen, you get to erase and reword as you go along, pretty much the way you can in longhand. Now I can't even write a two-line memo without going to the computer instead of reaching for a pencil!

Why does an author use a computer? The two reasons I can think of are that (1) a computer makes the author's job easier and (2) the publisher wants to use the disk to typeset the manuscript. Let's look at these two scenarios.

In the old days (last year), you (the author) did all your typing on a typewriter. You revised it, retyped it, read it again, and maybe had some additional changes for which you retyped patches. Then you sent it to the publisher, who sent the manuscript to readers for more changes; then you had to revise some more and retype some more—sometimes a lot more. But along comes a computer (or even a word processing machine that does no calculations) and your revisions become a snap. Do you want to move a whole section into another chapter? Simply indicate the beginning and end of what you want to move and move it! Do you want to change "Frederick" to "Sally" throughout? Search and replace! Do you need an index? A table of contents? Would you like to store long medical words as two-letter abbreviations? Depending on the machine and the program, you can do all this and much more. You still print out a manuscript, but any time you have to make a change, it's a snap to do.

What happens at the publishing company? Well, I (the publisher) am going to send your manuscript for composition. Virtually all composition today is done on disk; in other words, I'm going to have the compositor rekey onto a disk the same thing you've already typed and refined. The problem, of course, is that the compositor may create new errors and will take time doing something that's already been done. But if you'll give me your disk, I can have the compositor call up your manuscript on their screen and run it through their photo-typesetting machine. If I can use repro of lower quality than what I can get from a phototypesetter, I can simply print your manuscript on a laser printer that reads PostScript programming (my repro will then look very much like standard typesetting but at a lower resolution). Of course, nothing is quite that easy or else it would be done all the time. Here are some of the things that make the process more complicated:

- The disk must contain formatting codes so that the phototypesetter or the laser printer will know what's a main head and what's a footnote.
- Some subject matter, such as math and grammar texts, are too complicated to convert from home computer to phototypesetting.
- If a heavy editing job is required or expected, the existing disk will need a lot of repair.

How much work should the author do on the disk after writing the manuscript? Here are some of the factors the publisher must consider:

- Do I trust the author to put in already-approved copyeditor's changes? Is the author sloppy and likely to miss some? Will the author decide now not to accept things that she or he has already approved?
- If the author inputs the changes and I use the author's disk, do I have to pay higher royalties?
- Do I want to take up an author's time with inputting changes, which is something someone else can do?
- Should the author input typesetting codes, or is that still the compositor's job?
- If I have the copyeditor input the changes, my composition bill goes down but my copyediting bill goes up. How do I reconcile the difference if my company amortizes composition costs but not copyediting costs?
- Is doing all the compositor's work up front going to substantially reduce my composition bill? Should I think of inputting changes as a way to reduce typographical errors instead of saving money?

Probably lots of other questions will occur to the publisher and may have occurred to you too.

How do copyeditors work in the electronic age? They can still work the traditional way, of course (and happily copyedit hard copy without ever knowing whether it came from a typewriter or a computer), or they can use the disks themselves.

Like many authors, many copyeditors now have computers. Chances are they use them for simple word processing, the same way an author does. But some copyeditors actually edit on the computer. Here's the way it works. Let's say that you have an IBM or an IBM clone. The author worked on a similar machine. Your first question must be, What software did the author use? If you have a hard disk with WordPerfect installed and the author used Microsoft Word, you should ask for a copy of the author's software and install it yourself. (Several years ago, some code was written into software that prevented it from being copied more than a certain number of times. After all, the software manufacturer wants to sell copies, not have them given away by people who make their own copies. But nowadays most software is not protected by copyright; in fact, the first instruction in the documentation is almost always, "Make a backup of each disk and keep the original in a safe place.") If you have two floppy disk drives (almost no one tries to work with only one), put the author's software copy (once you get it) in drive A and the manuscript in drive B; what's in drive A can, of course, vary from manuscript to manuscript. First you have to learn a bit about the particular software program, but they all come with Help files, and they're generally very intuitive.

What happens if you have an Apple and not an IBM? You'll have to wait for a project by an Apple author unless the publisher wants to convert the disks so that you can be the copyeditor for that project.

OK. You have the author's disk—the manuscript—in one disk drive and the software in the other. What next? It's hard to imagine an author saying, "Be my guest. Just make whatever changes you want. I trust you." The author wants to see what you've done so she or he can react to it. No problem! There are text-editing programs, such as Red Pencil or For Comment, that allow you to make changes and call attention to them on the disk. Authors can simply check the changes on the screen the way they would normally check handwritten changes on the manuscript.

If you are the author, you'll probably want to skip the hard-copy stage and just edit on the screen. Start at the beginning, scroll through the document, and make changes as you go along. Take advantage of your computer's scrolling function to go back and check for reiteration and parallelism. It may sound like a lot of work when you're used to reading papers instead of screens, but you get used to it. If you know you used a certain word and want to change it, make use of the search-and-replace function. But please be careful. Before you answer "Yes" or "OK" when the computer asks, be sure you're replacing exactly what you want to replace and not some other form of the word. I wrote a long memo recently in which I wanted to use all capital letters to describe the design process. My computer globally replaced all caps for lowercase whenever it saw "design," and I ended up with a lot of "DESIGNer" and "DESIGNing" that I had to fix by hand. If your documentation doesn't explain exactly what to do, call the software support number given in your how-to book; the groups I've dealt with, WordPerfect and Word, have been very, very helpful.

Does all this equipment save money? Well, the material can be practically rewritten without worry—as long as it's done at the word processing stage. It's not put onto a floppy disk in a phototypesetting unit until it's pretty close to final. What's more, corrections can still be made as needed on the phototypesetting machine's disks before reproduction copy is turned out. Compare this with the old way of setting type with hot metal, where the manuscript was literally translated into characters cast from molten metal.

Newspapers have been using computerized text editing longer than other publishing interests. Newspaperpeople edit their stories on VDT's—video display terminals—until they're satisfied with the finished product. Their systems are so extensive that they can relay stories around the world via satellite to other news offices that have the same system. If you've seen a TV show or a movie that takes place in a newspaper office, you've seen editors writing on a VDT.

If you are both the author and the desktop publisher, think of yourself as that newspaper writer. You wouldn't want your daily to print an article that's full of errors, would you? Why, then, desktop-publish a book with typos (typographical errors), inconsistencies, bad grammar, misspellings, and poor transitions? The self-publisher (often, but not always, a desktop publisher) has a responsibility that the author never had: The author got a copyeditor (whether she or he wanted one or not!), but the self-publisher has to go it alone. You may be able to sell that book without copyediting it, but what about your next book? I've read desktop-published books and magazines that were filled with problems. I'll never buy another book by the same publisher, nor renew my magazine subscription.

That's a short introduction to computer use. But you're interested mostly in that job I called "editor"; what are those editing jobs?

Acquisitions Editor

This term is used only within textbook publishing. The acquisitions editor (also called the *sponsoring* or *procurement* editor) is the person who actually finds the author to write the book. In trade publishing, agents send in promising manuscripts to publishers; many manuscripts also come in "over the transom" (that is, unsolicited and direct from their authors). But in textbook publishing the editor visits college campuses to find a particular academician willing to write a manuscript to order. In some fields, such as law and medicine, editors attend professional conventions in the hope of finding prospective authors. Often an acquisitions editor will sign a contract with a textbook author on the strength of just an idea; the manuscript is then written and developed over time. Sometimes the acquisitions editor, with the help of independent reviewers, will assist the author in the development of the manuscript, and sometimes a developmental editor will be used.

It is rare that an acquisitions editor is well versed in the field in which he or she publishes; too many subjects are handled by one editor. In very technical areas the publisher probably has outside consultants or series editors (people hired to comment on all books in a series) who are experts in the discipline. These people read the manuscript, help the editor make the decision to publish, and suggest improvements in the content or approach.

Developmental Editor

If substantive work (or "development") is needed on an el-hi (elementary/high school) or college textbook manuscript, it is done by a developmental editor before the manuscript is put into production. Developmental editors sometimes actually work with the author to write the manuscript. Usually they study the competing works carefully to see how other authors treated a particular topic. Sometimes they rewrite a manuscript for a different grade level, or they hire a freelance writer to do so. Occasionally they venture out into the marketplace to find out what kind of book is needed. Sometimes they are specialists in the subjects they edit. If sense and substance are missing, developmental editors may add it or show the author how to do so. Developmental editors may copyedit the manuscript themselves, but always in a separate run-through after developing it.

Editor

Trade publishing has its developmental editors, too, but they're called simply *editors* or *line editors*. A good copyeditor may be all that a trade book needs, but more often there will be an editor as well. Sometimes this is the person who found the book; at other times it will be a line editor who reads the manuscript for organization and content and directs the author to rewrite where necessary. Maybe the line editor will also handle production. In trade publishing the editor is sometimes called a *senior editor* to distinguish him or her from a copyeditor. The trade editor may help the author develop the manuscript (fiction or nonfiction) from an outline or a draft. It's this editor who suggests to an author that a fictional character be more fully developed. Normally the editor is not as alert to mechanics and fine detail as a copyeditor is.

Managing Editor

You're probably most familiar with the term *managing editor* as it relates to newspaper publishing. Recall some of the famous managing editors you may know of: Ben Bradlee of the *Washington Post,* Seymour Topping of the *New York Times,* or Charlie Hume of the fictional *Los Angeles Tribune* in the "Lou Grant" TV show. In newspapers the managing editor may be responsible for stories from all the departments: city, art, finance, and so forth. The managing editor picks the story to be headlined and decides where in the paper each story will appear. She or he reviews all copy for content and style. Sometimes the managing editor's job is divided instead among several other editors, but always there is someone to review the writers' material.

In book and magazine publishing the managing editor may be more of a manager than an editor. Usually in magazines the managing editor will pick the articles to be included and often will annotate them with suggestions for the writer. Managing editors in book publishing companies frequently oversee the production process but do not actually read the manuscripts as they come in, although the conscientious ones may sample them for quality at some stage.

Production Editor

The production editor is usually the first main contact in the *production* process; by the time the manuscript gets to a production editor, all content questions should have been resolved. On magazines, books, or corporate brochures, the production editor copyedits the manuscript or arranges to have it copyedited; gets the author's approval of copyediting; sends the manuscript for composition; checks or proofreads proof; has corrections made to proof; deals with art and design, sometimes even designing the manuscript herself or himself; and arranges for printing the final product. The favorite way of describing the job of production editor in want ads is "Manuscript to bound book." Usually a staff job, production editing is often considered the most interesting and varied job in publishing.

Because editing and the production process are essentially the same job in newspapers, the term *production editor* is limited to jobs involving books, magazines, and corporate publications.

Proofreader

Let's look at the distinction between copyeditor and proofreader. Here's a quick production course: A manuscript—any manuscript, whether a newspaper article or a 2,000-page medical textbook—consists of typed or handwritten words on a page. You can make as many changes as you want on that page and it won't cost a dime. *Proof* is manuscript that has been set into type (even on a typewriter, if that's the form the final product is to take). It can be in the form of galley proofs, which are long strips of paper containing all the text in order, with no footnotes, tables, or artwork in place; or page proofs, which show exactly how each page in the finished book or article will appear. Whatever form proof takes, it is visually the same as it will appear in its final printed form; usually the publisher has paid to get the manuscript set into type. Adding just a comma to a line of type in proof—let's say a line as long as the lines on this page— can cost $5 or even more (1989 prices—tomorrow's may be higher!).

To understand why proof changes are so expensive, we need to look at the composition process. A compositor sitting at a keyboard rather like a typewriter keyboard types every character in the manuscript, along with format codes that describe how the printed page will look. Because the operator types every single character in the manuscript in order, it doesn't matter if the character is part of the original typed material or was handwritten in place by a copyeditor.

Today, as I indicated earlier, virtually all composition is done by computerized methods; the characters typed are transferred to a disk that drives a phototypesetting, or photo-output, unit. This machine translates the characters and formats to images that can be digitized (usually) to look exactly as they will appear when the material is printed. The output from the machine is either positive paper (called *repro* or *camera-ready copy*) or positive film (i.e., black type on clear acetate). A photocopy of this output is called a *galley,* and that's what the proofreader reads.

Here's where the correction cycle begins. If I want to change the phrase "the river" to "the winding river" at the end of a line, the line will still begin in the same place, but how am I going to fit in all those extra letters? I'm not. If I'm lucky, "the winding" may fit (if the line was loose to begin with), but "river" is going to move to the next line, and whatever was there may have to move over—and so on for each line in the paragraph until everything fits. So every line has to be retyped on the keyboard and re-output on the photo-output machine.

Sound expensive? It is. But it gets worse. What happens if I make that change in pages? Now all art, tables, and footnotes are in place, and there are a certain number of lines on a page. If I add that word "winding," I may need an extra line in the paragraph to fit it in, and that alters the number of lines on a page. "It's only one line," you may say, but good bookmaking (or magazinemaking) dictates that facing pages align, that footnotes go on the same page as their references, that a certain number of lines appear below a heading at the bottom of a page, and so on. *Now* the compositor has to cut the offending type out of the page and delete space around artwork or headings or make some other kind of change to fit in the extra line occasioned by my addition of "winding." But what about the lines that were on that page and that no longer fit there? They have to go on the next page, and so on. So the compositor cuts up *that* page, and the process continues.

How much did my "simple" correction cost? In galleys, probably about $2, assuming it was right at the end of the paragraph. In pages, well, if a whole chapter or article had to be repaged because a line was added at the beginning of the material, maybe $100!

In hot metal, corrections *are* cheaper than in computer typesetting, but use of hot metal is now rare. Assuming only one line has to be reset, an added comma may cost only $1—*only*! But multiply that by one comma on every page in this book and you can see why corrections can be expensive.

So proof is the final result of manuscript; in proof no changes should be made that can be avoided. The proofreader is looking only for typographical errors or actual mistakes, not ordinary niceties. The copyeditor marks changes right in the body of copy, because the compositor must set every character (remember that a character is a letter, number, or symbol) in sequence. The proofreader marks changes in the margins of the proof; that way the compositor can just glance at the margins to find those lines containing changes. It will do very little good to hide corrections within the line of proof if the compositor doesn't happen to spot them.

Chapter 12 describes the proofreading process in detail.

Fact Checker

Magazines usually have two or three staff people who do nothing but verify the information in article manuscripts. In some houses fact checkers plan to move up to become proofreaders or copyeditors; in others their job is so important that they specialize in it. Fact checkers frequently also handle permissions (see Chapter 10).

Copyeditor

I've saved this job for last, even though that's not strictly where it goes in the production process, because this book, after all, is about copyediting. It is very important to draw the distinction between copyediting and the other kinds of editing so that both the copyeditor and the publisher are in agreement about the copyeditor's responsibilities (we'll cover these in more detail in Chapter 3). Some companies, for example, expect copyeditors to do some developmental work, or rewriting, or writing, or something else. Whether you get a staff job or a freelance job, always be sure you know what's expected of you. Unless you have the publisher's permission—or blessing, sometimes—you should not attempt to turn a sow's ear into a silk purse. It is the publisher, not the copyeditor (unless the publisher asks you), who determines how much and what kind of work needs to be done on a manuscript. Nothing irritates a publisher more than a copyeditor who calls in after accepting an assignment as routine and says, "This manuscript is awful. It needs to be completely rewritten." The copyeditor should merely suggest; the editor or the author is the final arbiter of whether a change should be made. Copyediting means doing what the publisher wants, whether you agree with it or not. That's why you won't get any "rules" in this book— just suggestions of ways to handle things.

Now that we've taken a look at the production process and the jobs in it, let's look at the prerequisites for copyediting.

Prerequisites for copyediting. Anyone interested in pursuing a career in copyediting, whether full-time or freelance, must have a *good sense of grammar and punctuation.* If you flunked English grammar in high school or couldn't care less whether there should be a comma after an adverbial clause, you should think again about becoming a copyeditor. Good writing skills alone do not qualify you for a copyeditor's job (although they certainly might for one of the other editorial jobs discussed earlier).

Basic knowledge of English grammar is only the tip of the iceberg. I get dozens of résumés from English majors—and English teachers— every year, but when I correct their copyediting tests, I seldom see that they understand what is required of a copyeditor.

If you recall that a copyeditor must know *what to look for,* you have an indication of the problem. *Being observant,* then, is another prerequisite for copyediting. If you have ever mispronounced a word by adding, omitting, or transposing a letter, you must learn to be more observant. When I first moved to San Francisco, I thought the Strybing Arboretum was the Stybring Arboretum; it just sounded better to me. There is a publisher named Putnam and a publisher named Pitman; don't confuse the two. Putnam is a county in New York where I lived for many years. It is not, as some believe, Putman County.

Being observant means being able to say, "I saw that word spelled differently back about fifty pages, near the bottom of the page," and being able to go back and find and correct it. Or knowing that you've seen the word three times before instead of just two.

Curiosity is the third prerequisite. Curiosity in copyediting takes two forms: simply wondering if something is the case and hunting around for it in a variety of reference books, and looking up the spelling of every word you're not sure of. A good copyeditor can't resist the challenge of finding the correct answer to an obscure question; but if you're not curious enough even to check a dictionary for a word you're not sure of, you can't really claim to be a copyeditor at all.

Several years ago I taught a series of weekly classes in copyediting for the staff of my publishing company. In one of the early sessions I explained that I look up every word I'm not 100 percent sure of. The example I gave was *transferred*. I told the class that as many times as I look up that word, I just can never remember it and have to look it up again each time I encounter it. The following week I asked if anyone had been curious enough to look up how to spell *transferred*. Only one person had. What's particularly interesting about that story is that that woman went on to become managing editor of a large corporate publications department (earning much more than I ever will!). You *must* be curious enough to reject the idea that if it's in print, it must be OK.

Let me show you what I mean.

mustache	acknowledgement
benefited	sulphur
resistence	programmed

A copyeditor probably knows already that *resistence* is misspelled; it should be *resistance*. But what about the rest? You've certainly seen them in print this way, but haven't you seen them spelled differently as well?

English—or at least American—spelling is a challenge for even the best copyeditor. *Webster's Third New International Dictionary* has several pages of rules in the front for various grammatical topics, and it devotes a full page just to rules for spelling words ending in *-ed* and *-ing*! Although "rules" do exist (such as this one: For one-syllable words ending in a consonant preceded by a single stressed vowel, the final consonant is doubled before a suffix), there are so many rules and exceptions to rules that no copyeditor would want to rely solely on them. Even in its spelling section *Webster's* refers to many rules and exceptions. It is always best to refer to a good dictionary (see the bibliography) for the proper spelling of words with suffixes. Accord-

ing to its explanatory notes, *Webster's* generally gives variant
spellings of the same entry in alphabetical order ("benefited or
benefitted"); it considers the variants equal. Can you assume, then,
that if the entries are not in alphabetical order they should be considered arranged in order of preference? I certainly think so. Thus in
America *kidnapped* and *programmed* are the preferred spellings, even
though (also in America) it is normal to use the single-consonant style
before the suffixes *-ed* and *-ing* (*canceled, traveling*). Although the
following list (except for *resistance*) is neither correct nor incorrect,
then, it does show the most common way of spelling these words
in this country—at least according to *Webster's.*

mustache	acknowledgment
benefited	sulfur
resistance	programmed

The important thing, of course, is not that you use these spellings
(except for *resistance!*), but that you use the same spelling for the same
word each time it appears—and the same principle to spell similar
words.

Spellings change over the years, which is why a publisher asks you
to stick with a particular dictionary and why you must constantly
look up words in it. Don't feel bad if you look up the same word 200
times. Someday you may not have to look it up anymore, or maybe
you always will. The goal of a copyeditor is not to be a perfect speller,
but to know those words one can't spell perfectly. I know how to
spell certain words: *friend, recommend, science,* and a few others.
I don't know how to spell *transferred,* and I look it up every time
I write it. But after looking up *resistance* dozens of times, I now know
how to spell it and have put it in my column of known words.

There are some other prerequisites for copyediting, too, depending on the type of work you're interested in and on the publisher's
needs and expectations. Some publishers place strong emphasis on
neatness, others on the quality of your queries, still others on your
knowledge of production. Most companies do not require all things
of all copyeditors; they will dole out the work based on each copyeditor's strengths (and weaknesses).

One attribute that is popular with most companies and is mentioned by both *Chicago Manual* and *Words into Type* is the *ability
to use words properly.* You may have no trouble using words when
you write, but can you recognize poor phrasing in someone else's
writing? Once again that prejudice comes up: "But it's in print."

Many years ago the *New York Times* splashed a banner headline
across its second section:

New Yorkers Are Busy, But Not Too Busy To Ignore
The Problems of Strangers

Think about that for a minute. Don't worry if it takes a while; it didn't faze New York either. We *know* what it means: Even though New Yorkers lead hectic lives, they are willing to take some time to help others. But is that what it says? Not on your life! The problem, of course, is the word *ignore*. It's so readily available, unlike its opposite, *heed*, which was clearly intended.

Of course, knowing how to use words properly goes beyond simply being able to recognize sentences that say something other than what is really meant. *Style* is this broader area and is discussed in detail in Chapter 6.

A copyeditor must be a patient, careful, reflective person. She or he has to evaluate a sentence on several levels at once, for content, grammar, readability, and so on. A copyeditor must have a sense of the language and an interest in playing with language.

There are levels of copyediting, too. I am grateful to the Philadelphia book packaging firm Editing, Design & Production, Inc., for the following descriptions of editing (read *copyediting*) level, which, according to EDP, have been drawn from a number of sources:

Light Editing (usually for readings or tearsheet manuscripts)

When you request a Light Edit of your manuscript, EDP will perform the following operations. We'll correct faulty spelling, grammar, and punctuation, eliminate sexist usage (if requested*), and query dated references. We'll also make any revisions necessary to cross-referenced figure and table numbers. Reading copy will be *scanned* for cross-references and for missing material.

Regular Editing

When you request Regular Editing of your manuscript, we do the following: Your manuscript is edited for correct and consistent style in spelling, punctuation, hyphenation, capitalization, and grammar. We'll also check for consistency of numerals, abbreviations, alphabetical or numerical lists, and the use of italics. At your request, any material that's sexist, prejudiced, obscene, dated, or slanderous will be revised; otherwise, such material will be queried. We'll edit to improve word choice, transitions, and overall fluency, and to ensure consistency of in-text citations and end-of-chapter references. In addition we will: make certain art and text correspond; check numbering and completeness of references, footnotes, and bibliographies; add credit lines as stipulated; ensure agreement of table of contents with headings in text; mark callouts for all tables, figures, footnotes, and cross-references; ensure that headings

---

*Author's note: Notice here and below that the copyeditor or packager does not decide what is proper and what is not. We may not like it, but the publisher gives us the direction—not the other way around.

within each chapter are parallel in construction, number, and frequency. In addition, we will keep a thorough style sheet.

Heavy Editing

In addition to the services listed under light and regular editing, your manuscript will be edited to eliminate wordiness, triteness, confusing statements, vague generalizations, and mixed metaphors. Also, we will ensure the coherence, logic, and organization of your manuscript, and eliminate gaps, redundancies, jargon, and the use of the passive voice (if requested). We'll also make sure the tone and focus of your manuscript is consistent.

Copyeditor's responsibilities. In the preceding pages we've seen several definitions of copyediting and some examples of what a copyeditor is supposed to look for in a manuscript. Now I will list a copyeditor's responsibilities in general terms. Each duty is discussed fully in this book; so that you can have an easy reference point, I have included at the end of each listing the number of the chapter in which it is fully covered.

1. Correct punctuation and grammar (Chapter 4).
2. Be consistent in spelling, capitalization, and hyphenation (Chapter 5).
3. Make minor style changes (Chapter 6).
4. Follow an accepted, consistent bibliographic style (Chapter 8).
5. Query the author tactfully (Chapter 10).
6. Typemark or key the manuscript according to the publisher's requirements (Chapters 2, 9).
7. Prepare a detailed style sheet (Chapter 3).
8. Query apparent errors (Chapter 10).
9. Follow the publisher's instructions (Chapters 10,13).
10. Be alert to libel and permissions problems (Chapter 10).
11. Be aware of sense, organization, heading structure, and, in fiction, plot (Chapters 3,11).
12. Know how to handle art (Chapter 10).

Don't blindly adhere to any guide—not even this book—at the expense of clarity. Common sense plays an important role in copyediting.

Speed and pay. You should be able to copyedit between 3 and 10 manuscript pages an hour of almost any kind of material; for reprints, from 15 to 25 pages are possible. Most publishers expect at least 7 pages an hour; 3 is for people who need to do some developmental or content work. The number of pages per hour you do is the final number; it usually includes reading the manuscript twice, once for general impressions and once for details. So on a 300-page manuscript your first run-through may take 15 hours (20 pages an hour) and the second 25 (12 pages an hour). All told you spent 40 hours, for a 7½ page-per-hour final count. As a freelancer, that's what you would be paid for (assuming an hourly rate).

Most publishers expect freelancers to be able to copyedit from 150 to 250 pages a week; that's because they know that freelancers usually have more than one employer. Staff copyeditors usually handle at least 300 pages a week. Staff copyeditors on newspapers and weekly magazines must meet compositor deadlines, of course, so they have to handle as much material as there is within the time allotted.

Except on newspapers, where the pay approaches $900 a week, copyeditors, whether staff or freelance, can expect to make anywhere from $10 to $20 an hour. (Some, of course, make more, but $20 is considered the current maximum.) The average is from $11 to $15 an hour. If you think you'll be ripped off at $10 an hour, read Chapter 13, which explains why less is sometimes better.

Why copyedit? It's certainly not to get rich! Why, then, does anyone decide to be a professional copyeditor? Copyediting is not fun, it's hard work. That's not to say that many people don't enjoy their work, but they don't choose copyediting simply because they like to read. Why should you choose it?

Think about books and magazines and newspapers you've read. Were you ever bothered by spelling errors, improper syllable breaks at the ends of lines, inconsistencies? You bet you were, even if you didn't realize it at the time! You simply had a feeling something was wrong, even if you couldn't identify it. In the grand scheme of things, maybe it doesn't matter all that much, but if you have the power to make the written word more accessible, isn't that a grand responsibility? And if an author has something significant to say, the point may be lost—or the content diminished—if the material contains spelling and grammatical errors and other instances of carelessness.

Copyeditors are a special group of people. They cannot be satisfied with "It must be right; it's in print." They question everything. They know that Massachusetts is a commonwealth, not a state. They would know exactly how to address the pope if they met him. They don't mind going back over 1,000 manuscript pages because they have decided at that point to spell out numbers up to 100 after all. I hear of authors who complain about copyeditors: "They change my meaning"; "He was inconsistent"; "What was wrong with the way I did it?" But I hear of many more authors who discuss their copyeditors with awe: "You have the unenviable task of making my humble prose sound like Hemingway wrote it" (I really heard a business textbook author tell his copyeditor that); "She made the whole experience worthwhile"; "I want him on all my other books." Having your name in the preface of a book is certainly one reason to want to copyedit, but lots of us get our kicks from the challenge alone. To be able to set up tabular material to make it clear; to catch an error in an equation three pages back now that you see *this* equation; to realize before it's too late that the burly man with the thick red hair is suddenly described as thin and balding; that's what makes it all worthwhile.

The first step in copyediting, as in other crafts, is to master its tools, so we'll look at copyediting symbols next.

Copyediting and Proofreading Symbols

If you take a copyediting test and use the symbols from *Webster's*, you're a dead giveaway as a novice, no matter what you tell your potential employer about having copyedited Professor Hotchkiss's reports to the Bar so she wouldn't look like the literary idiot you know her to be. In the first place, the symbols in *Webster's* are *proofreading* marks, and they're handled differently from *copyediting* marks. In the second place, the typical compositor has become something of a mind reader over the years and can now read shorthand copyediting symbols. The more succinct your symbol, the less likely a compositor is to misinterpret it (and the more likely he or she is to take you seriously).

The purpose of this chapter is to explain how a copyeditor marks a change, not how a copyeditor judges whether a change is mandated. In Chapter 9 you will learn how the simple symbols can be used to make complex typographic changes, and in other chapters you will learn when changes are needed.

I said in the first paragraph that copyediting symbols are different from proofreading symbols. Well, they're not *that* different, but they are *used* differently. In Chapter 1, you will remember, I said that copyeditors work in the body of the text manuscript (and that proofreaders work in the margins of proof) because a compositor is setting into type every character in a manuscript. If one character has been crossed out and another one added, the compositor sets the character accordingly. In proof, however, the manuscript has already been set into type. With luck, very little of it is wrong, so no one is going through character by character to reset it. Instead, the compositor looks at the margins to see where changes have been marked. Those lines containing changes will be reset, but the rest of the standing type will be left as is.

In proof, errors can occur that can't happen in manuscript, so special symbols are needed that aren't needed in copyediting. For example, some dirt may get onto the film and partially obscure a letter so that in proof it appears broken. The proofreader will use the symbol for a broken letter and the compositor will fix it. In manuscript, of course, the copyeditor will just write the letter in properly! To make sure the compositor doesn't misinterpret the manuscript, a good copyeditor will of course do some extra marking. We will see in Chapter 9 that a copyeditor can help the compositor avoid errors.

Let's look at each symbol and how it is used. Refer to the inside front cover for the complete list. Symbols used only in proofreading are indicated with a circle in the outside margin, and more information about proofreading appears in Chapter 12.

DELETE ℒ

In copyediting, often this symbol is replaced by a horizontal line striking out the word or words not wanted. Either symbol is understood by a compositor. When crossing out any material, be sure to cross it *all* out, and only what is supposed to go. Probably most of the errors made in going from manuscript to type arise from incorrect deletion. If you are deleting many words, or part of one word and then several additional words, don't mark each one separately but rather cross them out with a continuous line. Mark with an arrow or a close-up symbol (see next section) from where you stopped to where you begin again; don't make the compositor check out every word to see if it belongs or not. Remember that the compositor is typing rapidly whatever he or she sees; whatever you can do to help out can only save time and money. For example, if you cross out several words and leave one word hanging at the end of the line, why not cross it out too and rewrite it in position? Why should the compositor have to hunt for it? And don't leave punctuation dangling by itself; cross it out and rewrite it where it belongs, as I've done in the third example.

Probably most of the errors made in going from manuscript to type arise from incorrect, ~~probably most of the errors in going from manuscript to type arise from incorrect~~ deletion. If you are deleting several ~~several~~ words, mark with and arrow.

Our heritage, ~~noble as it may be,~~ was in fact based on . . .

After three years, ~~(can you believe that it took that long?),~~ we were finally ready to . . .

► DID YOU NOTICE?

1. Use an arrow or close-up marks to indicate large areas of deleted copy.
2. Use a delete sign to get rid of a single letter, as in *and* in the first example.
3. Use either a delete sign or a horizontal bar to delete whole words or phrases.
4. Carry punctuation with the material that remains.

CLOSE UP⊃

The difference between this symbol and the delete-and-close-up symbol (see next section) is that nothing but space is being deleted. Mostly you will use this symbol if the author has typed two words that you're making into one, such as *wheel chair*. But if you have crossed out a couple of words, marking to close up is a good idea; you do this not because you're afraid the compositor is going to insert extra space but because you want to call attention to the fact that material has been deleted and to what should run in with (i.e., immediately follow) the previous material. Don't close up each word you're deleting, just the whole thing at one. (See previous examples.)

To make two words into just one, such as wheel chair or lamp post, even if they fall on sequential lines, just use a close-up sign.

► **DID YOU NOTICE?**

If you want to close up the last word of one line with the first word of the next, you don't need any special instructions, just the symbol.

DELETE AND CLOSE UP

This symbol is very important. It is not up to a compositor to read your mind (even though some do that quite well). If you take an extra letter out of a word, the compositor is not supposed to know that you didn't want two smaller words instead!

```
If you take an exxtra letter out of a word, the

compositor is not suppossed to know...


When/ever you remove an incorrect hyphen, be clear whether

you want two words or one word to remain.


Remember that if you take out several words from somewhere

within the sentence, it's a good idea to use a close-up sign

or arrow so the compositor doesn't have to,sit there and

hunt around for what's left.
```

► **DID YOU NOTICE?**

1. Although the symbol technically has two liaisons, you can get by with just the bottom one.
2. If you delete an entire word, you don't need the close-up symbol; the compositor won't put extra space between words. Thus you see that the close-up symbol alone (see the inside front cover) is not really used much in copyediting. The delete-and-close-up sign is far more frequent, as is the arrow shown in the third example and in the Delete section.

It is particularly important to mark end-of-line hyphens correctly. When a word has been broken into syllables at the end of a line, three possibilities exist for the word when it's set in type:

1. It never should have been hyphenated in the first place because

the word is really two separate words. In that case simply delete the hyphen; do not make any other marks. An example is

cash⤢

register

2. It may be one word. In that case, you need to ask yourself whether the word is hyphenated because the typist came to the end of the line or because the author considers it a hyphenated word. If the hyphen is added merely because there was no room to type the whole word on one line, you do not need to mark it for deletion. But if the compositor will not be able to tell whether the result should be a hyphenated word or a single word, mark appropriately. Here are examples.

copy⤢

edited   posi-

tioned

You may know that *copyedited* is one word, but the compositor won't.

3. The result should be a hyphenated term, such as *high-powered rifle*. Now you'll need to indicate that the hyphen should remain. There are four ways to do this: Insert a close-up symbol after the hyphen; insert a slash after the hyphen; write a caret below the hyphen; or underline the hyphen. The compositor will recognize any of the four methods.

copy-⊃   copy- /   copy-̭   copy‗

CARET⋀

A caret (Latin for "there is lacking") is used to add something to a line. If you wish to replace one word with another, simply write the new word above the deleted one. You don't need to use a delete sign and a caret; that's overmarking. If, however, you are adding simply a character or two, particularly in the middle of an existing word, you must use the caret. Close up the added characters to the beginning or end of a word. If you're adding several words, include them within a brace to identify clearly where the insert ends and where it is to go (but don't bracket just one word or a few letters).

Please note that if you replace one ~~phrase~~ with ~~a different~~ *word*
~~one,~~ do not use a delete sign and a caret; simply write *another* *(the new word)*
above the deleted one. If you are simply adding a character or
two, use a caret; close up the added letter to the beginning
or end of the word but not in the middle.

Whenever your additional couple of characters could stand
alone, always identy clearly that they close up within
the word.

▶ DID YOU NOTICE?

1. When you cross out something and replace it with something else, carry any punctuation with it. Do not expect the compositor to hunt for a comma or period several characters away.
2. When adding several words, be careful to use a brace that encompasses the entire addition, and position the brace properly.
3. If a word was missing a letter or two, double-check that you've added them in the right order and position. Witness the letter combination *identy*, meant here to be *identity*. Do not fall into the common trap of adding *it* after the *n*. If you do, by the way, don't blame the compositor for following suit. Try it.

SPACE

Most compositors will insert space if you simply draw a vertical line between the two words that have been incorrectly closed up, but a space mark ensures it. By tradition, a space mark indicates word space, that is, the same amount of space that goes around all words in the line. If for some reason you don't want that much space, use the vertical line without the space mark. Don't make your mark too deliberate, or it will appear that you want a line drawn; just slap it in there. In mathematics composition, by the way, space around pluses and times signs and all the other symbols is always marked that way, for thin space. We'll look at math editing in Chapter 11.

By tradition, a space mark indicates word space.

In math editing, the equation 2+5=7 is marked with
thin spaces.

► DID YOU NOTICE?

1. Rather than take the chance of being misunderstood, I wrote the space mark in place instead of just a vertical in the first example.
2. In math editing, be careful that your thin space marks can't be misinterpreted as vertical bars.

EM SPACE □

An em space is the true width of a type size; in 10-point type an em space is 10 points wide. The symbol is used frequently in graphic design and also plays an important role in mathematics (which will be discussed in greater detail in Chapter 11 when we look at mathematical copy). In nontechnical copy you will rarely have to use it; the designer will call for it instead.

Spaces larger than 1 em are identified by writing the number of ems inside the box: ②. This system is preferable to drawing a series of boxes, such as ⬜⬜, because to some people that might look like a "one" inside a box, or 1 em.

EN SPACE ▨

An en space is half the width of an em space. The symbol is used strictly as a design choice, with no other meaning. Usually it is the amount of space between a period and the first word in a list (for example, "1. Publishing"). See Chapter 9 for further discussion of typemarking.

PARAGRAPH ¶

If the manuscript has been typed with a paragraph indent, you needn't mark each paragraph individually. But if you want a new paragraph where none now exists, you must make your intentions clear.

```
                                        ¶
We discuss typemarking further in Chapter 9.ᴧTo make a

paragraph where there wasn't one, use the paragraph symbol.


    No symbol is needed if the paragraph indent is already

typed properly.
```

NEW LINE ⌐

Although this symbol appears mainly in mathematical copy, it comes up under special circumstances elsewhere. Use the symbol between the two lines you wish to form, and be sure to indicate how the second line is supposed to stand relative to the first, whether flush left (see next section), at a paragraph indent, or at some other indent. This symbol is discussed in more detail and with examples in Chapter 9.

FLUSH LEFT

Be careful how you use this symbol. After a displayed item, such as a heading, poem, or equation, copy *can* begin flush left. But most other times copy will simply run in with whatever came before it once the intervening material, such as a figure, has been taken out of the manuscript; it will be merely a coincidence if in the final product that particular line is in fact flush left. We will see in Chapter 9 how typemarking must be thought out carefully, and at that time I will give examples of the use of this symbol.

FLUSH RIGHT

This symbol is used infrequently and then usually only graphically. It is used mostly in math, for positioning of equation numbers, but it also shows up in some display, such as to place an author's name at the end of the preface. Rarely will you choose on your own to use the flush right position, but you may have to mark some items for the publisher's benefit.

RUN IN

If there is an opposite to paragraph indent or flush left, this is it. This symbol tells the compositor to continue immediately after the last line of type set; it says nothing about any other position on the page. If you want, say, extra space before continuing, you must say so.

> The symbols we've just discussed are the ones regarding positioning of type on the page. They are—
>
> 1. paragraph,
> 2. new line,
> 3. flush left,
> 4. flush right, and
> 5. run in
>
> Each time you use one of these symbols, ask yourself this question: Have I told the compositor everything I must about positioning? In other words, are your instructions clear and complete?

Comp: display this sentence w/ space above + below

The equation is

$\underline{x} = \underline{z}$

1. Those displayed words can't just run in together; they have to have punctuation after them. Always remember to follow through with your instructions.
2. You don't have to instruct the compositor to get rid of space; the run-in instruction automatically deletes the space that was typed below the display.
3. To be sure the compositor understands what you want, it never hurts to put an extra comment in the margin, circled so it won't be set.
4. You don't have to use those long run-in marks; half ones will do, as in the example at the top of this page. Just be sure your marks aren't so small that they look like commas.

STET... *stet*

The word *stet* is Latin for "let it stand." Although this mark appears most frequently in proofreading, you will write the stet symbol if you have deleted something that you shouldn't have and for some reason can't reinstate it clearly yourself. Do not use the dots by themselves; insert the circled word *stet* in the margin as well.

Normally you use a stet symbol if you cross out a word and replace it, then decide you'd rather have it the way it was typed originally. To avoid confusion over whether the erasure is supposed to be there or not, you stet the typed version after erasing or removing what you had written in.

 Normally you use a stet symbol if you ~~cross out~~ a word.

TRANSPOSE ⌒

In its simplest form this symbol is used to transpose two letters. It can also reposition whole words or phrases. When a word or phrase must move to a new line, however, it is best to circle it and move it with an arrow.

The transpose symbol isn't only used to transpose letters. It is frequently used also to reposition words. There is a special transposition symbol that can be used to alter and reposition more than two phrases or words.

▶ DID YOU NOTICE?

1. When a word or phrase is moved to a different line, circle it and move it with an arrow. You can do this even when the material that is moving falls in more than one line.
2. A special symbol leaves one word where it is and transposes the words on either side. See the last line in the example.
3. You must be careful when repositioning any word, phrase, or letter that you put it in the right place. *Reread carefully* the revised word or phrase with the transposition done.

SPELL OUT ◯

Digits below 21 (in English) and very common abbreviations that have been typed in manuscript can be circled to mean "spell out." Do not expect the compositor to know how to hyphenate 131 when it becomes all words, or where the capital letters go in the spelled-out version of Ph.D. (or even how to spell it out). But U.S. and U.N. and 4 are easily spelled out by the compositor; rather than crossing out the number or abbreviation, you can circle it. If the abbreviation comes at the end of a sentence, remember to leave the final period.

```
In the (U.S.) we use the decimal system, based on multiples
of (10).
```

C̲A̲PITALS

To set anything into capital letters, underscore it three times. If you want to set a whole phrase in capitals, it is neater to underscore only the middle part of each word, rather than every character involved.

L⌿WERCASE

To make a letter lowercase, put a slash through it, slanting from upper right to lower left. To make an entire word or phrase lowercase, you need not slash each letter separately; slash only the first letter of each word, and the compositor will figure out that all the other letters are to be lowercase as well. (As a precaution, you can indicate the extent of the lowercasing with a horizontal overscore.)

```
capitals and lowercase

capital letters are marked with three underscores.

L⌿WERCASE letters are marked with a slash.
```

► **DID YOU NOTICE?**

1. You must be careful to capitalize or lowercase only those letters you want changed. In the example, the second sentence still begins with a capital letter.
2. Do not use a ruler to mark capitals; any 3 underscores will do.

SMALL CAPITALS

As you might expect, small capitals are simply a smaller version of capital letters. Except for design purposes they have limited use. By tradition, A.D., B.C., A.M., and P.M. are set in small caps; very little else is. Some companies use small caps or caps and small caps for their names, caps and lowercase for everyone else. For example, in *Newsweek*, references read NEWSWEEK; all other magazines appear in roman caps and lowercase. (In Chapter 11 I give a couple more examples of the use of small caps.) If you wish to set an entire word or phrase in small caps, underline it completely with two underscores.

Small capitals

SMALL CAPS are used for a few abbreviations, such as

A.M. and p.m.

► **DID YOU NOTICE?**

1. Both lowercase and capital letters can be changed to small caps the same way.
2. Watch that you underline the whole word or phrase. If you want caps and small caps—that is, an initial capital letter and the rest small caps—make sure you make this clear. Better yet, mark the capital letter with three underscores.

ITALIC

A single underscore indicates italic, or slanted, type. If the manuscript you have has already been set into type (such copy is called *tearsheet*), do not re-mark any italic that is already there. The compositor will follow copy, and only your markings will change copy. Be sure to underscore end punctuation as well as the word it follows; there *is* such a thing as an italic comma!

Unfortunately, there are exceptions to every rule. In some tearsheet, such as in grammar and spelling books, italic type may be used frequently and in the middle of words—to call attention to a spelling change, for example. If it will be difficult for the compositor to spot all the tearsheet italic, do mark each occurrence, and warn the compositor to treat all material—tearsheet and newly typed—as virgin copy that has been marked for italic. Do not use both methods in the same manuscript.

And then there's another exception, and that's to the "rule" about underscoring punctuation following an italic word. Sometimes large punctuation marks, such as the question mark and exclamation point, take the style of the sentence, not of the word they follow. You should discuss the publisher's preferences with your in-house contact before making a decision. Then mark each occurrence carefully.

ROMAN

Roman type is the usual type we see daily. It has no special slant or boldness. Any typographic differentiation you want to see has to be marked. In original manuscript, roman is usually indicated by circling the appropriate word when necessary. If you are working with tearsheet and want to change something that had been set in italic back into roman, underscore it and write "rom" (circled) in the margin (but see the exception given under Italic).

Italics and Roman

The use of an underscore indicates a change in the style of type in evidence.

 In *tearsheet* manuscript, an underscore tells the compositor to get rid of the italic (unless a covering memo gives other instructions). To be clear, it is a good idea to write "rom" in the margin.

Let's look at a few rules about roman and italic type.

1. Essentially, an underscore changes the style of type in evidence to its opposite, that is, italic to roman or roman to italic.
2. If they are to be anything but roman, parentheses should be set in the same type style as their *surrounding* copy, not in the style of the copy within them. Naturally, what is inside the parentheses could be in the same type style as what is outside.

Sitka (in this place), Alaska, was once a Russian settlement.

Many compositors and publishers prefer that parentheses *always* be roman.

3. In an italic passage, items that are to stand out, such as titles or words needing emphasis, are normally set in roman to differentiate them; however, it is best to check this style with the publisher.

4. Math *symbols* (plus, equals, etc.) are always roman. Math *variables* are always italic, regardless of the type style of the surrounding copy.

Be sure to take <u>x</u> + <u>y</u> = 0. [Correct]

<u>Be sure to take x + y</u> = 0. [Incorrect]

► DID YOU NOTICE?

1. If you want to keep part of a typed underscore and get rid of another part, draw a vertical line where you're dropping the underscore and delete the underscore where you want to. If you think your marks are unclear, write "ital" with an arrow to the part of the word you want to see set in italic.

2. To both italicize and capitalize a letter, word, or phrase, draw four underscores under it. Of course, you can draw the italic mark as shown in this section and the capital mark shown earlier:

Italics and Roman
≡   ≡   ≡

BOLDFACE 〜〜〜

The use of boldface (dark) type provides extra emphasis. Except in math and grammar, it is always a design feature, and you must check with the publisher before using it. To make a word boldface, draw a wavy line below it. In tearsheet, to remove the bold from a word, circle the word and write "lf" (lightface) circled in the margin. (Or follow the principle discussed under Italic.)

Boldface

Boldface is often used for emphasis, but if you have not been told to use it, use italic instead.

In tearsheet, get rid of (**boldface**) by circling the word and writing "lf" in the margin.

► **DID YOU NOTICE?**

1. To make a word both boldface and italic (in publishing jargon, "bold ital"), use an underscore and a wavy underline. To avoid confusion, put the underscore in first, with the wavy line below it. But be aware that not all typefaces contain a boldface italic style. Furthermore, not all desktop systems can support bold ital.
2. You must make a wavy underline beneath all symbols that are to be boldface. The normal style is for punctuation to be in the same face as the word it follows, but determine the publisher's preference before marking.
3. When using the symbols "bf" and "lf," be very neat. There is little difference between handwritten *b* and *l*.

PERIOD ⊙

Use the circle around a period only if you think it might be misconstrued otherwise. Such would not be the case at the end of a sentence. But when the compositor might wonder, "Is this a period or a pencil mark?" then you should circle the period for clarity. Another use of the circle is to turn a comma into a period; no other instruction is needed.

```
You don't have to circle every period in the manuscript⊙

just circle the ones that aren't clear or those commas you

want to make into periods.
```

► **DID YOU NOTICE?**

Remember to capitalize the next word if you make a comma splice into two sentences.

COMMA OR SUBSCRIPT ∧

In fact, this symbol is not just for commas but is used to put anything into what is called the "subscript position," that is, below the baseline of type. (No, a comma is not a true subscript, because it begins *on* the baseline of type.) Most often it will be a comma that you're dealing with. Compare the superscript notation that follows, and note that you can't turn a period into a comma simply by using the subscript symbol; you have to draw the comma too. Use this symbol *only* when the subscript or comma isn't already clear.

water H₂O

APOSTROPHE OR SUPERSCRIPT ∨

As with a comma, this symbol should be used only to clarify. Technically, an apostrophe is a superscript, and therefore it takes a superscript symbol; it appears completely above the baseline of type. Recall particularly that there is a difference between an apostrophe, a single quotation mark, a superscript 1, and the symbol for prime, feet, or minutes. Each must be marked distinctly.

Do not use a superscript symbol to put an accent on a letter. In manuscript just draw the accent in place; the compositor will set it in order. In proof, cross out one letter (an unaccented one) and write the correct (accented) one in the margin.

3′ (ft)

prime
f′(x)

pos
ʹ ʹ 'Cause I said so,ʹ ʹ Michèle replied.

► DID YOU NOTICE?

1. Don't mark all commas, apostrophes, and quotation marks—just the handwritten ones or the ones that may confuse the compositor.
2. Compositors know all the tricks; they will understand what you mean when you write "ft" or "pos."

COLON ⊙

Use an oval to make a colon clearer. Do not, however, use it to turn any other punctuation mark into a colon; you can circle a comma to make it a period, but circling a semicolon won't make it a colon. Instead, cross out the semicolon, write the colon in its place, and then draw an oval around it.

SEMICOLON

When you put the caret over the semicolon, be careful that the dot in the semicolon is still visible; otherwise it may appear that you want a comma. Note in this case that you are not putting the character into a subscript position; it is only by tradition that the subscript symbol is used.

If you wish to make a semicolon into a comma, don't put a delete sign through the dot. Instead write the subscript symbol over the dot.

```
Don't mark the dot with a delete sign↑ but rather draw the
subscript symbol over it.
```

QUOTATION MARKS ᵛ/ᵛ

Use the superscript symbol, but make your quotation marks clear—by drawing over them if necessary. As I said earlier, you don't have to mark them if they're obvious. But look at the following examples from fiction.

pos)
```
'' 'Cause I want to,'' she replied.
```

single)
```
'' 'A car'? Is that what you called this, Ted?'' asked Paula.
```

If you are working with a computer, check to see if it distinguishes between opening and closing quotation marks (both single and double) and if your printer can support such characters. In other words, just because you believe you're typing the correct version on your keyboard doesn't mean that that's what you'll see in print. Review the self-test supplied with your printer to see what characters it can produce.

► DID YOU NOTICE?

In typeset material there is a difference, both literally and typographically, between an apostrophe and a single quotation mark, although you can't see the difference in typewritten copy. Be sure to identify the one you want. I will discuss the use of an apostrophe in fiction copyediting in Chapter 11 and the use of single quotation marks in Chapter 4.

PARENTHESES ⊄/⊅

Be very clear when you write parentheses (called "parens" in publishing slang). Compositors have been known to mistake them for everything from brackets to 7's to 1's to d's to cl's. Some copyeditors put a slash (or two slashes) through a handwritten paren, which seems to work well.

BRACKETS ⌐/⌐

Make brackets neatly and square, and make them dark so that they look as if they're meant to be set. Some copyeditors use brackets to indicate something they wish to call to the author's attention. If you do that, write the brackets very lightly, and label them, as shown in the first example.

If the author has typed brackets by using underscores and slashes, write over them to square them off.

```
You must be sure to distinguish(for the compositor's sake)

brackets from typographical considerations[and also from

notes you're making to yourself.]
```

delete this?

▶ **DID YOU NOTICE?**

1. The brackets that appear in the first example are to call attention to material covering a particular span; using brackets is a lot easier than writing, "Delete everything from 'and also' to 'yourself'?" or some other code. But the brackets must be written in very lightly. As a precaution, you can always say, "Comp.: Don't set brackets" or, even better, erase or remove them before sending the material for composition.
2. Make a paren look like a paren, and slash it for good measure if you wish.

EM DASH $\frac{1}{M}$

The dash that we think of instinctively as a dash is in fact an em dash. Like an em space, it is about as long as a capital M in the typeface being used. Most authors type it as two hyphens with no space between them or on either side (although some desktop publishing systems do support both em and en dashes). Other authors type one hyphen with space on both sides. In either case, or in any other situation, most dashes of whatever length (we'll look at the other kinds in Chapter 4) have no space around them in the printed book. If space has been typed, mark to close up.

To mark a dash of any length, write the multiple over the dash and the standard beneath.

```
Notice than an em dash—a standard dash, that is—

is the length of 1 em in the typeface.
```

▶ **DID YOU NOTICE?**

At the beginning or end of the line, you need not mark to close up space to the material around the dash; the compositor will do it automatically.

EN DASH $\frac{1}{N}$

As you have probably guessed, the en dash is the length of a capital N in the typeface, the same length as an en space. It is used mostly to indicate range but has some other uses too, as we'll see in Chapter 4. You must be careful to distinguish it from an em dash, so write your N's and M's clearly.

HYPHEN =

In the printed book, a hyphen is shorter and fatter than any dash. Its most obvious use is to indicate a word break at the end of a line, but it also appears, of course, as part of the spelling of many words and phrases. (Spelling with hyphens is examined in Chapter 5.) If the author has typed a hyphen, you needn't mark it in any way, but if you insert one, always write it as shown in the heading preceding this paragraph. In addition, because you don't know where the compositor must break the line, you don't know if end-of-line hyphens typed into the manuscript will remain or be deleted. Some, of course, must remain because they're part of the spelling of the word. Those you must mark, such as by underlining the hyphen so that the symbol looks like the one preceding this paragraph. Other end-of-line hyphens are unnecessary to begin with, regardless of whether the typeset line ends the same way as in manuscript; those should be marked for deletion. The rest are there only because the author couldn't fit the whole word on the line; if the whole word could have fit, it would have been one uninterrupted word. (Of course, *if* the line ends at the same place in composition, the compositor will set the hyphen just as it was in the manuscript.) Remember from the caret discussion that you don't have to mark to delete the hyphens that the compositor wouldn't question. Look at the following examples.

```
com-positor

re-establish

arm-chair

high-powered rifle

talk-show
```

Suppose each of those hyphens appeared at the end of the line, with the rest of the word on the next line; which way would you mark each word? Did you get the answers I did?

```
                com-
positor         re-
establish       arm-
chair           high-
powered rifle   talk-
show
```

► DID YOU NOTICE?

1. There is no confusion in the first word, so you don't have to mark it at all.
2. It's a matter of style whether you delete or retain the hyphen in *reestablish;* the compositor would have no way of knowing, so you must mark your preference. The way I've marked the example makes the word *reestablish;* if you want to keep the hyphen, and some publishers do want to, mark it like this: `re=` `establish`.
3. If we want *armchair* to end up as one word, we must mark to delete and close up.
4. If we want to keep the hyphen in the typeset line, we mark it to stet, as in *high-powered.*
5. I can't think of any reason that *talk show* as a noun should have a hyphen, so I've deleted it. (*Note:* I did not mark to close up, or else I would have gotten *talkshow.*)

Now that you have learned the copyediting marks, practice them by marking the following excerpt from a story. This exercise requires only marking, not word or punctuation changes, which you will learn later. After completing the exercise, check your work against the correctly marked material that follows. If you missed any marks, can you understand what you should have done? If not, go back and read the sections on the ones you missed.

```
Ron turned, He eyed Martha acros the room. Oh, how how
calculating she looked. His eyes become firey as he glared
at him—her with her holier-than-thou attitude. He ap-
proached her cautiously. afraid but somehow afriad, ready
for the confrontation.
```

''Well, well, she smirked. ''Look who's back, tail between his legs.''

''Damn you!'' he shouted, so that everone in the restaurant could hear. ''How you dare act that way with me!''

She stood smiling athim. She finally had him Where she wanted him. This time he wasn't going to win the aregument. Outside, in the marking lot, it began again. ''All right-all right, We'll do it your way.'' But Marhta only laughed at him.

They got into her car. For a moment they said nothing. Finally she spoke.

''I'm willing if you are.'' ''Yes, let's try it. He agreed. He left her and returned to his own car.

A sign flashed lazily behind her retreating chevy: JOE'S bar and grill.

Ron smiled to himself. ''Well, JOE'S BAR AND GRILL,'' he thought, ''You've done it again.''

*   *   *

Ron turned He eyed Martha across the room. Oh, how how calculating she looked. His eyes became filmy as he glared at him her with her holier-than-thou attitude. He approached her cautiously, afraid but somehow not afraid, ready for the confrontation.

''Well, well, she smirked. ''Look who's back, tail between his legs.''

''Damn you!'' he shouted, so that everone in the restaurant could hear. ''How you dare act that way

```
with me!''
     She stood smiling at him. She finally had him where she
wanted him. This time he wasn't going to win the aregument.
Outside, in the parking lot, it began again. ''All right,
all right, we'll do it your way.'' But Manhha only laughed
at him.
     They got into her car. For a moment they said nothing.
Finally she spoke.
     ''I'm willing if you are.'' ''Yes, let's try it, he
agreed. He left her and returned to his own car.
     A sign flashed lazily behind her retreating chevy: JOE'S
bar and grill.
     Ron smiled to himself. ''Well, JOE'S BAR AND GRILL,'' he
thought. ''You've done it again.''
```

Beginning in this chapter, each chapter will end with the key points covered in the chapter (in Chapter 12, we give a list of rules instead). If you are charged with setting the copyediting style for your organization, you will be able to refer to the list of key points as a quick reminder of what your responsibilities are. If you need more information about a particular point, reread that section in the chapter.

► KEY POINTS IN THIS CHAPTER

Deletions
- Use an arrow or close-up marks to indicate large areas of deleted copy.
- Use a delete sign to delete a single letter; use a delete sign or a horizontal bar to delete words or phrases.
- Carry punctuation with remaining material.

Additions
- When adding several words, enclose the entire addition within a brace, and position the brace properly.
- Double-check the position of added letters and words.

Transpositions

- Move words between lines with circles and arrows, not with a transpose symbol.
- Reread carefully the revised word or phrase after you have made a transposition.

Capital and Lowercase Letters

- Carefully mark only those letters you want to change case.
- When marking caps and small caps, clearly mark exactly which letters are involved.

Italic, Bold, and Roman Type

- In tearsheet, leaving type as it was printed will give you the same style when it is typeset unless you make other arrangements with the compositor.

Period, Comma, Semicolon, and Colon

- Turn a comma into a period by circling it.
- Circling a colon makes it clearer; circling does not turn any other mark into a colon.
- Put a caret over a semicolon to make it clearer; be careful not to obliterate the dot.
- Do not delete the dot of a semicolon to make it into a comma; put a caret right through the dot instead.

Quotation Marks

- Differentiate between single and double quotation marks, apostrophes, and prime or foot signs.
- Draw over quotation marks in the proper direction to make them clear.

Hyphen

- You do not need to delete hyphens that the compositor will know are there only because the end of the line was reached in typing.
- If a hyphen at the end of the line may or may not be needed, depending on style, mark it properly for the compositor.

Em Space

- Draw a box and write inside the number of ems you want; do not draw a series of boxes.

chapter 3

Awareness Training

Did you ever read a book and later say to yourself, I remember noticing such-and-such about halfway through on a right-hand page about 2 inches from the bottom? Were you able to go back and find it?

Why is copyediting such a special kind of editing, quite different from writing? Why do publishers groan when they receive applications from people who want to become copyeditors and who point to their years of teaching or writing experience? Because writing is not copyediting. Many writers lack an essential ingredient in the copyeditor's makeup: awareness, the ability to remember the most minute details, such as where something was on a page or how something was spelled earlier. Awareness manifests itself in many ways, most notably in consistency. Copyeditors notice the most trivial inconsistencies and correct them; writers generally do not.

But more than that, a copyeditor has a wealth of information at her or his fingertips. Good copyeditors know that there is no Chief Justice of the Supreme Court—that instead the title is Chief Justice of the United States. They know that the Lutheran Church has pastors, the Methodist Church ministers. They know that one feels nauseated, not nauseous, and that Delaware's New Castle is two words, whereas the Newcastle in Texas is one.

"*I* don't know those things," you say. "How could I ever be a copy-editor?" Well, that's where awareness comes into play. Copyeditors don't actually know all those things either, but they are *aware* that there may be something wrong, something they don't know. They realize that they must question every word use, every mark of punctuation, every spelling, every fact.

Thus we come to the three most important rules of copyediting:

1. Be consistent.
2. Look it up.
3. It isn't right just because it's in print.

One of the most important concepts for you to learn as you begin copyediting is that you're not reading for enjoyment. Publishers are wary of applicants who say, "I love to read." Copyediting is *work*, not fun (although certainly many copyeditors enjoy their work, just as many professional baseball players enjoy theirs). People copyedit all sorts of material: A book on engineering or organic chemistry or cement mixing is not what the average person takes to the park on Sunday afternoons. But believe it or not, there actually are people who prefer copyediting those very topics rather than the next bestseller.

There is no substitute for awareness of what you read. Even though this book or another gives you lots of "rules," you're going to come up against things that aren't spelled out anywhere for you. But if you pay attention not just to the content of what you read but to the presentation as well, you will gradually learn what are and are not appropriate styles.

Before we discuss the three rules just given and some of the ways you can learn awareness, look at the following example. I've deliberately made it simple so you won't get discouraged. See how many inconsistencies and other problems you can find in it. Never mind grammar or style right now; we'll get to them later in this book.

```
Dorie called Sally three times this morning, but there was

no answer. The phone rang and rang, sometimes for 9 rings;

it became discouraging. Dory was furious....

    When Sally returned from her exciting adventure, the

telephone was ringing--br-i-i-ng, bri-i-ng, bri-i-ng--she

picked it up on the fourth ring. ''Hello?--she was out of

breath--''Sally speaking.'' But no one was on the line...
```

► **DID YOU NOTICE?**

1. Is it Dorie or Dory? We really don't know, but we can be fairly sure it's not both. But just because "Dorie" comes first, it's not necessarily correct. Which spelling is more frequent? If it looks like a toss-up, don't count them all! The author obviously had no strong preference. It would be best to query the publisher or author right away so that you can make the change throughout the manuscript; at least make a covering note for the author to pick one spelling when she or he reviews manuscript or proof.

2. Three times, 9 rings. We'll look more closely at number usage in Chapter 7. Here, there's certainly no good reason for the author to spell out "three" while using the digit "9." On the other hand, "fourth" (paragraph 2) is always preferable to "4th" in narrative.

3. What about those "bri-i-ings?" There is sometimes a good reason for spelling a made-up word one way one time and another way another time, but I can't think of a good reason here. Which way do you think it sounds?

4. How many dots, or points, count as points of ellipsis? (Points of ellipsis indicate that something has been left out.) Well, three if they're in the middle of a sentence, and four at the end of a complete sentence. Don't forget, one of those four is a period, and periods come right after the last letter. So the points of ellipsis at the end of paragraph 1 are fine, but you'll need another dot after paragraph 2. Watch where you put it. If you put it on the very end, which is easiest, be sure to close up the first dot to the word "line" to make it the period that ends the sentence.

5. Surely you noticed that "Hello?" needs an end quotation mark after the question mark!

6. I said not to worry about style, but you could at least question "exciting adventure." Is there any other kind? Remember, it isn't right just because it's in print.

7. Here's a toughy. There is clearly a relationship between the two paragraphs, but does one follow the other naturally, the way most paragraphs do? Isn't the second paragraph really from a different point of view? In fiction, sometimes a line of space marks a change of tone between paragraphs. As you read for fun, see if you can spot the ways an author of fiction puts back the time or changes speakers from one paragraph to the next.

STYLE SHEET

Now that you have an idea of what to look for when you copyedit, you're probably wondering how you're going to remember all those style points. The answer is by keeping a detailed *style sheet.* There are two kinds of style sheet: One is given to the copyeditor by the publisher and lists style points the publisher has already decided on (and perhaps the author has approved), and the other is created by the copyeditor while working through the manuscript.

The publisher's style sheet usually consists of one or more typed pages containing notes on "house" style. The copyeditor, more often than not, is encouraged to add specific style points to it. Sometimes an in-house editor, mostly for the author's benefit, creates her or his own style sheet. The editor points out the preferred style and then the way the author treated the term; the author then has the chance to approve the style sheet before the copyeditor starts to follow it.

House style should never supersede the author's style if that style is acceptable. At the very beginning of this book, you may recall, one copyeditor said he let the author get away with a lot. It is, after all, the author's book, and the author has the right to ask, "What was wrong with the way I did it?" Sure, sometimes the answer is, "Well, nothing, but you did it six different ways, and I just wanted to be consistent." But no copyeditor should try to put words into the author's mouth.

Some copyeditors ask, "Why not make authors aware of house style?" That may work for college textbooks and reference and medical books, but on the other hand, that's what the copyeditor's job is. Why make the author take time away from her or his specialty to do something that's someone else's job?

If the copyeditor makes up her or his own style sheet, chances are it will look something like the one in Figure 3.1. Publishers' requirements for style sheets vary from 20 or 30 terms per manuscript to 50 or 60 terms per alphabet letter, depending on subject matter. A 1,500-page math manuscript may have 50 style points, whereas a 250-page novel may have hundreds. You should discuss with the publisher an appropriate approach. In my experience, a style sheet similar to the one in Figure 3.1 works well most of the time. This type of style sheet is common in the book publishing industry. Sometimes the publisher provides a blank style sheet, but you can also make your own supply fairly inexpensively. Type four separate pages, 1 through 4. Pages 2 and 3 will have boxes for the letters of the alphabet. Pages 1 and 4 will have divisions you feel comfortable with: for example, Tables, Footnote Style, Abbreviations, and Typographic Style. Use as many such designations as you wish, but leave plenty of room for each. And don't assume that because you're copyediting fiction you will never need a box for Tables; you may not *always* copyedit fiction, and then you'll be stuck with a bunch of incomplete blank style sheets. The boxes most copyeditors use are shown on page 50.

AB	CD	EF	GH
IJK	LM	NO	PQ
R	S	TU	VWXYZ
Style Punctuation	Numbers Abbreviations	Footnotes Bibliographies Tables	Typography Miscellaneous)

Figure 3.1. A blank style sheet.

1. Numbers and Dates (when to spell out numbers; how to treat dollars and cents; how to spell fractions; whether to use a comma between month and year, etc.).
2. Abbreviations (when to spell out and when to abbreviate; acceptable abbreviations; use of periods in abbreviations).
3. Punctuation (usually pertains to set elements within a chapter or article and how they're treated; often whether to use a comma after *thus*, etc.).
4. Tables (how to key; use of abbreviations; treatment of totals).
5. Bibliographic Style (sequence; use of abbreviations).
6. Footnote Style (how to reference; sequence; use of abbreviations).
7. Typographic Style (amount of space marked in similar situations; when to paragraph; what words are marked for boldface).
8. Miscellaneous (special decisions you've made that you don't want someone to overrule).

The publisher may want the style sheet for the compositor, author, and proofreader later. The more points you include, the less likely someone is going to make a change that affects your copyediting as a whole. That's why the categories you include on the style sheet are so important.

Once you've chosen the topics for the style sheet and decided where they will go, draw boxes to separate each letter or topic, using heavy black pencil. Label each page in *nonphotographic* blue pen (available at any art supply store) according to where it falls: outside front, page 1; inside left, page 2; inside right, page 3; outside back, page 4. Fold a blank sheet of paper (it can be very small) and label it the same way to indicate how the final product should look, and take the materials to your local print or photocopying shop. Don't have your blank style sheets printed on fancy paper; do the job as cheaply as possible. Each 11″ × 17″ style sheet should cost you less than 35 cents, and it will aid you immeasurably.

Some people prefer to work with lined yellow pads, letting one page represent each letter and style point. Yellow pads can work well if you don't mind flipping through them to find the letter you need, and they are certainly more convenient if you expect to list lots of terms. You will have to learn from experience which kind of style sheet works best for you.

Preparing and Using a Style Sheet

As you copyedit, you must indicate on your style sheet *every* style point that may be treated more than one way. Copyedit slowly, and as you work, ask yourself, How else could I handle this word? If there's no other way, fine. If there is, however, put it on the style sheet. Also, put on a style sheet words that *you* can't remember how to spell.

Let's look at an example. The word *friend* can't be treated differently—no letter change, no hyphen, no capital letter. But the author *may* have requested that the word *acquaintance* be substituted wherever she had typed *friend*. If the publisher tells you that, then you would put it on the style sheet. Of course, such constraints on usage are rare; for the most part only spelling, hyphenation, and capitalization are noted. For example, the word *decision making* may look like this under D on your style sheet:

decision-making (adj)

decision making, maker (n)

The abbreviations ("adj" for "adjective," "n" for "noun") indicate the part of speech; you can make up any that work well for you, such as "pl" for "plural" or "ex" for "exception."

Unless you *know* how a word is treated (remember Chapter 1?), *look it up!* Even though it's in the dictionary, put it on the style sheet. After all, it's a lot easier for you to refer back to a foldout than to thumb through a 1,000-page dictionary. And think of the people who will later be referring to your style sheet: the compositor, author, and proofreader. List on the style sheet all your choices, and refer to it whenever a similar situation crops up in the manuscript. If you run across the term *list maker*, for example, you may remember *decision maker* from earlier in the manuscript. That is your goal: to remember that you've seen something similar before. But be careful: Similar words are often treated differently, so always check the dictionary first. Here are some similar words that are treated differently by *Webster's Third New International Dictionary.*

>   freshwater (n)
>   freshwater (a)
>   salt water (n)
>   saltwater (a)
>   groundwater (n)
>   rainwater (n)
>   surface water (n)
>   springwater (n)

Remember: LOOK IT UP!

Not just spellings go on the style sheet. Always indicate how you're treating numbers too. In the Numbers box you may have the following entries.

ten, // (meaning that you're spelling out numbers under 11 and using digits for 11 and over)

30¢ (not $.30)

7000 (not 7,000)

Also do a box for footnote and reference style. A simple method would be

Joan R. Author, "Title," *Journal* 7, 3 (Dec./1980), pp. 000 ≈ 000.

John Q. Writer, Title (City: Publisher, 1980), chap. 3.

The first example is a footnote for a magazine, the second for a book. Notice that I didn't try to generalize too much; I used "Dec. 1980" rather than "Month year," for example, so it would be clear that I want to abbreviate the names of months. If it's easier for you to extrapolate the style point from an actual entry, then use an actual entry. Whatever method you use, be sure you understand it when you refer to it later in your work.

Sometimes you'll want to include on your style sheet recurring phrases so that you're sure to use the same wording and punctuation each time. In college textbooks, for example, chapters often begin with learning objectives, and the first sentence is something like this:

```
After reading this chapter, you should be able to:
```

Now notice the difference:

```
After studying this chapter you should be able to:
```

In the second example, a word was changed *and* a comma dropped. As you copyedit, determine the prevailing style, note it on the style sheet, and be sure all similar situations conform.

Some copyeditors add to the entries on their style sheet the page number of the first occurrence. That way, if they decide to change something later, they need go back only as far as that page reference. My personal choice is to be sure the first time, which is easier said than done. Sometimes you're not aware until after the first several occurrences of a word that it's been treated more than one way. Thus it's obvious that you must read the manuscript at least twice. (Even if the publisher wants the manuscript back in batches, you can still read it twice.) On the second reading you can make whatever corrections are needed.

What to Look For

What are some of the points that you should be aware of? Let's look now at the areas of confusion. We've seen some of them already.

1. *General.* Be sure that appropriate style is followed (see Chapter 6). Look for repetition; if key phrases are repeated, such as the statement about learning objectives, note the correct wording on the style sheet. If ideas are repeated, should they be, or should one or more of the repetitions be dropped? Watch for the sense of head levels and for the phrasing of heads. Are they parallel? Is the second-level heading clearly subordinate to the first? Are certain words unnecessary? Check the heads against the table of contents.

2. *Spelling.* Be sure to spell the same word the same way each time it occurs. Spelling is a particular problem with foreign words and proper names. Note them on your style sheet. Are some foreign words supposed to be in italic? Tell the publisher what source you are using for spelling.

3. *Hyphenation.* Some words could conceivably be written in one of three ways: as one solid word, as two words, or as a hyphenated word. An example is *armchair.* In the United States that word is normally spelled as one solid word, although it occasionally shows up as two. In England it is frequently hyphenated. Include on your style sheet all terms that could be treated like *armchair,* and check back each time the term appears. Remember that you may want a term to be two words as a noun but hyphenated as an adjective; indicate your preference on the style sheet. Be aware that some terms are hyphenated according to usage within a specific field. Chapter 5 gives some rules for hyphenation.

4. *Capitalization.* If you capitalize a word on page 7, don't lowercase it on page 13. Write these words *clearly* on your style sheet. See Chapter 5 for some rules about capitalization.

5. *Numbers.* Decide between words and digits, or at least have a cutoff point above which you'll use digits, and then stick to it. Chapter 7 discusses the use of numbers.

6. *Abbreviations.* Which terms can be abbreviated successfully? How should cross-references be abbreviated? In some non-technical materials, units of measure should be spelled out. Indicate on your style sheet your choices or rules for abbreviating. See Chapter 7.

7. *Footnotes and references.* Once you have determined the basic bibliographic style, stay with it. Adapt it to take into account all the variations, but settle on one specific style. See Chapter 8 for standard bibliographic styles.

8. *Tables.* Treat column heads consistently, and key similar heads the same way from table to table. Make sure table source notes are always in the same place. Chapter 10 discusses tables more fully.

9. *Artwork.* Mark labels consistently for capital or lowercase letters. Treat similar figures the same. Use abbreviations consistently throughout the art program. See Chapter 10 for more about art.

10. *Person.* If the manuscript begins in the third person, keep it there; don't change to first person along the line.

11. *Typographic elements.* Are defined words set off in quotation marks, italic, or boldface? Do some lists begin with letters in parentheses and others with numbers followed by periods? How many ellipsis points should there be? Do some tables have vertical rules while others don't? Are hints for exercises sometimes enclosed within parentheses and at other times not? The designer makes decisions on typeface, type size, and position on the page, but *you* have to make these other decisions.

12. *Other.* Certain fields—for example, chemistry, medicine, and law—may have terms peculiar to the field (see Chapter 11). You may wish to list these terms separately on the style sheet. In fiction, pay attention to plot, noting characteristics of people and places on your style sheet. See also Fiction in Chapter 11.

If you read the manuscript word by word and note every single point on your style sheet, you will end up with a very consistent manuscript. You can also help yourself by copyediting similar materials together. Work on all tables at one time, watching for similarities and differences and making tables similar when they should be. Copyedit all footnotes together, catching differences in spelling, journal abbreviations, and treatment. Do all bibliographic entries together too. If the manuscript has elements common to all chapters, such as learning objectives or exercises, copyedit them all at once so that you can watch for differences in phrasing. Check the sequence of all numbers: tables, illustrations, exercises, bibliographic references, equations, and so on. Are any missing? Professional copyediting services often work this way; in fact, many people may work on the same manuscript, one doing footnotes, one tables, and so forth. That way they help ensure consistency.

AWARENESS OF A SPECIAL KIND

If you follow the rules I just gave you, you can be a good copyeditor. To be a great copyeditor you need a special kind of awareness, as I mentioned at the very beginning of this chapter. You need, in fact, to be a trivia buff. One of the best ways to pick up trivia is to read some of the excellent specialized style manuals on the market. You don't have to remember the information; just know where to go to get it if you need it. Become completely familiar with at least one of the books by Theodore M. Bernstein listed in the bibliography and with either the *New York Times* or *Washington Post* style manual and the *U.S. Government Printing Office Style Manual* (see the bibliography). Just be aware that there is a need to check the author's terminology and that there are books that explain the terms.

Let's see how consistent you are. In the following exercise adapted from an old play review, make the changes you wish, and note all style points on the style sheet (Figure 3.2) accompanying the exercise. Don't worry about grammar or punctuation or word changes here; this exercise is intended to test your awareness. There are really no right answers, but your style sheet should have as many points listed on it as mine does, even though your choices may be different.

> In this play about university people, Albee deals with a
> great moral truth; the play is not merely a show of
> degeneracy. George is in the History Department of a small
> New England college (''Martha tells me often, that I am <u>in</u>
> the History Department...as opposed to <u>being</u> the History
> Department'').[1] Martha, George's wife, is a boisterous
> woman, 6 years older than her mild-mannered (though not
> meek) husband, and the daughter of the college's President,
> whom she idolizes. The play's two other characters are
> Nick, a young Biology professor, and his giggly wife Honey.

AB	CD	EF	GH
IJK	LM	NO	PQ
R	S	TU	VWXYZ
Style Punctuation	Numbers Abbreviations	Footnotes Bibliographies Tables	Typography Miscellaneous

Figure 3.2. A blank style sheet for you to use for this exercise.

The action commences around 2 A.M. in the home of George
and Martha, following a party at the President's home.
Lusty Martha, it seems, has eyes for Nick, and she invites
the younger couple in for a post-party nightcap. Unlike
most plays, Who's Afraid of Virginia Woolf? adheres to
Aristotle's theory of drama: that the life situation of the
play should not last longer than the play itself. From this
point, then, we see recreated the lives of four people,
minute by minute.

Also unlike most conventional drama today, each act is
carefully named: ''Fun and Games'' begins when the guests
arrive. After being humiliated by Martha, George retaliates
in Act Two, ''Walpurgisnacht,'' or Witches' Sabbath. Not
content with his victory in Act Two, not only over Martha
but over Nick and Honey as well, George plans the coup de
grâce in the final act, ''The Exorcism.''

[1]Edward Albee, Who's Afraid of Virginia Woolf? (New York,
Atheneum, 1962), Act I.

Now here is my marked manuscript. Does your manuscript look
like mine? Look at my style sheet in Figure 3.3. Do you have the same
terms on yours?

In this play about university people, Albee deals with a
great moral truth; the play is not merely a show of
degeneracy. George is in the History Department of a small
New England college (''Martha tells me often, that I am in
the History Department/./././as opposed to being the History
Department''). [1] Martha, George's wife, is a boisterous
woman, (6) years older than her mild-mannered (though not

AB	CD coup de grâce	EF	GH Great Moral Truth
IJK	LM mild = mannered (a)	NO nightcap (n)	PQ president post-party (a)
R re-created	S	TU	VWXYZ
Style space ellipsis ftn ref. goes after quote	Numbers two characters six years Act Two Abbreviations 2 A.M.	Footnotes V Edward Albee, Title of Play (City: Publisher, 1962), Act One.	Miscellaneous history department (except in quote) "Walpurgis- nakht," or Witches' Sabbath

Figure 3.3. The style sheet I prepared for this exercise.

meek) husband, and the daughter of the college's President,
whom she idolizes. The play's two other characters are
Nick, a young biology professor, and his giggly wife Honey.

The action commences around 2 A.M. in the home of George
and Martha, following a party at the President's home.
Lusty Martha, it seems, has eyes for Nick, and she invites
the younger couple in for a post-party nightcap. Unlike
most plays, Who's Afraid of Virginia Woolf? adheres to
Aristotle's theory of drama: that the life situation of the
play should not last longer than the play itself. From this
point, then, we see recreated the lives of four people,
minute by minute.

Also unlike most conventional drama today, each act is
carefully named: ''Fun and Games'' begins when the guests
arrive. After being humiliated by Martha, George retaliates
in Act Two, ''Walpurgisnacht,'' or Witches' Sabbath. Not
content with his victory in Act Two, not only over Martha
but over Nick and Honey as well, George plans the coup de
grâce in the final act, ''The Exorcism.''

[1]Edward Albee, Who's Afraid of Virginia Woolf? (New York,
Atheneum, 1962), Act One.

► DID YOU NOTICE?

1. I put "history department" under Miscellaneous instead of in
the alphabetical listings. Furthermore, I did not list "biology."
There is no need to list all variations, as long as you can remember
one of them. If I had listed "history department" under H,
I would have had to remember that it was "history" I'd listed,
rather than biology, math, or something else. Here, I had only
to look up the miscellaneous terms.

2. It is not your responsibility to verify footnote references or actual wording of quotations unless that is part of your agreement with the publisher. Likewise, you needn't check whether First Avenue in Cincinnati is one-way or whether there are 473 steps leading up to some obscure church in Saint-Jean-Cap-Ferrat. On the other hand, the publisher will certainly think highly of you for making the attempt.

3. You will learn about numbers in Chapter 7, but for purposes of this exercise you should have noticed the three styles I wrote on my style sheet. Notice, too, that I changed the footnote style of referring to an act to agree with the text style. There were, of course, more numerical references in the passage than I have listed on my style sheet. I wanted merely to set down my style choices so that I would have something to refer to each time a numerical situation arose.

4. Something doesn't have to be wrong in manuscript to go on the style sheet. Many terms I listed were already correct, but just because they're correct here does not mean the author won't treat them differently later; I don't want to forget the correct choices when I see the incorrect ones later.

5. I put some terms on the style sheet for the benefit of the proofreader to come after me. "Nightcap" is such an example (well, it *could* be "night cap," couldn't it?).

If your style sheet isn't as detailed as mine, even for these three short paragraphs, you'd better be more careful. For a fiction manuscript of 250-300 pages, you should have at least 250 items on your style sheet; for nonfiction (except mathematics, which has very little prose), plan on at least 1 item every 5 manuscript pages. So for a 500-page manuscript you'd have a minimum of 100 items on the style sheet. Remember, the style sheet is meant not only to remind *you* of the style decisions you made on the manuscript; it also serves others who handle the manuscript after you.

After you've completed the style sheet, type it alphabetically, explaining any abbreviations you've used. At the end of the style sheet add miscellaneous style notes, such as how you treated footnotes and tables. Some publishers prefer having all terms, including numbers and abbreviations, in alphabetical order. Check with your publisher if you are in doubt about what style to follow.

The following is a retyped style sheet for a 250-page mystery manuscript. Notice how detailed it is and how easy it will be for the proofreader to check every style point. Read this style sheet carefully to see if you can understand why each entry is there. Then aim for such completeness in the style sheets you prepare.

STYLE SHEET FOR _____

n = noun, v = verb, a = adjective,

pa = predicate adjective, adv = adverb

aerie	booze-battered (a)
after-pub (a)	brick-and-tiled (a)
afterward	broadside
all right	bulleted
anesthetized	bullet hole (n)
armor-piercing (a)	bulletproof (a)
armory	bullshit
back alley (n)	burnt-out (a)
background	businessman
back lit (pa)	bust-up (n)
backup (a)	cabby
backwater	caliber
Bahrain, bahraini	car-bound (a)
bald-headed (a)	car parts
bank note	car wash (n)
best-known (a)	centerfold
best-looking (a)	chalk-circled (pa)
bigwig	chauffeur driven (pa)
black gold (a)	check
blackout (n)	chessboard
bluestocking	chiaroscuro
blunt-nosed (a)	civilization
bone-jarring (a)	close-up (n)
boot-black (a)	cloud-blistered (a)

cold-faced (a)

color

crimebuster

crisscrossed

cubbyhole

custom-made (a)

dark-suited (a)

dead-end (a)

deep-pile (a)

demi-bottle (n)

destabilize

dialogue

doberman pinscher

doom-laden (a)

double take (n)

downhill

dumb-assed (a)

earth-moving (a)

electric-powered (a)

ex-tent dweller

fast-buck (a)

favorite

felt-flat (a)

few-worded (pa)

fezzes

fiber glass

fine-tune (v)

fine-tuned (pa)

first-floor (a)

flyswatter

forecourt

forklift (a)

fresh-grown (a)

fresh-ish

Frisbee

frizzy-haired (a)

full-time (a)

gas-guzzler (a)

gatepost

good-bye

good-looking (a)

gray

groundwork

gruff-sounding (a)

gunfire

gunmetal (n)

half-collapsed (a)

half dozen

half-French

half-kilometer (a)

half-light (n)

half-made (a)

half-moon (n)

half past

half-strangled (a)

halfway (a)

hand-selected (pa)

handshaking (n)

hangdog (a)

harbor

headboard

headline-catching (a)

head-on (a)

headway

hee-hawing

hell

high-class (a)

high-headed (pa)

high-pitched (a)

high-ranking (a)

hightail

hippie

hit-and-run (a)

home-going (n)

honey pot (n)

honored

hood-lid (n)

horror show (n)

humor

humpbacked (a)

ice-cold (a)

ill-lit (a)

infrastructure

inland

inquiry

inshore

irrelevancies

kidney-shaped (a)

kilometer

Klaxon

label-less (a)

lamppost

large-built (a)

layout

left-wing (a)

leveled

light-blue-suited (pa)

liter

London-based (a)

Londonward

long-distance (a)

long-legged (a)

long-range (a)

loose-grit (a)

lovemaking

lunchtime

majordomo

makeup

maneuver

marveled

marvelous

matter-of-factly

metalwork

meter

midday

middle aged (pa)

mid-morning (a̲)

mid-pages

mild-angered (p̲a̲)

mild-paced (p̲a̲)

million-dollar (a̲)

modeling

monosyllables

mortar

motorized

mustache

nearby

neighbor

newspaper-sized (a̲)

newsstand

no-man's-land (a̲, n̲)

nonaligned

nonplussed

no-questions (a̲)

oceangoing (a̲)

offhandedness

once-over (n̲)

oncoming

one-way (a̲)

organize

other-worldly (p̲a̲)

out-of-date (a̲)

overgenerous

overheated (a̲)

pandora's box

paralyzed

pensioned-off (a̲)

percent

personalized

photo-surveillance

pickup (n̲)

potshot, potshotting

pox-ridden (a̲)

prearranged

prefecture

preseason (a̲)

pricey

punch-drunk (p̲a̲)

quarter-mile (n̲)

raincoat

rainwater

realize

resistance

right-hand (a̲)

riveted

runaround

run-in (n̲)

S-bend (n̲)

seaborne

sea gulls

seawall

seesawing

self-pity

semi

shortchange (v)

shortlist

short-sighted (pa)

sight line

signaled

single-handedly

six-pack

sizable

slipstream

smoking-rubber (a)

soft-spoken (a)

split-second (a)

stall-holder (n)

steel blue (a)

straw-colored (a)

sun-room (n)

super-rich (n)

surreptitiously

tail plane (n)

takeoff (n)

tape recorded (pa)

technicolor

Telex

tendentious

thin-faced (a)

third-floor (a)

three-point (a)

tight-focused (v)

tires

too-obvious (a)

touch-and-go (a)

toward

trafficked

traveling

turbaned

twin-engined (a)

two-hour (a)

underdone (pa)

under way (adv)

up-market (adv)

upward

U-turn (n)

Valium

verbalize

visualize

walkway

wall-to-wall (a)

warm-up (n)

well-swept (a)

west-facing (a)

whiskey

white-coated

white-knife (v)

white-sprayed (a)

whitewashed (a)

wickerwork

wide-laned (a)

wide-open (a)

windowpane

window seat

windshield

work load

worldwide (a̲)

ten-franc (a̲)

six-foot seven-inch (a̲)

five foot ten

four-thirty

M-thirty-eight

Numbers

seventies

fourteen

one hundred

six A̲.̲M̲.̲

eleven fifteenths

ten-foot (a̲)

fifty-year-old (n̲, a̲)

Miscellaneous

U.K.

Evening Standard

in dialogue, OK to say

Assistant Commissioner

Crime; in text, add ''of''

► DID YOU NOTICE?

1. This manuscript, according to the publisher, was written by a British author but intended for an American market. Thus many of the terms that seem to us to need no correction were actually nonstandard American English in the manuscript (such as *verbalize,* which was *verbalise*).
2. Many of the terms are simple misspellings, but the proofreader may want to look them up. So isn't it easier to provide them here, in a central place? A good example of a difficult word is *tendentious.*
3. Do you think the copyeditor looked up most of the words? Do you think all of these words were in the dictionary? Probably not. Most likely the copyeditor had to make up some of the words based on information about others.

ALPHABETIZATION

Somewhere in the material you copyedit you may need to alphabetize; maybe it'll be a bibliography, maybe word lists like the ones throughout this book. Maybe you'll be copyediting an index as one of your early assignments. If nothing else, you'll want to type your style sheet (like the one on the previous pages) in alphabetical order. You can handle that, right? You know that *t* comes after *s,* which comes after *r*. If it were that easy, the author would have done it correctly the first time!

There are two methods of alphabetizing: letter by letter and word by word. In letter-by-letter alphabetizing you alphabetize up to the first mark of punctuation and ignore spaces. (Hyphens do not count as punctuation in this system.) In the word-by-word system, you stop when you get to a space; entries beginning with initials precede all other entries. Can you think offhand of the best example of each system?

If you've ever had a hard time finding TWA in the phone book, you've seen word-by-word alphabetizing. Dictionaries and encyclopedias use letter-by-letter alphabetizing. Here are examples of each.

Word by Word	*Letter by Letter*
cc	cast
cast	cast about
cast about	castanet
cast out	castaway
castanet	caste
castaway	cast-iron
caste	cast out
cast-iron	cc

The second example is from a dictionary. Many indexers prefer this style too because, frankly, it's easier.

► DID YOU NOTICE?

1. In word-by-word alphabetizing, cc, being initials, precedes all other entries.
2. Letter-by-letter alphabetizing assumes that an entry ends at a period (or similarly strong mark) or comma.

► KEY POINTS IN THIS CHAPTER

Rules of Copyediting

- Be consistent.
- Look it up.
- It isn't right just because it's in print.

Style Sheet

- Keep a detailed style sheet.
- Add to the style sheet every item you might treat more than one way.
- Refer to the style sheet often.
- Allow the author's style to prevail.

What to Look for During Copyediting

- Headings should be parallel and follow outline style.
- Key repeated phrases should have the same wording each time.
- Spell, hyphenate, and capitalize the same and similar terms consistently.
- Follow rules for spelling out numbers as opposed to using digits and for using or not using abbreviations.
- Pick and maintain an acceptable bibliographic style.
- Mark art labels and table column heads consistently from piece to piece.
- Use italic and bold type properly and consistently.
- Check all numerical sequences.

Alphabetizing

- Word-by-word alphabetizing assumes that a word ends after all the initials.
- Letter-by-letter alphabetizing ends an entry at a period or comma.

C H A P T E R 4

A Review of Punctuation and Grammar

If you're considering copyediting as a full-time or freelance career, you probably have some interest in grammar and punctuation. Even experienced copyeditors occasionally need to review certain points. Certainly there are people better qualified than I to teach you grammar, but after checking hundreds of tests and projects, I can certainly give you some help on the tricky points. This chapter, then, is a review of punctuation marks and many of the grammatical points you may have forgotten or perhaps never really understood. Read it carefully and be sure you understand everything. If you need additional help, read the *Harbrace College Handbook* (see the bibliography). Do look for help: You're likely to end up working for a stickler like me.

Many of the "rules" given here are of course more like style preferences. It will usually be obvious which are preferences and which are not, but sometimes you may mistake a preference for law. Give some thought to these "rules," then; can you think of acceptable alternatives?

PUNCTUATION

Let's begin with punctuation.

Period

The period has three uses: to end a sentence, to separate letters in an abbreviation, and to indicate a typographic break.

Period Used at the End of a Sentence

1. Use a period at the end of a declarative sentence.

   John Lennon was murdered on December 8, 1980.

2. Use a period at the end of an imperative sentence.

   Don't go into the house.

   If the imperative is also an exclamation, use an exclamation point instead (see Exclamation Point).

3. Use a period at the end of an indirect question.

   He asked her where she was during the blackout.

4. Use a period at the end of a rhetorical question.

   May I suggest that you read the introduction before proceeding.

5. It is a matter of personal preference whether to use a period after incomplete sentences within a displayed list. However, if a complete sentence follows at least one item in the list, put periods after all items.

   Define the following:
   1. iambic pentameter. Give an example.
   2. epic poem.
   3. sonnet.

Period Used in Abbreviations

1. Use a period after a person's initials (unless current style dictates otherwise). Note that there is space after each period.

   John R. Smith
   E. A. Doe
   but JFK

2. Use a period after traditional abbreviations of state names but not after the Postal Service abbreviations of them. (Traditional abbreviations are seldom used now, however.)

   Calif. *but* CA

3. Use a period and no space in other common abbreviations.

   Ph.D.

Note: Some abbreviations take periods and some do not; see Chapter 7.

4. A period at the end of an abbreviation may be followed by any other punctuation mark except another period.

> Barbara got her Ph.D., then went to work as a clerk.
> Larry worked for British Leyland Ltd.

Period Used Typographically

1. Use a period after numbers in a displayed list.

   > 1. birds
   > 2. animals

2. Do not use a period following displayed headings, such as the headings in this book.
3. Use a period (if that is the style) in references to figure and table numbers. (See also Hyphen.)

   > See Figure 1.7.
   > In Section 4.7 we . . .

Period Used with Other Punctuation

1. A period goes inside an end quotation mark.

   > On leaving Corregidor MacArthur promised, "I shall return."

2. Do not use a period with an exclamation point or question mark.

   > Richard asked, "What should we do about the picnic?"
   > Lucas, R. *What Is the Nature of Life?* New York: Smith Press, 1980.

3. A period may go either inside or outside parentheses, depending on what is enclosed within them. If the enclosure is an independent sentence, it takes its own period. If the enclosure is not an independent sentence, the period goes after the close parenthesis.

   > I went out for lunch yesterday. (I try to get out once a week.)
   > I went out for lunch yesterday (for the first time in two weeks).

4. A period usually goes inside a single quotation mark; with philosophical terms it occasionally goes outside.

Define the concept of 'being'.

Note: This is philosophical usage only. Normally terms are enclosed within double quotation marks.

5. Use a period with ellipsis points if one would be used without them.

The train finally arrived, but it was too late. . . .

For further clarification, see the discussions of all the other punctuation marks mentioned.

Comma

The comma has many uses, which we will go into in detail. Many times you must simply use your judgment, but keep in mind that a comma often indicates a pause; if you would pause in speaking, put a comma in writing.

Comma Used in Compound Sentences

1. Usually use a comma before the conjunctions *and, but, or, nor, for, so,* and *yet* in compound sentences.

Zack walked slowly to the door, and Nancy followed behind.

Note: A compound sentence consists of two distinct sentences, each able to stand alone. Be careful not to confuse a compound predicate with a compound sentence.

Zack walked slowly to the door and went out.

Note also that there is no subject other than Zack; "and went out" is not a distinct sentence able to stand alone, whereas "Nancy followed behind" is.

2. You need not use a comma if the clauses that make up the compound sentence are closely related or if the second relies on the first for its sense. If a comma sounds better, use one.

I wanted to attend the concert but I couldn't.

Comma Used After Introductory Phrases and Clauses

1. Use a comma after an introductory adverbial clause.

When it rains, Howard gets depressed.

2. Use a comma after an introductory infinitive phrase.

> To get to First Street, take the L bus.

3. Use a comma after a long introductory phrase.

> Three years after the end of the Second World War, Bob still could not forget that day in Normandy.

Note: How long is long? If you would pause after the phrase, use a comma.

4. Use a comma after a short introductory phrase if confusion could exist without the comma.

> In 1911, 203 persons lived in Jonesville, Idaho.
> In general, situations such as these occur rarely.

5. Do not use a comma after an introductory phrase in an inverted sentence, one where the subject follows the verb.

> On the branches of the tree rested the remains of the season's first snowfall.

Comma Used Before Adverbial Clauses

1. Do not use a comma if the adverbial clause follows the main clause.

> Howard gets depressed when it rains.

2. If the adverbial clause following the main clause is introduced by a subordinating conjunction, such as *whereas, although,* or *because,* use a comma only if one seems necessary.

> Tracy attended the concert because her father asked her to.

In this example you will notice that a pause does not occur (remember that you put in a comma if you would pause when speaking); that is, a strong relationship exists between the two clauses. Sometimes, however, a comma is needed for sense; without a comma (without a pause), the sentence says something other than what the author means.

> Don't worry about the errors, because they'll be handled during the correction session.

If you omit the comma before *because,* the implication is this: Don't worry about them because of this; worry about them because of something else. That's not what this sentence means.

The word *because* is very tricky; each time it appears you should ask yourself whether you would pause before it. If you would pause, put in a comma. Usually, if the clause that introduces *because* is positive, you don't need a comma.

> I bought a new car because I drive so far to work every day.
> Harris couldn't afford a new car, because his paycheck wouldn't cover the financing.

Comma Used to Set Off Transitional and Special Elements

1. Use a comma after any parenthetical element that serves to break up the continuity. Within the sentence, use commas on both sides of the element.

   > Oh, how I hated her.
   > However, I was unable to come up with a solution.
   > Frank learned, for example, that honesty is the best policy.
   > Peter asked, among other things, whether his lover would be welcome at the party.

   If there is no break in continuity, there is no pause, so you can omit the comma.

   > Bob was consequently able to complete the project on time.
   > Thus Danny became the first of our group to amount to anything.

   There *must* be a comma after *however* except as an adverb ("however hard I tried, I couldn't hit the ball").

2. Use a comma to set off *etc.; yes* or *no* at the beginning of a sentence; and the conversational *well, now,* or *why.*

   > I inquired about mortgage costs, PMI, interest rates, etc., but I forgot to ask when the new development would be ready.
   > Yes, Paul is an outstanding choice for the role.
   > Now, what do you think of that?

3. Use commas to set off direct address.

   > Please, Arlynn, do come to the party.
   > No, thank you, sir.

4. Use a comma to set off titles or degrees.

   > Marie Winters, M.D.

Comma Used in a Series

1. Use commas to separate all elements in a series.

   Edward thought that the most important presidents were Kennedy, Nixon, Lincoln, and Madison.

Note: The comma before the *and* is called the series comma. Textbook publishers almost always use the series comma, magazine publishers almost never. The absence is also British style. Trade book publishers always follow the author's preference. Always ask the house style on the series comma.

   During the summer Susan visited British Columbia, Nova Scotia, and Newfoundland. [style with series comma]
   She waited an hour, tore up the invitation and stalked out of the room. [style without series comma]

2. Use a comma between coordinate adjectives if the word *and* logically could be read between them.

   The company is committed to hiring intelligent, aggressive people. [intelligent *and* aggressive]

3. Do not use a comma to separate an adjective from a word group.

   Marjorie stood on the shaky black platform. [not shaky and black]
   Edi eyed the group of sad, bored office workers.

4. Do not use a comma to separate an adjective from the noun it modifies.

   The company hires intelligent, ambitious people.

Comma Used with Antithetical Elements

An *antithetical element* contradicts the rest of the sentence or presents two parallel structures.

1. Do not use commas to set off elements in the *not to . . . but to* construction.

   We come not to praise Caesar but to bury him.
   I went to Lake Tahoe not so much to ski as to gamble.

2. Use commas to set off antithetical elements.

   Betsy, not Sue, was prom queen.

3. Use commas to separate interdependent clauses.

> The more you study, the higher your grade will be.
> The greater the effort, the greater the reward.

Note: In the first example I used a verb in the second clause although a verb is not essential. I did so because the two clauses are not technically parallel; the subject of the first clause is *you,* and the subject of the second clause is *grade.* I like the sound of the sentence better with a verb. Sentences such as these usually sound better one way, so you will have to use your judgment.

4. Do not use commas in short interdependent phrases.

> The sooner the better.

Restrictive Versus Nonrestrictive Elements

To continue with our discussion of commas, we need a definition of restrictive and nonrestrictive elements. A *restrictive* element is necessary for the sentence to make sense; it cannot be removed from the sentence, because it will tell you "which one" when such identification is necessary. Let's look at an example.

> The boys who attended the picnic are ill.

Which boys are ill? All the boys in the sixth grade? No, only the ones who attended the picnic. The sentence answers the question Which ones? and is restricted to only those boys.

A *nonrestrictive* element can be taken out of the sentence without changing the meaning. Such an element is surrounded by commas.

> My car, which is parked across the street, is a Ford.

What happens if that element is removed from the sentence?

> My car is a Ford.

The sentence is fine without it; it does not answer the question Which one? It is not restricted, the way the first example was, to *only those* or *only that.*

> Only those boys who attended the picnic are ill.

If you test each sentence to see if it's restricted to *only those* or *only that,* you'll be able to tell right away whether the sentence is restrictive.

Comma Used with Nonrestrictive Elements

1. Use commas around nonrestrictive elements.

The mouse startled Stan, who jumped up from his seat.
The mouse, which startled Stan, ran off into its hole.
O. J. Simpson, wearing his famous number 32, ran onto the field.

2. Do not use commas with restrictive clauses. In restrictive clauses, use *that* instead of *which.*

The mouse that is in the corner startled Stan. [only that mouse—not some other one]
The scarf that is on the bureau would look nice. [not the scarf in the closet]

There are some special cases of nonrestrictive elements—of elements that serve to clarify but are not needed. They are called *parenthetical elements.*

Comma Used with Parenthetical Elements

1. Use commas around parenthetical expressions.

Such a victory, the coach explained, was vital to morale.
They purchased cups, plates, fruit, bread, and so on, for the party.

2. Use commas before and after each element after the first in addresses and dates.

On May 24, 1973, in Vancouver, British Columbia, John Sterling fell in love.

3. Use a comma after the first name in an inverted bibliographic reference.

Clark, Susan, and John Winter. *The Psychological Effects of Drug Problems.* San Francisco: Book Lovers Press, 1981.

You must learn to use commas properly with parenthetical elements. When an educated person reads an article or a book, errors such as those with dates and states *glare.*

An *appositive* is a word or group of words that renames the noun or pronoun it follows. There is no verb between a noun and its appositive.

Comma Used with Appositives

1. Use commas around nonrestrictive appositives.

Robert Joffrey, one of the greatest choreographers of the century, died in 1988.

A great believer in civil rights, Derek Smith was appalled at the way Worthen had been treated.

2. Do not use commas with restrictive appositives.

My sister Sally is a writer. [my sister Sue is a doctor]
The playwright Shakespeare was a remarkable man.
[there *are* other playwrights]

Comma Used with Quotations

1. Generally use a comma to introduce or follow a direct quotation.

Elaine shouted, "Get out of here!"
"I can't make it," Jim whined.

2. Not everything within quotation marks is a quotation. Do not use a comma to set off material within quotation marks used as the subject, object, or appositive.

"Mayday" is the distress call for planes and ships.
Jeffrey always called her "Mata Hari."
The term "Mayday" is a distress call.

Comma Used with Other Punctuation

1. A comma goes inside the end quotation mark of a direct quotation.

"I'll be back," Cathy replied.

2. Do not use a comma with an exclamation point or question mark.

"Leave me alone!" Joan shouted at her ex-husband.

3. A comma never precedes an open parenthesis (except typographically; see Parentheses).

According to Miller (who should have known better), stars never shine in the rain.

4. A comma goes outside a single quotation mark only if the mark is used to indicate special usage, not if it is used in a quotation.

The concept of 'being', which we discussed earlier, is difficult to understand.

Note: This is philosophical usage only. Normally terms are enclosed within double quotation marks, and then the comma goes inside.

Semicolon

A semicolon is a weak period. It is used to separate but not conclude. If there is a direct relationship between two sentences, normally they should be separated by a semicolon instead of a period.

Semicolon Used in Place of a Comma and a Conjunction

1. If two independent clauses are not connected by *and, but, or, nor, for, so,* or *yet,* separate them with a semicolon.

   I returned to the dance; I didn't want to appear to be sulking.

2. Use a semicolon before an independent clause introduced by *hence, therefore, that is, however, then, indeed, for example, namely,* and the like.

   Alison attended the ballgame willingly; however, she never expected the team to win.

3. Do not use a semicolon to separate an independent clause from a dependent one.

   Alison attended the ballgame, which she never expected to enjoy.
   Come if you can, that is, if you want to.

Semicolon Used in a Series

1. Use a semicolon to separate items in a series if any of the items contains a comma.

   We invited Carolyn, who is always a laugh at parties; Kenneth, who gets hostile when he drinks; and Janet, mostly because Kenneth insisted.

2. Occasionally use a semicolon to separate items in a series if they consist of complete sentences.

   He gave Bill three instructions before the camp bus came: Don't go into the lake without a counselor; don't eat too much; and don't lose anything.

Semicolon Used with Other Punctuation

1. A semicolon goes outside an end quotation mark.

   Janie began singing "The Star-Spangled Banner"; she waited for the crowd to follow her.

2. A semicolon never precedes a parenthesis (unless the parenthesis is used typographically, as a design feature, or in mathematics).

> Michael was a fool (or so we'd heard); he should have known better.

Colon

A colon has three uses: to introduce a list, statement, quotation, or summary; to introduce a clause relating to the preceding clause; and to indicate typographic distinctions. In its normal usage, a colon says, "Here they are."

Colon Used to Introduce a List, Statement, Quotation, or Summary

1. Use a colon after the word *follows* or *following.*

> Each student is reminded to bring the following to the picnic: some food item to share, a beach towel, and clothes to change into after swimming.

2. Never use a colon after a form of the verb *to be.*

> The most important items to bring with you are a deck chair, radio, cooler, and beach umbrella.

3. Use a colon to introduce a formal or lengthy statement or quotation, or in headlines to introduce an idea.

> Lincoln paused before addressing the crowd: "Fourscore and seven years ago..."
> SADAT: WE MUST NOT GO TO WAR

4. If the second word group summarizes the first, introduce it with a colon.

> Joan pointed to her excellent driving record: forty years without so much as a parking ticket.

Colon Used to Relate One Clause to a Previous One

1. Use a colon to emphasize an explanatory relationship between two clauses.

> Al swims not for enjoyment: It is expected of him.

2. If the relationship seems minor, use a semicolon instead of a colon.

> Many people find swimming tiring; they prefer floating.

Colon Used Typographically

1. Use a colon between chapter and verse in references to the Bible. There is no space on either side.

   John 3:16

2. Use a colon between the hour and minutes in time designations. Again, there is no space on either side.

   4:10

3. Use a colon (space after but not before) between the volume number and page number in a bibliographic reference, even if the year appears within parentheses between the two (see also Chapter 8).

   Journal of Sociology 4 (1979): 325-339.

4. Use a colon between the city and the publisher in bibliographic references (see also Chapter 8).

   Indianapolis, IN: Bobbs-Merrill

5. Use a colon between a title and subtitle.

   Have you read "Growing Old: A Love Story"?

6. Usually use a colon in play dialogue, following speakers' names. Some publishers use a different typographic system for plays, which they will explain to you, but for isolated dialogue, the colon is normally used.

   CELE: Can't you be serious?
   MARY: I'm never serious.

   Follow the publisher's style for aligning or not aligning the colons.

Colon Used with Other Punctuation

1. A colon goes outside an end quotation mark.

   They came from everywhere to what Bruce called "the enchanted cave": from the mountains, from the beaches, even from the cities.

2. A colon never precedes a parenthesis (except typographically).

   Then they heard from Monroe (a scoundrel if ever there was one): "Anyone who won't pay the price proceeds at his own risk."

Question Mark

The question mark (also called the interrogation point) is used after direct questions. Sometimes these questions are nothing more than converted simple statements, and sometimes they are contained within declarative statements. Any time there is a direct question, there should be a question mark.

A question mark is also used to indicate doubt.

Question Mark Used After a Direct Question

1. Use a question mark after a direct question.

   How will I recognize you?

2. Do not use a question mark after an indirect question.

   He asked how he would recognize Teresa.

3. Use a question mark after a direct question contained within a declarative statement.

   All the time she wondered, Is it worth it?
   "How will I recognize you?" she asked.
   She asked, "How will I recognize you?"
   Is it worth it? was the problem.

4. Use a question mark after a converted simple statement.

   Go to bed *now?*

Question Mark Used to Indicate Doubt

1. Use a question mark within parentheses to indicate uncertainty about a fact.

   Bud said he was going to either Washington State (?) or Virginia.

2. A question mark used directly after a year within a range indicates a guess.

   The work of Chaucer (1340?–1400) is one of our greatest legacies.

Question Mark Used with Other Punctuation

1. The question mark is placed inside quotation marks, parentheses, or brackets if it is part of the enclosed material.

   "Where are you going?" Diane asked.
   If we leave tomorrow (that *is* the idea, isn't it?), we can probably return by next Tuesday.

2. If the material enclosed within quotation marks, parentheses, or brackets does not contain a question, but instead the main sentence is the question, then the question mark goes outside.

> Will you please sing "Begin the Beguine"?
> Can we leave tomorrow (after the mail comes)?

3. Do not use a period, comma, colon, or semicolon immediately after a question mark.

> John Jones, "Are We Ready for Twenty-First Century Art?" *Art Review* 8 (1979): 22–47.

Exclamation Point

An exclamation point should be used only to indicate an interjection or a high degree of emotion. Be careful not to overuse it.

Exclamation Point Used in Expressions of Emotion

1. Use an exclamation point to indicate emotionally laden imperatives.

> Attention!
> Get lost!

2. Use an exclamation point to express surprise.

> I can't believe it!
> What a catch!

3. Do not use an exclamation point after mild exclamations.

> What a nice person she is.

Exclamation Point Used with Other Punctuation

1. The exclamation point is placed inside quotation marks, parentheses, or brackets if it is part of the enclosed material.

> "Watch out!" yelled Will.
> Alice (naturally!) wore a costume made of cigarette butts.

2. If the material enclosed within quotation marks, parentheses, or brackets does not contain an exclamation, but instead the main sentence is the exclamation, then the exclamation point goes outside.

> Stop singing "The Yellow Rose of Texas"!
> You can't mean that (I hope)!

3. Do not use a period, comma, colon, or semicolon immediately after an exclamation point.

John Jones, "Success!" *Psych. Review* 8 (1980): 22–27.

Parentheses

Parentheses are used to set off parenthetical material or are used typographically to enclose numbers or letters acting as subdivisions.

Parentheses Used to Set Off Material

Use parentheses to enclose material not necessary to the sense of the sentence.

It is a fact of life (unfortunate, to be sure) that people grow old.
According to Darwin (1809–1882), species adapt and make their own way.
That year the gross national product (GNP) exceeded $2.5 billion.

Parentheses Used Typographically

1. Use parentheses to enclose letters or numbers introducing items in a list.

He expected her to (1) come from a good family, (2) be able to talk intelligently, and (3) be reasonably attractive.

2. An end parenthesis can be used with a letter or number within display only, not within running text.

He expected her to
1) come from a good family
2) be able to talk intelligently
3) be reasonably attractive

Such a use, however, should be a design decision; among other possibilities are double parentheses, a slash, or a period.

3. Use parentheses in mathematics according to standard mathematical usage. (For some of the uses of parentheses in mathematics, see Chapter 11.)

Parentheses Used with Other Punctuation

1. Within a sentence, place any comma, period, colon, or semicolon after the end parenthesis, not before the opening one. (The exception is when a parenthesis is used typographically or mathematically.)

According to Darwin (1809–1882), species adapt and make their own way.

2. Question marks and exclamation points go before or after the end parenthesis, depending on whether the material enclosed in parentheses is the question or exclamation or whether the sentence itself is.

> Jonas (can you believe it?) actually swam all the way to shore (the north shore)!

3. Place a period either inside or outside parentheses, depending on what is enclosed. If the enclosure is an independent sentence, it takes its own period. If the enclosure is not an independent sentence, the period goes after the close parenthesis.

> I went out for lunch yesterday. (I try to get out once a week.)
> I went out for lunch yesterday (for the first time in two weeks).

Brackets

Brackets have three uses: to enclose parenthetical material; to enclose editorial comments or explanations; and to make typographic distinctions, particularly in phonetics and mathematics.

Brackets Used to Enclose Parenthetical Material

1. Use brackets to enclose publishing information that falls within parentheses.

> This play is one of the best examples of Restoration comedy. (For further discussion of this topic see John Jones, *Restoration Comedies at Their Best* [New York: Williamson Press, 1980], pp. 14–40.)

2. Use brackets to enclose parenthetical material that falls within parentheses.

> This play is one of the best examples of Restoration comedy. (For another fine example, read *Chariot's Delight*, by Arthur Rogers. [Rogers was actually a nineteenth-century playwright who wrote in Restoration style.])

Brackets Used to Enclose Editorial Comments or Explanations

1. Use brackets to identify a person, place, or thing not clear from a quoted sentence.

Blaise told *News* magazine, "They [the president's staff] act before they think."

"It [our reliance on foreign oil] will be our undoing," she added.

2. Use brackets to enclose the word *sic* in quoted material. *Sic* (Latin for "thus") is used to let stand an error that appeared in a quotation.

She read Dale the article from the paper: "Hoffman hit a fool [sic] ball behind home plate, according to the *Winston-Salem Chronicle.*"

3. Use brackets to comment on quoted material.

"After World War II, *no person was safe from war.*" [Italics mine.]

Brackets Used Typographically

1. Use brackets to set off phonetic transcriptions.

The word *be* written phonetically is [bi].

2. Use brackets for "continued" lines.

[To be continued]
[Continued from page 81]

Note: Parentheses can be used for this purpose instead of brackets.

3. Use brackets to set off reference numbers to a bibliography (see Chapter 8).

According to Smith [2], . . .

Note: Here, too, parentheses can be used instead of brackets.

4. Use brackets in mathematics according to special rules (see Chapter 11).

Brackets Used with Other Punctuation

1. Use punctuation with brackets in the same way as with parentheses.
2. Do not use punctuation with "continued" lines.

Quotation Marks

There are two kinds of quotation marks, double and single. Both kinds are used to set off quoted material. In America, double quotation marks are used for the main quotation; if that quotation includes another quotation, single quotation marks are used for the quote within a quote. (In Britain the situation is normally reversed.) We will discuss double quotation marks first and then briefly deal with single quotation marks.

Double quotation marks are used to set off quoted material, to identify certain titles, and to set off specially used words.

Double Quotation Marks Used with Quoted Material

1. Use quotation marks to set off dialogue. To be dialogue, there must be a speaker and a verb of saying.

   "What's the use?" asked Maria.

   In dialogue, each speaker change begins a new paragraph.
2. Use quotation marks to set off quotations.

   Shakespeare's Polonius urged his son, "Neither a borrower nor a lender be."

3. Do not use quotation marks if a long quotation is displayed (i.e., set off) rather than run into the text.

   According to his calculations,

   By the year 2000, the United States will have a population of 280 million, and the world's population will be 6.8 billion. California by that time will have over 29 million people, and even the smallest state, Rhode Island, will have 1.7 million inhabitants. There will be almost no oil available for U.S. consumption, and food shortages will abound. It will not be a pleasant time.

Double Quotation Marks Used to Identify Titles

Use quotation marks to set off titles of articles, songs, poems, essays, short stories, and TV shows.

   Nora sang "I Could Have Danced All Night" in the revue.

Note: Use italic (without quotation marks) to identify plays, periodicals, books, and works of art.

Double Quotation Marks Used in Special Sense

1. Use quotation marks to set off popular words or phrases from quoted material.

   Is there really "liberty and justice for all"?

2. Use quotation marks to indicate irony or to single out a phrase, but be careful not to imply irony where there is none.

> He took us to see his "apartment," a twelve-room flat in his mother's villa.
> The "bottom line," in this sense, is that without expenses there will be no growth.

3. Use quotation marks in translations of foreign words.

> Such a system is a *plutocracy* [Greek *ploutos,* "wealth"].

4. Use quotation marks around nicknames or slang.

> She was a "floozie."
> Stan "The Man" Musial was one of the greatest baseball players of our time.

5. Do not use quotation marks around nicknames used in place of a name.

> Red Smith was at the club tonight.

6. Do not use quotation marks with the term *so-called.*

> Tish's so-called boyfriend was at the dance with Judy.
> The so-called manifest destiny policy sent Americans into the West in the 1830s.

Some authors use quotation marks to set off words used as words, or words being used in a technical or other special sense, although most publishers prefer italics.

> A "binary dump" is a dump of the computer's memory in binary form.
> A *binary dump* is a dump of the computer's memory in binary form.

Double Quotation Marks Used with Other Punctuation

1. Generally, periods and commas go inside quotation marks.

> "I'm going out now," Lynn said.

2. Colons and semicolons go outside quotation marks.

> First the teacher read "Ode on a Grecian Urn"; then our class discussed it.

3. The question mark, exclamation point, and dash go inside quotation marks if they are part of the quotation; otherwise they go outside.

Have you heard Bruce Springsteen's song "Hungry Heart"?
"Wait—" she stammered. "Don't go yet."

Single Quotation Marks

Single quotation marks are used to set off quotations within
quotations. All punctuation rules that apply for double quotation
marks apply for single ones as well.

Louis asked, "Have you ever heard a more stirring rendition of 'America the Beautiful'?"

(For further discussion of quotations, see Capitalization in Chapter 5, Permissions in Chapter 10, and Fiction in Chapter 11.)

Dash

There are four kinds of dash: en, em, 2-em, and 3-em.

En dash. An en dash is half the width of an em dash. It is about as
wide as a capital N in the typeface being used. It is used mainly to
indicate range or to replace a hyphen in a compound adjective
containing two words or a hyphenated word. (It is also used
typographically; see Hyphen.)

En Dash Used in Ranges

1. Use an en dash to indicate inclusive page numbers, times or
dates, and references.

pp. 336–338
during the decade 1960–1969
Chapters 4–6

2. Do not use an en dash in place of *from . . . to* or *between . . . and.*

between 1960 and 1969

En Dash Used in Compound Adjectives

1. Use an en dash if one term in a compound adjective consists
of two words or a hyphenated word.

post–World War II recession
high-income–low-income ratio

2. Do not use an en dash in simple compound words.

the Taft-Hartley Act
an input-output analysis

Because an en dash is used within a single term, no other punctuation is used with it.

Em dash. An em dash is about as wide as a capital M in the typeface being used. It is used to set off parenthetical material, to indicate faltering speech, and, typographically, to introduce a name. These uses make it the most common kind of dash.

Em Dash Used to Set Off Parenthetical Material

1. Use an em dash in place of a comma to set off material already containing commas.

   My three brothers—David, Rick, and Art—are trying out for the football team.

2. Use an em dash to indicate breaks in thought.

   I can—I must—do it.

3. Use an em dash to introduce a summarizing thought.

   To win the game and bring the trophy back to Chicago—that was our aim.

4. Use an em dash to set off an element needing emphasis.

   Some workers—plumbers and electricians, for example—have successfully organized.

Em Dash Used to Indicate Faltering Speech

1. Use an em dash to indicate an interrupted thought in dialogue.

   "What in—" he began, but he never finished.

2. Use an em dash to indicate faltering speech.

   "But—you're—you can't be serious!" cried Judi.

Em Dash Used Typographically

Use an em dash to introduce a name following a displayed epigram or quotation.

   "Life is a circus."—Jacques Lichine

Em Dash Used with Other Punctuation

1. Do not use a period or a comma with an em dash.

   "Hold it just a min—" he began.
   Carol started to speak. "I'll just bet you—"

2. An em dash follows a question mark or exclamation point if the material enclosed within dashes contains a question or exclamation.

> "My baby—oh dear!—my baby is trying to fly!"

When you edit, be careful not to overuse the dash. But you should be aware that some authors, particularly novelists and poets, are fond of dashes. To these people, all those dashes may be an integral part of the story they have to tell, and you should resist the temptation to delete them.

Other dashes. A 2-em dash indicates missing letters, and a 3-em dash a missing word. As such, these dashes appear only in transcribed material, where it was not clear what word was intended, or in fiction, to denote a missing word. (A 2-em dash may also be used to represent a chemical bond.)

> John J—— is probably the murderer.
> According to the account, the travelers began their journey in July at Mount ——— and reached the village of Lazare in mid-September.

If an entire word is missing, or if only the beginning or end of a word is missing, leave normal word space before or after the dash. If the middle of a word is missing, there is no space around the dash.

> "D——n you!" she screamed.

A 3-em dash is used in bibliographic entries to indicate that the author of a work is the same as the author of the immediately preceding work.

> Lucas, R. *What Is the Nature of Life?* New York: Smith Press, 1980.
> ———. "Why We Lost the Vietnam War." *Soc. Rev.* 16 (1980): 112–113.

Hyphen

The main use of a hyphen is in syllabication, which, being the responsibility of a proofreader, not a copyeditor, we will not discuss until Chapter 12. It is also used in compound words, a topic discussed in Chapter 5. There is one other use for a hyphen, and that is a typographic one, namely, to indicate a number for reference. (In place of the hyphen, an en dash or period may be used.)

> Section 3-15
> Figure 4-2

Because a hyphen is used internally, no other punctuation is used with it.

Slash

Most often a slash, also called a *solidus, diagonal*, or *shilling*, is used in mathematical copy (see Chapter 11). It is also used to indicate options, to mark the end of a line of poetry within text, or to stand for *per*.

Slash Used in Options

> Explain how to repair a radio/TV/tape deck.

Slash Used to Set Off Lines of Poetry

> One of Dickinson's most famous poems begins, "Because I could not stop for Death/He kindly stopped for me."

(See also Poetry in Chapter 11.)

Slash Used in Place of Per

> 15 cm/min [15 centimeters per minute]

Points of Ellipsis

Points of ellipsis are three dots separated by thin space. (In Europe the dots are usually not spaced, and there is no space between them when they appear in French, Spanish, or other European languages.) In mathematics the dots are often centered vertically on the line (see Chapter 11), but normally they appear on the baseline, just like a period. In dialogue, points of ellipsis indicate uncertainty; in quoted material they indicate missing material. When they come after the end of a sentence, the ellipsis points are preceded by a period. Otherwise there is space on either side of them.

Ellipsis Points Used to Indicate Uncertainty

> "I suppose I could go...," pondered Ellen.

Ellipsis Points Used to Indicate Missing Material

> "My fellow Americans... Ask what you can do for your country."

Ellipsis Points After End of Sentence

> We wanted to go to Europe in the spring, but we'll just have to wait. ...

Apostrophe

An apostrophe has three uses: to form certain plurals, to form contractions, and to indicate possession.

Apostrophe Used to Form Plurals

1. Use an apostrophe to make letters and numbers plural.

   Mind your P's and Q's.
   Molly got 80's in all her subjects.

2. Use an apostrophe to form the plural of a word used as a word.

   The sentence has two "and's."

3. Use an apostrophe to form the plural of an abbreviation.

   There are several Ph.D.'s in my office.
   There are two YMHA's in the city.

4. Do not use an apostrophe to form the plural of years.

   During the 1960s there was considerable student unrest.

Apostrophe Used to Form Contractions

1. Use an apostrophe to indicate one or more missing letters in a contraction.

   We'll go soon.
   There's no time like the present.

2. Use an apostrophe to indicate missing numerals in a year.

   the class of '81

3. Use an apostrophe to indicate missing letters in dialogue.

   "I went 'cause I felt like goin'," Julie countered.

Apostrophe Used to Indicate Possession

1. Do not use an apostrophe with the pronouns *his, hers, its, ours, yours, theirs,* or *whose.*

   The cat licked its paw.

Note: Be careful not to confuse *it's* with *its, who's* with *whose,* or *you're* with *your.* The terms with the apostrophe are contractions, not possessives. *It's* always means *it is* or *it has; who's* always means *who is* or *who has;* and *you're* always means *you are.*

2. For simple possession, see Chart 4.1.

Chart 4.1. A Guide to Forming Possessives

	Singular	Plural
Not ending in s	*Add 's*	*Add 's*
	day's end	men's shoes
	my brother's wife	children's clothing
	the horse's mouth	
Ending in s	*Add 's*	*Add '*
	Yeats's poems[1]	ten cents' worth
	Dickens's novels[1]	witches' sabbath
	Nicholas's suit	citizens' rights
		the Joneses' possessions
	Add '	
	Mars' wrath[2]	

1. Or delete the final *s* if you prefer.
2. Classical Roman and Greek names ending in *s* traditionally do not take another *s* after the apostrophe. Some sources also recommend that the biblical names Jesus and Moses take an apostrophe only.

Note: To form the possessive singular of any noun, add *'s* to the singular. If the singular already ends in *s*, you may add just the apostrophe (*Mr. Jones' car*), or you may add *'s* (*Mr. Jones's car*). To form the possessive plural of a noun, first write the plural. Then, if the plural already ends in *s* (*boys*), add just an apostrophe to the word (*boys'*). If the plural does not end in *s* (*women*), add *'s* (*women's*).

3. For double subjects, use the possessive with the second noun only.

> John and Ed's house is for sale.

GRAMMAR

You have probably had your fill of grammar over the years, and you probably understand most of the rules well. But many copyeditors and writers find certain areas difficult. This next section, then, is just a review of the tricky points. I'm not going to define parts of speech (I assumed you knew them when I wrote the punctuation section). All I'm going to do is touch on those areas of grammar where copyeditors and writers seem to have difficulty. You'll notice that some of these rules depend on other, more obvious rules of a familiar kind. I offer these without explanation.

Comma Splice

You've always known that you're not allowed to make a comma splice (i.e., to connect two complete sentences by a comma), but are you aware that you may be making the most common kind?

1. Use a semicolon, not a comma, before *that is, moreover, nevertheless, for example,* and the like, when the expression precedes an independent clause.

> It looks like rain today; therefore the picnic will probably be canceled.
> Tom and he seemed very popular; that is, they were always surrounded by people.

2. When a dependent clause follows a transitional expression, a comma is a strong enough break.

> Among the most common grammatical errors is the comma splice, that is, the run-on sentence.

Sentence Fragment

Fortunately, few people interested in copyediting as a career have difficulty in recognizing sentence fragments. The main difficulty for copyeditors is when to accept them in informal writing. Naturally you must use your judgment. If the fragment sounds OK, then leave it.

> Where should I begin? At the beginning.
> I'm probably not a very good writer. Which is unfortunate under the circumstances.

Note: This last example in particular could be done better if the dependent clause were preceded by a comma or a dash, but in very casual writing it might pass.

One-word replies are almost always acceptable in writing.

> What am I getting out of this? Nothing.

Parallelism

In its broadest sense, parallelism provides a pleasant sense of form and structure. Notice how beautifully parallel this passage from Shakespeare's *Julius Caesar* is:

> The fault, dear Brutus, is not ‖ in our stars,
> but ‖ in ourselves

If you can write that way, or copyedit others that way, so much the better. But you must be aware of parallel structure in more specific ways.

1. Within a sentence, make all clauses and phrases parallel.

> The work of a copyeditor is <u>to correct</u> spelling, capitalization, and punctuation; <u>to use</u> proper grammar and punctuation; and <u>to do</u> a variety of production-related tasks.

Note that each phrase is introduced by an infinitive in this example.

2. Be sure that your connecting words form complete phrases.

> Her house is as big as, if not bigger than, Malvina's. [*as big as* Malvina's; *bigger than* Malvina's]

3. Be sure that words such as *either* or *only* modify the proper phrase. Determine whether the sentence is parallel where the word is currently placed.

> Either she is crazy or she is lying.
> She is either a cheat or a liar.

4. Notice in the following sentence (from *Webster's Third*) how the position of the word *only* changes the sentence.

> I hit him in the eye yesterday.

> Try putting *only* in each of the eight places in the sentence.

> Only I hit him in the eye yesterday.
> I only hit him in the eye yesterday.
> I hit only him in the eye yesterday.

And so on. Each time, ask yourself, What word does *only* modify? Then it becomes very simple to position the word correctly.

Verb Tense

Normally tense is not a problem to people who are interested in copy-editing, but one situation does occur rather often.

> I would have liked to have gone.

How many times have you used that expression? The problem is, it's incorrect. Unless there is another clause to come that expresses "before such and such," a simple infinitive will suffice.

> I would have liked to go.
> I would have liked to have gone before I retired.

Also note that the past perfect tense (*had* ——) should be used to show an action completed before another past action.

> I *had eaten* my lunch when Henry *called*.

Verb Number and Agreement

1. The verb number should agree with the subject in inverted sentences beginning with *there* or *here*.

There were three dogs in the park.

2. A linking verb agrees with its subject.

Broken bo<u>nes we</u>re the result of the skiing accident.
The re<u>sult of the skiing accident wa</u>s broken bones.

3. With collective nouns, use a singular or plural verb, depending on sense. If the collection is acting as a single group, use a singular verb; if the individual members of the collection must be considered, use a plural one.

A majority of the group favors the new rule.
A number of people are planning to attend.
He doesn't think a million dollars is enough for
the project.

Verbs with Neither *and* Either

In an *either. . .or* or a *neither. . .nor* construction, use a singular verb.

Neither Joanne nor Marian was at the game.

Note that if two singular nouns are joined, the verb is singular, but if two plural nouns are joined, the verb is plural.

Either the Yankees or the Orioles are favored.

If one plural and one singular noun are involved, the verb agrees with the noun nearer to it.

Splitting Infinitives and Verb Phrases

It used to be that you could never split an infinitive without some strict grammarian coming down hard on you. That's not so true these days, although we are still advised to avoid splitting infinitives or other phrases. When you see a split infinitive, ask yourself, Could the modifier go anywhere else without sounding awkward or changing the meaning? If not, leave it alone!

He seems to really want the puppy.

If you don't split the infinitive here, what will you do with *really*? To say "He really seems to want the puppy" is not the same; he really *wants,* not really *seems*!

Normally adverbs should come after verbs, but occasionally, as with split infinitives, they will sound better between the verb and the auxiliary. Both these examples are correct.

She was singing beautifully when he interrupted.
Roy had been properly warned about the permit.

Pronoun Agreement

There are two areas of difficulty with pronoun agreement. Let's look at the cases in each area.

Pronouns with Multiple Nouns

1. If two nouns are joined by *and,* normally the pronoun will be plural.

    John and Marty sold their house.

2. If two nouns are joined by *or, nor, together with, in addition to, as well as,* or the like, normally the pronoun will be singular.

    Charlene, together with Winnie, brought her lunch.

3. If both male and female are involved, it is normally better to recast the sentence.

    Clayton couldn't start his car, and Elizabeth couldn't start hers either.

Pronouns Replacing Each *or* Every

1. Do not use *they* or *their* to replace a singular noun, with the possible exception of *everyone,* which can be considered plural under certain conditions.

    Everyone agreed that they were enjoying the play.

2. When replacing a singular noun with a pronoun, do not use *he* to include male and female. Use masculine and feminine pronouns as alternates, recast the sentence in the plural, or rewrite the phrase.

    Each person should supply his or her own books for the course.
    All persons should supply their own books.

Adverbs

The only real difficulty with adverbs is when they modify such verbs of sense as *see, taste, sound, feel,* and *smell.* Normally these verbs take adjectives, not adverbs.

    I don't feel good.

That's correct, even though it sounds as if it should be *well.* To feel well means to have tactile sense or coordination.

Prepositions

By now you have probably used some version of this saying a hundred times to prove a point, but at the risk of repetition, I offer it to anyone who hasn't heard it.

> "That is the sort of English up with which I will not put."
> —Winston Churchill (said to someone who did not believe in ending sentences with prepositions)

In fact, there is no good reason not to end sentences with prepositions, unless by so doing you are causing confusion or losing a point.

> That's a fine note to end on.

is no worse than

> That's a fine note on which to end.

—and certainly more to the point. But, and I love this example from Bernstein's *The Careful Writer* (New York: Atheneum, 1979), you would miss the point in this case:

> He felt it offered the best opportunity to do fundamental research in chemistry, which was what he had taken his Doctor of Philosophy degree in.

I think you can see the difference.

Speaking of prepositions, there's one more real trouble spot, and that's the word *like.* Now, *like* is correct as a preposition but not as a conjunction. As a conjunction ("Winston Tastes Good Like a Cigarette Should") it should be replaced by *as.*

As a preposition, *like* must take an object.

> She walks like a duck.

In this example, *like* precedes a noun (*duck*) that is not followed by a verb, so it is OK; it is a comparison. In fact, whenever *like* takes an object, whether it be a noun or a pronoun, it is correct as a preposition. As a conjunction, however, *like* causes all sorts of problems because the term that follows it is not an object but a subject.

> She walks like me.
> She walks like I do.
> She walks as I do.

The first example—subject, verb, preposition, object of the preposition (a pronoun in this case)—is OK. The second example is not OK, because *like* has been used as a conjunction (note that *I* is a subject, not an object). The third example, while stilted, is OK: The conjunction preceding *I* (which is in the subjective case because it is the subject of *do*) is not *like,* but *as,* which really is a conjunction. I think the best rule with *like* is to rewrite the sentence without it if you're not sure whether you're using it correctly. In informal writing, of course, such as in this book, *like* appears even as a conjunction; leave it if it would sound awkward if changed.

Objective Case

Here we have another situation where the cure is worse than the disease. Because the objective case often sounds so bad, people tend to use the subjective case (also known as the nominative case) as the object of a preposition. The best test of which case is correct is to remove one element of the object and see how the resulting sentence sounds.

> This air is not good for us nonsmokers.
> This air is not good for we nonsmokers.
> This air is not good for us. [sounds OK]
> This air is not good for we. [sounds ridiculous!]

Thus, the correct sentence is the first one.

> The note was sent from her to me.
> The note was sent from her to I.
> The note was sent to me. [sounds OK]
> The note was sent to I. [huh?]

Thus, the first choice is correct.

Be on the lookout for authors who believe that the subjective *I* sounds better than the objective *me.*

Dangling Modifiers

From way back when I was a kid, I still remember this example from my grammar book:

> Flying around the room, I saw two birds.

Every time I'm not sure whether I have a dangling modifier on my hands, I think of that example and can tell immediately. Each time you come across a prepositional, adverbial, or other phrase, ask yourself, What does this phrase refer to? If it's referring to the wrong subject, rewrite.

> After being carefully tested, we judged the car to be a
>   good buy.

Who or what was carefully tested? We want to say that the car was tested. The sentence as it is now written has *us* being tested. To be correct, we must rewrite.

> After being carefully tested, the car was judged to be a good buy.
> After we tested it carefully, we judged the car to be a good buy.

That's actually the hardest kind of dangling modifier to notice; it's so prevalent that we've come to believe it's correct. Remember: Ask yourself what your subject is.

The Subjunctive Mood

Fortunately we use the subjunctive mood very little in English. The only time it really shows up is in conditional phrases or wishful thinking.

> I wish I were rich.
> If I were rich, I would buy a yacht.
> If he were more sensitive to my feelings, he wouldn't treat me that way.

After a wish or a condition contrary to fact, use *were* rather than *was.* Yes, there are other instances where the subjunctive is used, but you will usually know just by sound whether they're OK. Here are some examples.

> The judge demanded that the prisoner be sent back to her cell.
> He asked that he be allowed to hold the baby again.
> We urged that the committee take immediate action.

Now let's see how well you've learned the material in this chapter. In the following sentences, make the appropriate changes, using the correct copyediting symbols. There may be more than one right answer for some of the exercises, so when you check your answers against mine at the end of the chapter, just be sure you can see how I got my answers and why I marked them as I did. Also, some of the exercises may be correct as written.

EXERCISES

1. It was not known how the boys got to the deep, ship channel estuary.

2. He was the subject of an intense, nationwide search.

3. ''The quake measured 5.3 on the ricter scale.''

4. After the parade, (which lasted until noon) they went to the coffee shop.

5. He asked where I was going?

6. The total is the same or greater than that in Exercise 27.

7. According to Dessa who ran yesterday's meeting, the outlook for the new fiscal year is grim.

8. Will you please send me a copy.

9. ''Please stay awhile!'' Marilou begged.

10. Lisa suggested that the team (1) work on defense, (2) learn to hit, and (3) a new manager.

11. I wish I was dead!

12. The hit song <u>Moon River</u> came from what movie?

13. Arresting the suspect, Pat was questioned by the policeman.

14. Near the beach lived a hermit.

15. Let's put some really tough items on the scavenger hunt list, for example, a 1931 calendar and a punctured tire.

16. My sister, Karen, is smarter than my sister, Catherine.

17. A complete search of the area turned up only one clue, a cigarette with lipstick.

18. ''How can you call my idea ''ridiculous?'' asked Eric.

19. Johnson's book which is on the bestseller list for the first time this week is about elves and leprechauns.

20. I made the trip, because I wanted to.

21. He waited....but no one came.

22. The trip will be very expensive, therefore I cannot go.

23. After reading Chapter 10, the plot became clearer.

24. Karl's parents live in Hagerstown, Maryland in a very large apartment.

25. They got the bad news after the game (which Fillmore High never should have lost): Dare would need an operation.

26. Either Clarissa was a genius or else insane.

27. Sharmon would have liked to have kept Rich on the staff.

28. Who's cat is that?

29. This meat tastes like garbage.

30. Its better to be safe than sorry.

31. Karryll wasn't wealthy; however she always seemed to have money to spend.

32. The argument is between Kathy and he.

33. A big problem around my neighborhood are all the stray dogs.

34. The meat tasted so badly she couldn't swallow it.

35. A number of people were at the party.

36. A majority of the class were in favor of the new textbook.

37. Each player should make his move carefully.

38. Read pages 43–61.

39. Rose's and Mark's car was in an accident.

40. How peaceful the house is tonight!

Answers

1. It was not known how the boys got to the deep, ship channel estuary.

2. He was the subject of an intense, nationwide search.

3. ''The quake measured 5.3 on the ricter [sic] scale.''

4. After the parade, (which lasted until noon), they went to the coffee shop.

5. He asked where I was going?.

6. The total is the same ^as^ or greater than that in Exercise 27.

7. According to Dessa, who ran yesterday's meeting, the outlook for the new fiscal year is grim.

8. Will you please send me a copy.

9. ''Please stay awhile!'' Marilou begged.

10. Lisa suggested that the team (1) work on defense, (2) learn to hit, and (3) ^hire^ a new manager.

11. I wish I ~~was~~ ^were^ dead!

12. The hit song ^"^Moon River^"^ came from what movie?

13. Arresting the suspect, Pat ~~was~~ questioned ~~by~~ the policeman.

14. Near the beach lived a hermit.

15. Let's put some really tough items on the scavenger hunt list; for example, a 1931 calendar and a punctured tire.

16. My sister, Karen, is smarter than my sister, Catherine.

17. A complete search of the area turned up only one clue: a cigarette with lipstick.

18. ''How can you call my idea ^''^ridiculous?^''^ asked Eric.

19. Johnson's book, which is on the bestseller list for the first time this week, is about elves and leprechauns.

20. I made the trip, because I wanted to.

21. He waited...but no one came.

22. The trip will be very expensive; therefore I cannot go.

23. After ~~reading~~ ^I read^ Chapter 10, the plot became clearer.

24. Karl's parents live in Hagerstown, Maryland, in a very large apartment.

25. They got the bad news after the game (which Fillmore High never should have lost): Dare would need an operation.

26. Either Clarissa was a genius or else~~,~~ ^she was^ insane.

27. Sharmon would have liked to ~~have kept~~ ^keep^ Rich on the staff.

28. Who⌢se cat is that?

29. This meat tastes like garbage.

30. It's better to be safe than sorry.

31. Karryll wasn't wealthy; however,^~^she always seemed to have money to spend.

32. The argument is between Kathy and ~~he~~ ^him^ ⊙

33. A big problem around my neighborhood ~~are~~ ^is^ all the stray dogs.

34. The meat tasted so bad~~ly~~ she couldn't swallow it.

35. A number of people were at the party.

36. A majority of the class ~~were~~ ^was^ in favor of the new textbook.

37. Each player should make his or her move carefully.

38. Read pages 43-61.

39. Rose⸓ and Mark's car was in an accident.

40. How peaceful the house is tonight⌣! ⊙

► KEY POINTS IN THIS CHAPTER

Period

- Use a period after a person's initials and in common abbreviations; do not use periods in Postal Service abbreviations.
- A period goes inside an end quotation mark.
- Do not use a period with an exclamation point or question mark.
- A period goes outside the end parenthesis unless what is enclosed within parentheses is an independent sentence.
- Use a period with ellipsis points if one would be used without them.

Comma

- If you would pause in speaking, use a comma before a conjunction in a compound sentence.
- Do not use a comma before a conjunction in a compound predicate.

- Use a comma after long introductory phrases.
- Use commas to set off transitional, parenthetical, and antithetical elements.
- Use commas to set off appositives.
- Use a comma to set off a nonrestrictive element.
- Ask the publisher whether you should use the series comma.
- Use a comma between coordinate adjectives if you could insert *and* between them.
- Use commas to set off dates and states used as appositives.
- A comma goes inside an end quotation mark.
- Do not use a comma with an exclamation point or question mark.
- A comma goes after a close parenthesis, not before an open one.

Semicolon

- Use a semicolon to join two independent clauses not connected by a conjunction.
- Do not separate an independent clause from a dependent one with a semicolon.
- Use semicolons to separate items in a series if one or more of the items contains a comma.
- A semicolon goes outside an end quotation mark.
- A semicolon goes after a close parenthesis, not before an open one.

Colon

- Use a colon to introduce a list, statement, quotation, or summary.
- Use a colon to relate one clause to a previous one.
- A colon goes outside an end quotation mark.
- A colon goes after a close parenthesis, not before an open one.

Question Mark and Exclamation Point

- A question mark or exclamation point is placed inside the end quotation mark, parenthesis, or bracket if it is part of the enclosed material; it is placed outside otherwise.
- Do not use a period, comma, colon, or semicolon immediately after a question mark or exclamation point.

Parentheses and Brackets

- Parentheses are used to set off material. Brackets are used to set off material within parentheses.
- Punctuation goes after the close parenthesis or bracket, not before the open one.

Quotation Marks

- Do not use quotation marks if the extract is already displayed typographically.
- Use quotation marks for titles of songs, poems, short stories, and TV shows; for nicknames; to indicate irony; and (if preferable to italics) to set off words used as words.
- Do not use quotation marks with the term *so-called.*
- Commas and periods go inside the end quotation mark; semicolons and colons go outside. The question mark, exclamation point, and dash go inside if they are part of the quotation.

Dash

- An en dash is used in compound adjectives or to indicate range.
- Do not use an en dash in place of *from . . . to* or *between . . . and.*
- An em dash is used to set off parenthetical material or faltering speech.
- Do not use a comma or period with an em dash.

Hyphen and Slash

- Use the hyphen as part of the spelling of a word.
- Use the hyphen to break a word into syllables at the end of a line.
- Use the hyphen in compound terms.
- Use the slash, not the hyphen, to indicate options.

Ellipsis Points

- Use ellipsis points to indicate uncertainty, missing material, and an incomplete thought.

Apostrophe

- The apostrophe is used to form certain plurals, to form contractions, and to indicate possession.
- Do not confuse *it's* with *its, who's* with *whose,* or *you're* with *your.*
- For double subjects, the possession goes on the second noun only.

Sentence Structure

- Use a semicolon, not a comma, before a connecting word if both clauses are independent.
- Use sentence fragments in informal writing only.
- Make all parts of the sentence parallel; be sure that connecting words form complete phrases.

Verb Forms

- Use the past perfect tense only to show an action completed before another past action.
- Use the subjunctive mood to indicate condition contrary to fact.

Prepositions and Objective Case

- Do not use *like* as a conjunction, only as an object of a preposition.
- Do not use a subjective pronoun as the object of a preposition.

Verb Number and Agreement

- The verb number agrees with the subject in inverted sentences beginning with *there* or *here*.
- A linking verb agrees with its subject, not the predicate.
- Choose a singular or plural verb to accompany a collective noun, depending on sense.
- Use a singular verb with *either...or* or *neither...nor*.

Split Verb Phrases and Dangling Modifiers

- If the sentence sounds better when you split an infinitive or a verb phrase, do it.
- To avoid having a dangling modifier, be sure you know what the subject of the prepositional, adverbial, or other phrase is.

Pronoun Agreement

- Use a plural pronoun to replace two nouns joined by *and*.
- Use a singular pronoun to replace two nouns joined by *or, nor, together with, in addition to,* and the like.
- If both male and female are involved, recast the sentence.
- Do not use *they* or *their* to replace a singular noun.
- When replacing a singular noun with a pronoun, do not use *he* to include male and female.

Spelling, Capitalization, and Hyphenation

Chapter 3 stressed the importance of consistency in copyediting. This chapter will examine the importance of consistency in the treatment of individual words.

The rules given in this chapter have been drawn from several style manuals. The problem with style manuals is that they give a lot of rules and then start listing exceptions. One style manual will tell you always to do something, and another will tell you never to do it. So the rules I give you in this book are simple and fairly consistent. Don't worry if the publishers you work for have preferences different from mine. But in the absence of other instructions, you'll find my suggestions simple to follow. They can aid you in your work and are a handy reference. Your main concern, of course, should always be consistency.

SPELLING

In its broadest sense, spelling includes capitalization and hyphenation. After all, to describe the way a word is spelled is to take into account all characters from the first to the last, and that includes capital letters and hyphens. For simplicity, however, I've chosen to treat each of the three areas—spelling, capitalization, and hyphenation—individually.

I'm not going to give you a bunch of spelling rules. As you've probably already realized, in English there are a lot of exceptions anyway. The only sure way to spell properly is to keep a dictionary close at hand while you work. Remember Chapter 3? Look it up!

Of course, some words are easier to spell than others. Those words become familiar to you and no longer pose a problem. (To a 7-year-old, however, even those words may be difficult.) If you are a doctor, you have in your daily vocabulary many words that the rest of us never use; you probably know how to spell them too. The words that we seldom write are those that we don't remember how to spell, even though they may be found frequently in the materials we read. Because, when we read it, we know what the word is supposed to be, we don't bother to see if all the letters are there and in their proper order. Occasionally we find a word that doesn't look quite right, so we look it up. Sometimes it is correct and sometimes it isn't. But we seldom bother to remember the correct spelling.

There's also a problem with words we pronounce incorrectly to begin with. I told you earlier about my mispronunciation of the Strybing Arboretum, and I spelled it the way I pronounced it. I always assumed that someone who ran a restaurant was a *restauranteur.* But a friend pointed out that the correct word is *restaurateur.* We're used to hearing and reading things one way, and we assume that that way is correct.

Many books publish lists of commonly misspelled words; this one is no exception. I can't tell you if these are the *most* common spelling problems, but I can tell you that I always have difficulty with them, and so do the copyeditors whose work I see. I verified them in *Webster's Third,* using the first choice. As I said in Chapter 1, the first choice these days is just the more common one (or even the one that comes first alphabetically), but in previous editions of *Webster's* it was the outright preference. Consequently, most publishers still prefer it. In any case, the main thing is consistency. Your dictionary may use different spellings for some words, but if you use the same dictionary always, you will start to see a pattern. Try to commit these words to memory. If you're not good at that, at least *remember what words are on this list.* Then, when you do come across one in a manuscript, you'll know that you have to look it up to see how it's spelled. The words with asterisks are the ones that can be spelled only one way; the others are preferred variants.

accommodate*	all right*	benefited
acknowledgment	amoeba	bouillon*
adviser	analogue	canceled
afterward	bandanna	catalog

consensus*   labeled   privilege*
cookie   liaison*   programming
descendant   lightning*   reconnaissance
despicable*   liquefy   resistance*
diagramming   millennium*   restaurateur
disk   misspell*   salable
ecstasy   mustache   separate*
embarrass*   naphtha*   siege*
fluorescent*   newsstand*   skeptic
foresee*   nickel   subpoena
fulfillment   numskull   sulfur
gauge   occurrence*   supersede
glamour   parallel*   theater
guerilla   pastime*   totaled
harass*   percent   toward
idiosyncrasy   picnicking*   weird*
indispensable*   pipette   whiskey
inoculate*   precede*   woolly
judgment

Spelling, in the sense dealt with so far, does not affect meaning. But what about other words that, when misspelled, can cause a great deal of trouble? What about homonyms? These are pairs of words that sound the same or nearly the same although they are spelled differently. The following list gives the spelling and meaning of some common homonyms.

accept (take)   baloney (nonsense)
except (omit)   bologna (lunch meat)

advice (noun)   breath (noun)
advise (verb)   breathe (verb)

affect (influence)   calendar (list of dates)
effect (result)   calender (make paper smooth)

all ready (prepared)   capital (city)
already (previous)   capitol (building)

altogether (completely)   cloth (noun)
all together (in total)   clothe (verb)

ascent (rise)   complement (complete)
assent (consent)   compliment (praise)

desperate (full of despair)   perquisite (privilege)
disparate (distinct)   prerequisite (precondition)

discreet (prudent)   principal (chief)
discrete (separate)   principle (rule)

ensure (make sure)   stationary (fixed)
insure (underwrite)   stationery (paper)

Some words are spelled one way as one part of speech and another way as another part of speech or in a different tense.

glamorous   phosphorus (n)
glamour   phosphorous (a)

mucus (n)   transferable
mucous (a)   transferred

And what about foreign terms? Always look such words up in a reliable dictionary, and use appropriate accents (a good rule is to use the accented version of a word if *Webster's* gives it, even if it's the second choice). Some common examples of accent-laden foreign words are

naïve
papier-mâché
résumé

Also check whether the publisher wants ligatures (œ), and accents on capital letters (RENÉE). And above all, spell foreign words and names consistently (*ü* or *ue*?).

What do all these lists point out? That you must look up every word you can't absolutely swear you know how to spell. Look at the first list again for a minute. Why does *programming* have two *m*'s but *diagraming* only one? What about *numskull*? It comes from *numb*, right? Well, it does, but it doesn't keep that final *b*. And if *harass* has one *r*, surely *embarrass* must. But it doesn't!

This whole section only goes to prove how difficult English spelling is and how careful you must be. Yes, as I said in Chapter 1, there are a few rules that help, but they're not the answer. The only suggestion I'm going to give you is that unless the word is an accented foreign one, you use the first choice in *Webster's*. The first choice is normally the difference between American and British spelling. Thus in America we write *traveled*, while in England they write *travelled*. That's a subrule, but don't take it too literally. In America we normally have a single consonant before the suffixes *-ed* and *-ing*, as in *labeling* and *canceled*. But as usual, as you saw with *programming,* the rule doesn't always hold (in England, by the way, it's spelled *programing*!).

Just remember: Look it up!

EXERCISES

Correct the misspellings and variants in the following sentences, using the first variant in *Webster's Third*. (Some sentences are correct as written.) Use correct copyediting marks. If you use the dictionary instead of your own recollections, you won't make any errors.

1. Margaret was transferred by her company.

2. Shelley was very knowledgable about the legal precedent.

3. When arrested, Scott offerred no resistence.

4. The preceding announcment was paid for by Citizens for Garner.

5. His pronounciation left alot to be desired.

6. Her absenses were not unnoticed by the principal.

7. Claudia's licence was suspended after she practised parking--on the police cheif's front lawn.

8. Isn't it wierd how irridescent jewelery sparkles?

9. I often go to the zoo to feed bananas to the guerillas.

10. Ruth's small son is very mischievous.

11. One lateness is permissable.

12. Her personnel opinion of him wasn't so high.

13. You must have some definite plan.

14. Lois wrote the date on the calender.

15. Willie had travelled many miles with that despiccable human being.

16. The picture sat nobly on the mantelpiece.

17. Rain forced cancellation of the concert.

18. It was an Independence Day celebration to be remembered.

19. He was publically ridiculed.

20. Charlie had to much of a committment to quit without warning.

Answers

1. Margaret was transferred by her company.

2. Shelley was very knowledgable about the legal precedent.

3. When arrested, Scott offerred no resistance.

4. The preceding announcment was paid for by Citizens for Garner.

5. His pronounciation left alot to be desired.

6. Her absenaes were not unnoticed by the principal.

7. Claudia's license was suspended after she practised parking--on the police cheif's front lawn.

8. Isn't it wierd how irridescent jewelery sparkles?

9. I often go to the zoo to feed bananas to the guerillas.

10. Ruth's small son is very mischievous.

11. One lateness is permissable.

12. Her personnel opinion of him wasn't so high.

13. You must have some definite plan.

14. Lois wrote the date on the calender.

15. Willie had travelled many miles with that despicable human being.

16. The picture sat nobly on the mantelpiece.

17. Rain forced cancellation of the concert.

18. It was an Independence Day celebration to be remembered.

19. He was publically ridiculed.

20. Charlie had to much of a committment to quit without warning.

CAPITALIZATION

When should you capitalize the first letter in a word? We all know that sentences begin with a capital letter. What else does? This section looks at three broad areas of capitalization: word groups, words within titles and headings, and special nouns.

Word Groups

1. Use a capital letter after a colon only if what follows the colon is a complete sentence.

   Tony's advice was simple: Be yourself.
   Kim brought some wonderful foods to the picnic: cheese, champagne, fruit, canapés, even dessert!

Note: Some writers prefer to capitalize after a colon only if the colon is followed by two or more sentences, or to capitalize a complete sentence after a colon only if it's a major thought.

2. Use a capital letter to begin a complete sentence within a sentence, even if no colon precedes.

   What he wanted to know was, What was going to happen?

3. Capitalize a single word used as a complete sentence within a sentence.

   His answer was Yes.

   or

   His answer was, Yes.

Note: Some writers prefer to lowercase single-word sentences.

4. Capitalize the first letter of sentence fragments within dialogue.

   "Rowing must be fun," I commented to Sheryl. Then I added, "If you like that sort of thing."

5. Lowercase the first letter of words within a quotation or dialogue that acts as the predicate.

   We were taught to "sow our wild oats."
   "Rowing must be fun," I commented to Sheryl, "if you like that sort of thing."

6. Capitalize or lowercase (consistently!) parallel sentence fragments used as questions.

   Will this system work for mechanics? for teachers? for doctors?

or

> Will this system work for mechanics? For teachers? For doctors?

7. Normally lowercase complete sentences within parentheses in the middle of a sentence.

> Terry was afraid (he was always afraid of something) to leave before Trudy got home.

8. In displayed lists, normally lowercase incomplete sentences.

> Define the following:
> 1. iambic pentameter
> 2. sonnet
> 3. epic

Titles and Headings

1. Capitalize all nouns, verbs, adjectives, adverbs, and pronouns, regardless of length.
2. Capitalize a preposition if it contains five or more letters, if it is the first or last word of the title or heading, or if it is part of the verb.

> Going Through Changes
> Stepping Out
> Out of Nowhere
> Adding Up Our Losses

3. Capitalize articles and conjunctions if they contain five or more letters, if they are the first or last word of the title or heading, or if they follow a mark of punctuation.

> A Clear Picture
> And Fiddling While Rome Burns?
> Dylan Thomas, The Voice of the Turtle
> Richard Nixon: A Leader in Our Time

4. Lowercase the infinitive *to.*

> How to Win Friends and Influence People

5. Capitalize the following special words: *As, If, Once, Than, That, Till.*

> Older Than Noah
> She Says That It's Over

6. Capitalize all elements of a hyphenated compound.

> Twentieth-Century Playwrights
> Consciousness-Raising Sessions
> A Quasi-Stellar Radio Source
> Bigger-Than-Life Murals
> Pint-Sized Problem
> Made-Up Names
> English-Speaking Nations

Note: Often you see the second word of a compound lowercased, but I always capitalize it just because it looks better.

7. Capitalize the second number in hyphenated numbers except in street addresses.

> Twenty-First Birthday
> Forty-second Street

8. Lowercase or capitalize parts of foreign names according to usage. Newspaper style guides or the GPO Manual are good sources to check.

> Von Braun's Legacy
> Werner von Braun's Legacy
> Samuel Du Pont and His Family
> E. I. du Pont de Nemours & Co.: Still Going Strong

9. When in doubt about capitalizing a word in a title or heading, write it both ways and decide which looks better!

Special Nouns

There are so many individual cases of capitalization that I cannot cover them all here, nor is there a need to: *Chicago Manual* has an excellent chapter, "Names and Terms," that goes into capitalization in great detail. The GPO Manual also is very helpful here. In this section I will simply combine many of the common rules and give some general examples; it is up to you to check on individual situations.

1. Capitalize professional titles when they precede names, but not when they follow them or are used alone.

> Governor Connally
> Pierre Trudeau, prime minister of Canada
> the pope

Note: The news magazines capitalize *President* and *Pope;* you should check the house style of any publisher you work for.

2. Capitalize terms denoting parts of the world but not terms used merely to give direction.

   the Mideast
   eastern Rhode Island

3. Capitalize common geographical nouns or adjectives when they appear as part of the proper name but not when they stand alone.

   Sahara Desert
   the desert

4. Capitalize generic terms used as part of a name except when they appear in the plural to describe two or more names.

   the White Mountains
   the junction of the Ohio, Allegheny, and Monongahela rivers

5. Capitalize words derived from proper names unless those words have taken on a special meaning.

   Roman
   roman numerals
   french fries

6. Capitalize trade names. Be very careful here; many of the words we use daily are in fact trade names. Always check the dictionary; if the word is capitalized there, you must capitalize it also. In doubtful cases, such as *ping pong*, always check two or three current dictionaries or style guides.

   Xerox (photocopier)
   Valium (tranquilizer)
   Mah-Jongg (a Chinese game)
   Scotch tape (cellophane tape)

7. Capitalize full names of religious groups, political organizations, and other organized groups, but lowercase shortened citations or adjectives derived from these names.

   the State Department; the department
   a Presbyterian
   the Republicans
   the State of New York; New York State; the state
   the U.S. Army; the army
   Parliament; parliamentary

8. Capitalize names of acts, historic events, battles, doctrines, and so forth, but lowercase common nouns referring to these terms.

   the Renaissance; the Middle Ages saw a renaissance
   the Taft-Hartley Act; the act made it illegal
   the Civil War; war is hell

9. Capitalize references to specific chapters, figures, tables, exercises, and the like, in a book, but lowercase words referring to a general part of the book.

   in Chapter 3; in this chapter
   read Appendix A; in the appendix

It is important to realize that the rules I've given here are extremely general and provide merely a hint about how to decide when a capital letter is needed. As you become familiar with house styles and style guides, you will learn new rules and perhaps even some that clash with mine. It will be your decision—with your employer's help!—which rules to follow.

EXERCISES

Capitalize the following sentences or phrases using the rules given in this section or following a style guide. Use the correct mark for capital and lowercase letters. (Some sentences are correct as written.)

1. the president of the United States
2. Pope John Paul II
3. the mid-atlantic states
4. the Catskill and Smoky Mountains
5. Her reply was simply yes.
6. Look at Table 5.
7. The boat was made of fiberglass.
8. Was it Poor Richard who said, ''early to bed''?
9. Read A View From The Bridge.
10. We had Brussels sprouts for dinner.
11. Bud asked, ''How can you be so stupid?''
12. His son wanted to be a marine too.
13. Mario Cuomo, Governor of New York State

14. Polonius had some advice: neither a borrower nor a lender be.

15. Such creatures disappeared during the ice age.

16. an army sergeant

17. I'll take the case all the way to the Court of Appeals.

18. the Jarvis initiative, or proposition 13

19. Presley: the Man and the Myth

20. Read the Article ''Willie Nelson: the Red-headed Stranger.''

Answers

1. the president of the United States

2. Pope John Paul II

3. the mid-atlantic states

4. the Catskill and Smoky Mountains

5. Her reply was simply yes. [also OK as originally written]

6. Look at Table 5.

7. The boat was made of fiberglass.

8. Was it Poor Richard who said, ''early to bed''?

9. Read A View From The Bridge.

10. We had Brussels sprouts for dinner.

11. Bud asked, ''How can you be so stupid?''

12. His son wanted to be a marine too.

13. Mario Cuomo, governor of New York State

14. Polonius had some advice: neither a borrower nor a lender be.

15. Such creatures disappeared during the ice age.

16. an army sergeant

17. I'll take the case all the way to the Court of Appeals.

18. the Jarvis initiative, or proposition 13

19. Presley: the Man and the Myth

20. Read the Article ''Willie Nelson: the Red-headed

    Stranger.''

HYPHENATION

Compounds are those words that consist of combinations of words, or of words with prefixes or suffixes. Compounds can be almost any part of speech; they aren't restricted to nouns and adjectives, although that is how we see them most often. Compounds may be one word (*bookstore*), two words (*civil rights*), or a hyphenated word (*go-between*).

In this chapter, please note, when I speak of hyphenating, I am referring to how a word is spelled. The hyphen has another use, of course, but that is in syllabication, which is something for proof-readers, not copyeditors, to be concerned with. We will look briefly at syllabication in Chapter 12.

Many compounds do appear in the dictionary, but it is time consuming to look them up. And dictionaries are not always consistent! The GPO Manual (see the bibliography) has an excellent section on compounding, and of course the rules in this book can also help you to make choices. Common sense, too, can sometimes help. But common sense, of course, is based on some knowledge you have stored away somewhere. That's what I'm attempting to do in this section: give you that knowledge so that common sense can take over later.

One-Word Compounds

First we'll look at one-word compounds. These might be nouns, adjectives, verbs, or just about anything else. Their common characteristic is that they are made up of two words or of a complete word plus a prefix or suffix. Remember that the newly formed compound need not be a noun either.

Historically, compound words begin as phrases of two or more words; then they get hyphenated; finally, they may be closed up to make one word. If you compare American words to British words, you can see this tendency: The British hyphenate many of the words we treat singly, such as *arm-chair*. As you read British materials, watch for this "unusual" (to Americans) hyphenation, and picture the same word as it would occur in American literature. Would it be one word? Probably.

Do not try to close up to a single word all the hyphenated compounds you don't find in the dictionary or style manual. Many terms are peculiar to a field, and usage in the field dictates their spelling. Follow copy or query the author or publisher if you can't find such words in print.

Now let's see the rules for one-word compounds. As usual, I've compiled this list from several sources (remember, the GPO Manual is most helpful here) and have tried to keep the rules simple and consistent.

1. Two nouns that form a compound noun are treated as one word when the first noun in the new term consists of one syllable and when one of the nouns loses its accent.

   fireplace
   bedpost
   salesperson

2. A verb and adverb used to form a compound noun are treated as one word unless confusion might result.

   layoff
   makeup
   slowdown
   run-in (what's a runin?)

3. Nouns beginning and ending with certain words are almost always treated as one word. The complete list is too long to provide here, but here are a few examples.

Nouns Beginning with Book-	*Nouns Beginning with* Wood-
bookstore	woodwork
bookseller	woodcarver
bookcase	woodbin

Nouns Ending with -Berry	*Nouns Ending with* -Man
elderberry	fireman
strawberry	salesman
blueberry	policeman

4. Compounds that are used as personal pronouns are one word.

   herself
   oneself

5. Words such as *everywhere, anything,* and *somebody* (in any combination) are treated as one word unless they apply to a particular person or thing.

   anyone; any one thing
   someone; some one thing

6. Compounds containing a prefix or suffix are normally treated as one word. (For the chief exceptions, see rule 7 of Hyphenated Compounds.)

> antislavery
> predawn
> fishlike
> tenfold
> reestablish

Two-Word Compounds

Open compounds (two-word compounds) are combinations of words considered as single concepts. They are usually nouns, but they may also be used as adjectives or verbs. Normally such two-word adjectives remain open. Neither element in an open compound loses its accent during compounding.

> civil rights; civil rights leader
> blood pressure
> high school; high school student
> real estate; real estate deal
> common denominator

Certain two-word compounds are hyphenated when used as adjectives, and some are even made into one word. The GPO Manual is the best source of information about such words.

> common law; common-law marriage
> salt water; saltwater taffy

Hyphenated Compounds

All compounds that aren't treated as one or two words are hyphenated. In this section we look at when and when not to hyphenate.

Hyphenated compounds can be nouns, adjectives, or even verbs. Adjectives are the most common, however, so let's start there.

All the rules that follow apply to *preceding* adjectives. Predicate adjectives are not normally hyphenated, except as noted.

1. Hyphenate the combination of an adjective or noun plus a past participle.

> red-haired girl
> long-legged beauty
> water-soaked ground

2. Hyphenate the combination of a noun plus a present participle.

decision-making body
back-breaking chore
labor-inducing drug

Not all words ending in *-ing* are present participles. *Gerunds* are *-ing* words used as nouns; usually a compound consisting of a noun plus a gerund is left open.

book publishing company
word processing system

3. Hyphenate the combination of a number plus a unit of measure used as an adjective.

1,500-meter race
4-minute mile
18-year-old son
50-cent tip

Do not hyphenate terms used with *percent* or a dollar sign.

15 percent tip
$100 million deficit

4. Generally hyphenate compounds beginning with the following words, whether they are preceding or predicate adjectives: *quasi-, cross-, self-, all-,* and *half-.*

quasi-judicial decision
self-righteous snob; he certainly was self-righteous
all-encompassing study; the study was all-encompassing
half-timbered houses; the houses were half-timbered

5. Hyphenate compounds ending with *-odd.*

Twenty-odd people attended.

6. Treat as one word adjectives ending with *-like* unless the root is a proper name or ends in *-ll.*

starlike
berrylike
businesslike
Hitler-like
ball-like

7. Do not hyphenate compounds beginning with prefixes unless the root is a proper name, a number, or a compound word, or if an incorrect homonym results.

reaffirm
nonessential
posttest
subordinate
un-American
pre-1945
re-cover [to cover again]
non–high-energy [note use of en dash]

8. Hyphenate the combination of an adjective and a noun.

   high-energy wave
   red-letter day

9. Do not hyphenate the combination of two nouns used as an adjective.

   cathode ray tube

10. Do not hyphenate names of chemicals used as adjectives unless chemists hyphenate them as nouns. Do not hyphenate foreign phrases for any reason unless they contain hyphens in direct quotation.

    carbon monoxide poisoning
    the a priori ruling

11. Do not hyphenate the combination of an adverb ending in *-ly* plus an adjective.

    readily available drug
    badly written essay

12. Hyphenate compounds beginning with *well-, ill-, better-, best-*, and the like unless they are already modified or are used as predicate adjectives.

    well-known writer
    very well known writer
    she is well known

13. Hyphenate compound adjectives all of whose members are colors.

    blue-green water
    reddish-orange leaves*

---

*Some style manuals suggest leaving as open compounds those terms whose members are not equal.

but

shocking pink dress
pale blue sky

14. Hyphenate spelled-out fractions.

three-fourths majority

15. Hyphenate permanent compounds (those words so standard as
to be found in dictionaries) used predicately.

The house was old-fashioned.

Hyphenated nouns are less frequent than hyphenated adjectives.

1. Hyphenate two nouns of equal value used as a compound noun.

dinner-dance
soldier-statesman

2. Hyphenate relationships compounded with *great-* and *-in-law.*

great-grandfather
sister-in-law

3. Hyphenate all compound nouns beginning with *self-.*

self-consciousness
self-reliance

4. Hyphenate words ending in *-elect* unless the root is a compound.

mayor-elect
his daughter-in-law elect

5. Hyphenate special phrases according to the dictionary or common sense.

Johnny-come-lately
go-between
cat's-eye

Hyphenated verbs have come into use mostly as slang or in the
most casual writing. Hyphenate a verb that was originally a noun
or is similarly made up.

to road-test a car
to make-ready a printing press
to fine-tune the process

Remember that hyphens are not whimsical additions to words;
they are used to aid the reader in understanding. If by following one

of the rules given here confusion is introduced, then rewrite the sentence. And be sure you can differentiate between a hyphenated adjective and a compound noun.

> *compound noun:* a slow moving van [a moving van traveling slowly]
> *hyphenated adjective:* a slow-moving van [a van—any van—moving slowly]

Hyphens to Avoid Confusion

A few words are hyphenated merely because without the hyphen the reader will have to pause to figure out what the word is.

> an un-iced drink [uniced]
> an un-ionized compound [unionized]
> a pre-image [preimage]

EXERCISES

Using the rules of this section or the dictionary where appropriate, hyphenate the following exercises. Remember to use proper copy-editing symbols. (Some sentences are correct as written.)

1. Martin was considered something of an elder statesman.

2. A fire was going in the wood burning stove.

3. The freckle faced boy sat in the rocking chair.

4. A slow-down was inevitable.

5. Her blood sugar level was low.

6. He practiced self restraint.

7. Do the Pre Test on page 1.

8. Any thing you can do to help will be appreciated.

9. The scene looked like a picture post card.

10. He was a hard riding cowboy.

11. The new figures show an 11-percent increase.

12. The ex GI was honored.

13. Her great great grandmother is still alive.

14. Ask the secretary-treasurer for the books.

15. She likes to catch fire flies in a jar.

16. She was the laughing-stock of the town.

17. He likes being the bread winner.

18. She had a reputation for being a fast talking person.

19. He tried to cross ventilate the room.

20. Rita was a highly-gifted pianist.

Answers

1. Martin was considered something of an elder statesman.

2. A fire was going in the wood-burning stove.

3. The freckle-faced boy sat in the rocking chair.

4. A slow⌒down was inevitable.

5. Her blood sugar level was low.

6. He practiced self-restraint.

7. Do the Pre-Test on page 1.

8. Any⌒thing you can do to help will be appreciated.

9. The scene looked like a picture post⌒card.

10. He was a hard-riding cowboy.

11. The new figures show an 11-percent increase.

12. The ex-GI was honored.

13. Her great-great-grandmother is still alive.

14. Ask the secretary-treasurer for the books.

15. She likes to catch fire⌒flies in a jar.

16. She was the laughing⌒stock of the town.

17. He likes being the bread⌒winner.

18. She had a reputation for being a fast-talking person.

19. He tried to cross-ventilate the room.

20. Rita was a highly-gifted pianist.

► KEY POINTS IN THIS CHAPTER

Spelling

- Look up every word you can't swear you know how to spell.
- Use the first choice in *Webster's Third*.
- If *Webster's* gives an accented version of a word, even if it's not the first choice, use it.

Capitalization

- Capitalize a complete sentence after a colon, or a complete sentence within a sentence.
- Lowercase the first word of a sentence fragment that acts as a predicate within dialogue, but capitalize otherwise.
- Lowercase incomplete sentences in displayed lists.
- Lowercase complete sentences within parentheses in the middle of a sentence.
- Within titles and headings, capitalize all nouns, verbs, adjectives, adverbs, and pronouns; articles and conjunctions that start or end the title, follow a mark of punctuation, or contain five or more letters; and prepositions that start or end the title, follow a mark of punctuation, are part of the verb, or contain five or more letters. Capitalize all elements of a hyphenated compound and the second number in hyphenated numbers (except in street addresses). Lowercase the infinitive *to*.
- Capitalize or lowercase proper nouns according to usage.
- Capitalize titles of respect when connected to a name, not when used alone.
- Capitalize terms denoting parts of the world but not terms used to give direction.
- Capitalize common nouns and adjectives when used as part of the proper name but not when they stand alone.
- Capitalize generic terms used as part of a name except when they appear in the plural to describe two or more names.
- Lowercase words derived from proper names if those words have taken on a special meaning.
- Capitalize trade names.
- Capitalize full names of organizations, but lowercase shortened citations or adjectives derived from those names.
- Capitalize names of acts, events, battles, doctrines, and the like, but lowercase nouns referring to those terms.
- Capitalize references to specific chapters, figures, and so forth, in a book, but lowercase words referring to a general part of the book.

Hyphenation

- Look up simple compound words in the dictionary.
- Two-word compounds, which are combinations of words considered as single concepts, are normally open.
- Hyphenate the combination of an adjective or a noun plus a past participle, as well as the combination of a noun plus a present participle. Generally do not hyphenate the combination of a noun plus a gerund.
- Hyphenate the combination of a number plus a unit of measure used as an adjective; do not hyphenate when the combination is not an adjective.
- Do not hyphenate compounds beginning with a prefix unless the root is a proper name, a number, or a compound word, or unless a false homonym results.
- Do not hyphenate compounds ending with the suffix *-like* unless the root is a proper name or ends in *-ll.*
- Hyphenate compounds beginning with *quasi-, cross-, self-, all-,* and *half-,* as well as compounds ending with *-odd.*
- Hyphenate compounds beginning with *well-* and the like when they precede the noun and are not already modified.
- Hyphenate the combination of an adjective and a noun except when considered as a single concept.
- Do not hyphenate the combination of two nouns as an adjective, nor names of chemicals used as adjectives.
- Do not hyphenate the combination of an adverb ending in *-ly* plus an adjective.
- Hyphenate compound adjectives all of whose members are colors.
- Hyphenate spelled-out fractions.
- Hyphenate permanent compounds used predicately and other permanent compounds according to the dictionary.
- Hyphenate two nouns of equal value used as a compound noun.
- Hyphenate relationships compounded with *great-* and *-in-law.*
- Hyphenate words compounded with *-elect* unless the root is a compound.
- Above all, if by following a rule for compounding you introduce confusion, rewrite.

C H A P T E R **6**

Style and Word Usage

What is style? Style consists of more than just sentence structure and word usage. Whether or not you use a comma in a compound sentence indicates part of your style. Whether you spell out numbers or use digits instead is a matter of style. Even which words you choose to capitalize is part of style. Some elements of style are the copyeditor's concern; we've already looked at spelling, capitalization, and hyphenation, and in the next two chapters we'll look at other areas. In this chapter, however, we're going to concentrate on the two main ingredients of style: sentence structure (syntax) and word usage, including stereotyping.

Before you get carried away, remember that the author is boss; always keep the author's ego in mind, and be sensitive to the author's own style. Don't impose your own style on the author's work, but do feel free to make suggestions that will enhance the work, correct the errors, and make the material consistent and readable.

Fiction authors are especially likely to resist changes in their style; after all, to them style is as important as story. Established authors probably get away with practices that others don't. If you find grammatical errors in descriptive text, ask the editor if you should feel free to correct them; don't do it otherwise.

SENTENCE STRUCTURE

Certainly no element more completely defines an author's style than the way she or he strings words together. Some authors use long words and sentences; others write series of short declarative sentences. Some authors have a formal style, others a chatty one. What kind of style does Hemingway have? What about Faulkner? What style do you use when you write?

The "rules" given in this section should not be considered carved in stone. Forms that are technically correct may often sound pedantic; a correct style is one that suits the subject. Often a conversational tone is desirable. Maybe your author didn't read your favorite style manual before writing the manuscript you're working on. That's an author's prerogative, and you're not in a position to change everything in the manuscript to conform to a particular set of style rules. But where a sentence could be made clearer or more potent, feel free to suggest changes. And if you add your own material, for whatever reason, at least keep the following points in mind to guide you.

1. *Use the active voice.*

In the active voice, the subject is acting; in the passive voice, the subject is being acted upon. Here is an example of the active voice.

Joan threw the ball.

Now here is that sentence in the passive voice.

The ball was thrown by Joan.

Conceivably there are conditions under which the passive version of the sentence would more exactly describe the author's intention. If I wanted to make the point that the ball was thrown by Joan and not by José, I might want the passive voice. But certainly you can see how much crisper the sentence is when written in active voice.

Be sure, then, to keep in mind your subject and the point of the sentence. If you have a paragraph describing the ball in great detail and all of a sudden you change your subject to Joan, you may confuse the reader. I can't tell you always to change from passive to active— or never to. I can only caution you to listen to the sentence and decide which is more appropriate under the circumstances.

Changing voices presents a particular problem when we work with scholarly books. Look at the following sentence.

It was found that oxygen burns.

How would you change that sentence to active? Well, you could say, "Scientists found that oxygen burns," but is that true? An author may very well argue that point. Maybe "chemists" or "students" or "Joseph Priestley" is what the author had in mind. Or what about this sentence?

> It was learned that President Roosevelt had polio.

Learned by whom? President Roosevelt? Mrs. Roosevelt? Congress? The country? All of them, to be sure, but which one in this sentence? Yes, maybe you'd be able to tell from the context:

> The country became worried: It was learned that President Roosevelt had polio.

But you are not the author and can't put ideas into the author's head, so you should not attempt to rewrite sentences like that. If you have a real problem with comprehension, by all means query the author: "When *who* learned?" If, however, the sentence seems clear and direct in the passive voice and you fear weakening it by changing it, then leave it alone. Eventually you will get a feel for when the passive voice is actually more appropriate; the sentence will simply sound better.

2. *Use positive statements.*

Can you see the difference between these two commands?

> Don't go outside.
> Stay in the house.

The second one doesn't leave much room for doubt, does it? If I were 6 years old and heard the first command, I think I'd do my best to find a way to skirt the issue.

Positive language is more definite than negative language, and consequently it is clearer. Here is an example of a negative idea.

> Adam wasn't fond of opera. He found it boring and he didn't like not being able to understand the language.

Now look at the sentence cast in positive language.

> Adam hated opera; it was boring and incomprehensible.

Note that by "positive" I mean that the language is more concrete and words such as *didn't* and *not* are gone; Adam's feelings about opera haven't changed!

I'm sure you know by now that you can't go through a manuscript looking for negative sentences to change. But you can look for negative sentences that lack punch and suggest ways to recast them.

3. *Use concrete language.*

Fiction writers rarely use abstract language; they know that their readers can visualize scenes more easily if specific and concrete words and ideas are used. A good fiction writer does not write, "Jason was a tall man." Instead she or he writes, "At nearly seven feet tall, Jason towered over his friends."

Then why is it that nonfiction writers often use vague language that makes the reader go back and try to figure out what's happening? Small-town newspapers have a habit of letting weak stories go by; the reporter didn't want to risk offense, so she or he tried to avoid getting to the point. Watch for sentences such as the following one, and offer suggestions for changing them.

> Weak species usually seem to have a relatively shorter life expectancy rate than stronger species.

Sure, you know what the sentence says, and there's really nothing wrong with it, except that it has a lot of "out" words—words that give the author an out—that don't tie the author down to being specific. Wouldn't it have been more effective to say something along these lines?

> Only the strong survive.

Clearly, this example makes a nice rhetorical point; in some journals it would be overkill. But doesn't the original sentence remind you of when you had to write a 200-word paper and you wanted to stick in as many "out" words as possible? A compromise sentence might be

> Strong species usually live longer than weak ones.

Watch for vague sentences; authors who think they're sounding erudite by not getting to the point are merely being annoying.

4. *Delete unnecessary words.*

Many of the expressions we use frequently contain words we could do without. Not only do extra words cloud the issue, they also take up space, and rarely can a publisher afford the extra columns or pages needed to accommodate those needless words.

Here are some common examples of phrases containing needless words.

Original Version	*Revised Version*
the real reason is that	because
this is a story that	this story
in spite of the fact that	although

because of the fact that	because
no doubt but that	no doubt
in order to	to

The following phrases have been revised to delete unnecessary words.

Original Version	*Revised Version*
There are three types of virus known.	Three types of virus are known.
Gary's father, who is a vegetarian,	Gary's father, a vegetarian,
The opera house, which was the scene of	The opera house, the scene of
What needs to be done is that a thorough search must be made.	A thorough search must be made.

Of course, you must decide whether the words or phrases *are* unnecessary. In some cases they may be making a particular point, or they may be needed for mood. Look at these examples.

> There once was a king who promised his daughter in marriage to the first man who could climb Devil's Mountain.

It wouldn't sound the same as

> A king once promised...

Likewise, the sentence

> What I really want to do is finish the race in less than 3 hours.

may not be equivalent to

> I really want to finish the race in less than 3 hours.

Can you see why not? Can you tell that the first speaker is expressing some doubt that it can be done, while the second sees no real difficulty? Before you make changes like these, ask yourself if you will be changing the meaning. Better yet, ask the author if the changes can be made. And whatever you do, don't change the tone of the passage.

5. *String phrases together if they belong together, but don't make sentences unwieldy.*

Hemingway may have gotten away with a lot of short, choppy sentences, but most readers feel more comfortable with an occasional prepositional phrase or compound sentence thrown in. Consider the following sentence.

> It was a pleasant day. Therefore I decided to take a walk.

Now, doesn't it sound more cohesive when written like this?

> Because it was a pleasant day, I decided to take a walk.

For variety, join some sentences by beginning with a subordinate clause, as in the example just given, and join others with conjunctions.

> It started to rain, so I turned back.

6. *Whenever possible, do not use indefinite words without a specific antecedent.*

An antecedent is a word or phrase that precedes the noun or pronoun now replacing it. What does *this* refer to? Often it refers to the idea or word that came immediately before, but sometimes it does not, and then its antecedent is unclear. Look at this example.

> Katy rarely attended church. This caused her parents great anguish.

Granted, it's not difficult to tell what *this* refers to, but maybe the statement would read better this way:

> That Katy rarely attended church caused her parents great anguish.

Or perhaps this:

> Katy rarely attended church. This omission caused her parents great anguish.

In any event, when you come across an indefinite word standing alone, such as *it, these, that,* or *this,* ask yourself, Is the meaning clear? Can there be any doubt what *this* refers to? If there is, then clarify the sentence. And if you can't figure out how to clarify the sentence, a *real* problem exists! Watch for authors who use *this* to refer to the content of several previous sentences, as in this example:

> Following the deaths at City Hall, thousands mourned the slain mayor and supervisor. Candlelight services and memorial gatherings were common. People grieved openly and shared their grief with strangers. This went on for months.

Well, what are you going to do with that sentence? Unless you are sure you understand the passage and can suggest a rewritten version *in the author's own style*, query!

7. *Do not change from one person, gender, tense, or voice to another if you intend no change in meaning.*

Read the following paragraph.

> A publisher's greatest resource is his or her authors. Authors make a publishing company; without them the company is just a company—a widget manufacturer, if you will, or a doodad factory. Authors bring life to the company, something that widgets and doodads don't. A publisher would do well to recognize its dependence on this life.

What's wrong? A subtle change in pronoun gender, from *his or her* in the first line to *its* in the last. Such changes are not easy to spot, especially when you're concentrating on the *would* in the last line. There's nothing wrong with *would:* A mood change is called for in moving from the indicative to the conditional. Watch carefully for such changes—correct and incorrect—when you copyedit.

Here's a common example of a subject change.

> All citizens should vote. If you do not, you are...

You may have noticed some subject changes in this book. Sometimes I say "a copyeditor must," sometimes "you must." That's because sometimes I'm giving "rules" for copyeditors to follow and sometimes I'm explaining something to you. Is it clear when I'm doing one or the other? When you copyedit, be sure that subject changes are warranted; if they're not, get rid of them.

8. *Use language properly.*

Later in this chapter we'll look at some words that are frequently misused, but right now I'm talking about the proper use of words in relation to other words. Ask yourself, What is the author saying? Is that what she or he *means* to say?

> John and Marge had such a romantic evening; they literally waltzed on air most of the night.

Not unless they repealed the laws of physics, they didn't. You can literally waltz the night away, but you can't waltz on air.

> Unquestionably, the best book on this subject is Dorian Read's *Dance and Dancers.*

Not so! I would question that. I can't question facts—which book is the bestselling, the largest, the most expensive—but I can question what is best. Best is opinion, not fact. In the example, then, you should change "Unquestionably" to "Possibly" or "Arguably."

Watch out for nonsequiturs and mixed metaphors. Remember: Ask yourself what the author intended, then write it that way.

Changes you make in style should always reflect the original style of the material. Don't go grouping sentences just for the heck of it, and don't make other sweeping changes either. Word changes for clarity: fine. Changes in sentence structure for variety or clarity: good. But always be sure that the style remains the author's.

SEXISM, RACISM, AGEISM

In recent years more emphasis has been placed on protecting the feelings of minority groups: women, ethnic groups, the elderly. Particularly in nonfiction writing, and specifically in textbooks, unintentional slurs were frequently made against minority groups.

It is not my intention to censor, nor can it be yours. In textbooks, however, censorship is common and often desirable; ethnic slurs of even the most innocent kind must be removed from the books our children learn values from. There is also movement toward eliminating sex stereotyping and ageism from schoolbooks, and this trend is good.

But you will still come across written materials that have references you don't like, because, after all, people should be able to write whatever they want. What should you do if you find a racist comment in something you're editing? Don't change it. Ask the publisher for her or his policy. Then perhaps point out the offending passage to the author. Perhaps it was an oversight, and the author would be embarrassed if it found its way into print. There is a difference, for example, in referring to "Jack, a black from South Carolina" and "Jack, a black man from South Carolina." Intentional or not, the effect of the second example is a put-down. So *ask*. But you don't have the right to determine what some other person's morals should be and whether he or she should refrain from bigotry.

Ageism is a form of intolerance directed toward older people. It implies that just because of age, an older person is not able to function as well as a younger one. How true is that really? Older people may lack the speed and endurance of the young, but they may be just as active. Have you ever watched a tennis match between two 60-year-old celebrities? It wears me out just thinking about it! A person's brains, likewise, do not deteriorate just because the eyesight or hearing may fade at a certain age. Watch for ageist references, and point them out to the author or publisher.

Sexism, of course, is the area of most concern these days. Although we were always told to treat ethnic minorities with respect, we were also subjected, wherever we went, to references to *he* that included both men and women. Well, I'm here to tell you that *he* does *not* include women; *he* refers to men and *she* refers to women. Getting rid of sexism means changing not only our thought patterns but our language patterns as well. No longer is *salesman* an acceptable word for men and women who sell. No longer can we say *lady poet* without implying that a woman poet is somehow inferior to a man poet.

Most publishers want to be nonsexist, but they don't want to put words in the author's mouth. They say that if the author has made no attempt to be nonsexist, the copyeditor should not overdo the changes. Authors are gradually learning to make their prose nonsexist, but it's not always easy for someone who has always thought of men as principals and women as teachers. And it's not just male authors who think this way. I once saw a manuscript authored by two women who referred throughout to authors as *he!* Copyeditors must be on the lookout for sexist references, and they should point them out to the publisher if they feel awkward telling the author. Sexist references fall into two main categories: sexist language and sex stereotyping.

Sexist Language

It is not always possible to correct sexist language, but there are some things that can be done. Here are a few hints.

1. Recast sentences into the plural to avoid references to *his or her.*

Original Version	*Revised Version*
The student should do his homework each evening.	Students should do their homework each evening.

2. Alternate references to *his* and *her.* This method works well in certain subject areas, such as child development, where it would be awkward or impossible to always use plural or *he or she.* Thus one paragraph can describe a child as *she* and another as *he.*
3. Do not characterize professions by sex.

Original Version	*Revised Version*
the male nurse	the nurse
the authoress	the author
a girl Friday	a personal assistant [or aide]

It may also be convenient to indicate sex by a pronoun: "The writer sent her manuscript to the publisher." And frequently it doesn't matter what the person's sex is anyway.

4. Avoid, wherever practical, words that use the suffix -*man* in the traditional sense of "male."

Original Version	Revised Version
salesman	salesperson
fireman	fire fighter
foreman	supervisor

However, this generalization doesn't always work. Although *firewoman* is certainly not common, *policewoman* is, and perfectly acceptable. Other words are simply too new to be appropriate at this time. A *midshipman* right now can be male or female; with luck, in a few years there will be another word. And what about *freshman*? That word may never change. Why should it? Don't invent words just for the purpose of eliminating the -*man* suffix everywhere it appears. But do be sensitive to women's participation in all areas.

5. Never draw parallels using nonparallel words.

Original Version	Revised Version
man and wife	husband and wife
men's room, ladies' room	men's room, women's room
men and girls	men and women; boys and girls

6. Except in dialogue, query all put-downs of women, such as "the little woman" (would you say "the little man"?), "I'll have my girl get it," or "my helpmeet." *Wife, secretary, lover,* and *friend* are perfectly acceptable words. Fortunately, the problem of put-downs comes up seldom in writing; unfortunately, it occurs far too often in speech.

Stereotyping

When you copyedit, think about the pictures being painted by the author. Are they complete, or have some groups been omitted? Are they stereotypical? Are women the nurses and men the doctors? Women can take any position they wish: telephone installers, judges, even homemakers. So can men; they can be nurses, teachers, and yes, even homemakers. Blacks and whites and Hispanics and everyone else can hold jobs in all areas. Old people and young people can be useful members of society.

Be alert when you copyedit. Do not allow any group to be left out by virtue of language or stereotyping. An entire segment of the population may feel that such-and-such book or article or brochure is not intended for them. Elimination of sexism is so important in el-hi publishing, in fact, that the copyeditor may be asked to keep a running tally of references to boys and girls to be sure they're equal. But as I've said throughout this section, you make changes in sexist, ageist, or ethnic stereotyping and language *cautiously,* and then only with the approval of the publisher.

WORD USAGE

Using words properly is, as we've just seen, an important part of style, but so is using the proper words. I'm not going to provide an exhaustive list of words commonly misused and tell you what words should have been used instead. Many excellent books on word usage already exist, and I recommend that you buy at least Theodore M. Bernstein's *The Careful Writer* (see bibliography). The bibliography lists many additional usage books that you should become familiar with. I've picked out only a few words that create problems. I use them to illustrate that many words we use with abandon are in fact used incorrectly. We all must look up words we're not sure of (and be wary of those we *are* sure of!). Become familiar with the usage guides listed in the bibliography; then when you come across a word, you'll think to question it.

a, an. You learned the distinction between *a* and *an* a long time ago, but now that you're a copyeditor, you have to take the lesson a step further. When an indefinite article precedes a letter, number, symbol, or acronym, you first pronounce the term and then decide which article it takes. The same goes for words beginning with *h* or with a *u* sound.

> a union
> an ugly child
> a historic event, an historic event [but be consistent]
> an honor
> an X and an O
> a 0 (zero)
> a NY cabbie (a New York cabbie)
> an NYU student (an en-why-you student)
> an AFTRA member
> a NATO (*not* an en-ay-tee-oh) country

above, below. These words have their place, but they should not describe the position of material on the page. In manuscript, change them to *preceding, following,* or some other non-committal term. When the page is made up, the material will rarely be "below" or "above"—it may even be on a different page.

adverse, averse. Adverse is an adjective meaning "unfavorable" or "harmful." *Averse* is also an adjective, but it never precedes a noun; instead it appears as a predicate adjective meaning "opposite" or "opposed."

affect, effect. Affect as a verb can mean "to cultivate" or "to influence." *Effect* as a verb means "to put into effect."

> The decision affected millions.
> The commission will try to effect the decision.

Effect as a noun means "result." *Affect* as a noun is essentially obsolete except as a technical term in psychology, where it means "conscious emotion."

> We are wondering what the effect of the cutbacks will be.
> The patient was depressed, showing little affect.

aggravate, irritate. These terms are almost always used incorrectly. We often say, "He really aggravates me," when we mean, "He irritates me." *Aggravate* means "to cause to worsen"; *irritate* means "to anger."

> His cold aggravated his weakened condition.
> She irritates me no end.

all right. This phrase is *always* two words.

> "Alright" is most certainly not all right.

a lot. Also two words.

> "Alot" is not all right.

any, any other. "Smoker's Delight tastes better than any cigarette." Is Smoker's Delight a cigarette? "Smoker's Delight tastes better than any other cigarette." Is Smoker's Delight a cigarette? Simple, huh? There's no excuse for mistakes here.

anymore. My favorite misused word. *Anymore* (as one word, please note) may not be used with a positive statement, only with negative ones.

> She doesn't sleep much anymore.

With questions or positive statements, *nowadays* or *these days* or *still* should be used instead.

> Do you play tennis still?
> She sleeps a lot these days.

as to. I would like to see this phrase stricken from the English language. *Concerning* or *about* or nothing at all will almost always work.

> I am not clear about [*not* as to] his motives.
> She was uncertain whether [*not* as to whether] she could attend.

cannot. Always one word, but it can be made two words if another word intervenes.

> Can you not see what's happening here?
> I cannot help liking him.

compose, comprise. These terms are very tricky. The whole comprises the sum of its parts; the parts compose the whole. There is no passive voice to *comprise*; thus you cannot say *is comprised of*, although you can say *is composed of* or *consists of*.

> Parliament comprises the House of Lords and the House of Commons.
> Parliament is composed of the House of Lords and the House of Commons.
> The House of Lords and the House of Commons compose Parliament.

continual, continuous. *Continual* means "continuing for a time with no breaks" or "recurring often"; *continuous* means "continuing forever" (well, nothing is forever, but you get the idea).

> The rain was continual for 4 days.
> Horseguards watch Buckingham Palace continuously.

couple, couple of. New Yorkers notwithstanding, the correct phrase is "a couple of dollars." You can, however, say, "a couple more people."

data, datum. Why it should be so hard to remember that *data* is plural, *datum* singular, I don't know. In fact, the data are indisputable.

deprecate, depreciate. Another frequently misused pair. You know that *depreciate* means "to lessen in value"; did you know that *deprecate* means "to pray away"? That's right, *deprecate* means, literally, "to wish for removal of" and is a synonym for *disparage; depreciate* is a synonym for *belittle.*

> Dr. Jones depreciated the corporations in her speech. [belittled]
>
> Dr. Jones deprecated war in her speech. [wished it would go away]

Here is the definition of *deprecate* from *Webster's Third:* "to disapprove of often with mildness." You would do well to become familiar with this definition.

discreet, discrete. The distinction between these two words is easier than you may think. *Discreet* means "prudent," *discrete* means "separate." The noun *discretion* comes from *discreet.*

> Darlene told Melissa the secret because Melissa was always discreet.
>
> The house has three discrete units.

ensure, insure. If you *ensure* something, you make sure of it. To *insure* means to take out insurance on.

farther, further. Farther applies to actual distance, *further* to degree or extent.

> I ran farther than my sister.
>
> I can go no further in my concessions.

Note that in the second sentence *further* is not physical distance but rather extent.

fewer, less. Fewer refers to number, *less* to quantity or extent.

> The new stadium holds fewer spectators than the old one did.
>
> Richard earns less money than Bryan does.

healthful, healthy. Something *healthful* is good for you; *healthy* describes your health.

historic, historical. Like other pairs of -*ic,* -*ical* words, the shorter form usually implies more significance. A historic building had some great moment of history connected with it; a historical building is merely old.

hopefully. Edwin Newman set the future of this word back several decades when he declared that it was totally inappropriate at the beginning of a sentence. Too many of us use *hopefully* incorrectly. It is an adverb meaning "with hope"; it does not mean "I hope." If you mean "I hope," say it.

I hope we will be able to start practice on time.
Hopefully, we will be able to start practice on time.
[We will start practice on time and will feel hopeful about our performance—but that's probably not what you mean]
We work hopefully for the senator's reelection. [we hope he'll be reelected]

important, importantly. Here's another one. *Importantly* is, like *badly*, rarely correct. The expression is *more important*, not *more importantly*, as an author once pointed out to me.

More important, I was able to learn something.

irregardless. Do I really have to tell you there's no such word? The word is *regardless*. That doesn't mean that there's no such words as *irrespective*, though; that's the word you mean when you say *irregardless*.

last, latest. Last means "final"; *latest*, "most recent."

lend, loan. Very simply, *loan* is a noun, *lend*, a verb.

Please lend me some money. I'll repay the loan shortly.

liable, likely. Liable means "responsible for"; *likely* means "possible."

proved, proven. The past participle of *prove* is now considered *proved. Proven* does, however, have a place as an adjective.

The theory was proved by scientists.
He is a proven winner.

raise, rise. Raise is a transitive verb; it requires an object. *Rise* is intransitive.

I rise at 7:00 every day.
I thought he was going to raise a ruckus.

reason is because. Something happens because *or* for a reason, but not both. After *reason is*, use *that* and not *because*.

The reason I can't attend is that I'll be on vacation.
I can't attend because I'll be on vacation.

so . . . as. Use this construction only in a negative sense; otherwise use *as . . . as.*

Ed was not so well liked as Will.
Michael is as handsome as Larry.

Even in negative construction, *as . . . as* can be used in informal writing.

Ed was not as well liked as Will.

towards. Never, never, never in America! There should be no *s* on the end of *toward, backward, afterward,* or *forward* in this country, although some authorities are shockingly tolerant of this British usage.

while. While means "during"; avoid using it in place of *whereas* or *although.*

Nero fiddled while Rome burned.
Whereas Jeanie is smart, her sister Georgie is a genius.
Although Claude has letters in three sports, no pro team has scouted him.

who, whom. Who is the nominative case, *whom* the objective; everyone knows that. The problem arises when the word is followed by another phrase.

Give the present to whoever shows up first.

Whoever is the subject of its own clause, and that clause is the object of the preposition *to.* The example, then, is correct.

He'll give the present to whomever he chooses.

Whomever is the object of its own clause ("he chooses whomever"), which in turn is the object of the preposition *to.* So this sentence, too, is correct.

Remember: This list is intended solely to show how even the most common expressions are misused. If you become familiar with one (or several) of the style guides listed in the bibliography, you are on your way to becoming a better editor. But at the very least, you must always look up words and constructions to be sure you're using them properly. If you are copyediting something of current concern, be sure to use a newspaper guidebook, to avoid, for example, calling an emerging nation a "third world nation."

A FEW MORE WORDS ABOUT STYLE

At the beginning of this chapter I said that even the use of a comma in a compound sentence is an indication of style. That's because the rules of grammar—which include rules for the use of the comma—apply to formal style. Deliberate rejection of grammatical rules indicates informal style. That's not necessarily a bad thing; it all depends on the material. Textbooks certainly must follow formal style to be understood. But fiction, and particularly dialogue, need not adhere rigidly to the rules of good grammar. A character in a play might say, "It's one of my favorite all-time songs," when what she really means is, "It's one of my all-time favorite songs." The meaning is not lost. In formal writing, however, the author—and the copyeditor—must pay attention to such items as word order. They will notice that a job is "well paying," not "well paid." We all make such slips in our everyday language and even in the writing that we do for pleasure, so fictional characters can make them too. But we must avoid them in formal writing.

Now do the exercises to see how well you understand the principles of this chapter. I've made them short so that you can spot the problems quickly. Look up any word usages or constructions you're not sure of. And remember that what is acceptable in fiction may not be acceptable in the more formal type of writing that concerns us here.

Answers follow the exercises. If your answers are different from mine, fine—if you can defend them. (Some sentences are correct as written.)

EXERCISES

1. It wasn't hard to understand why Wilhemina was well liked.

2. I don't get around much anymore.

3. Mark each entry in the third column with a T or a F.

4. He wondered what effect the new policy would have.

5. There are nine planets known at this time.

6. If a nurse wants to make more money, she has to strike.

7. Wallace, who was a presidential candidate in 1968, was later paralyzed.

8. The moon continually affects the tides.

9. He quit the commission in spite of the fact that they were making progress.

10. The mayor lost a lot of support because she often deprecated minorities.

11. Hopefully the Giants will have a better season next year.

12. Five nations have an SEATO membership.

13. A teacher who does not have the respect of his or her students should resign, and he or she should find another line of work.

14. A good author literally tries to paint pictures in readers' minds.

15. President Kennedy was assassinated in 1963.

Answers

1. It was easy to understand why Wilhemina was well liked. [positive sentences are clearer and stronger than negative ones]
2. I don't get around much anymore. [fine as is, with *anymore* in a negative construction]
3. Mark each entry in the third column with a T or an F. [you need *an* before the sound *F* makes]
4. He wondered what effect the new policy would have. [that's right—*effect* means "result" here]
5. Nine planets are known at this time. [the revised sentence is less wordy, and it doesn't change the meaning]
6. If nurses want to make more money, they have to strike. [who said only women are nurses?]
7. Wallace, a presidential candidate in 1968, was later paralyzed. [get rid of the extra words]
8. The moon continuously affects the tides. [remember that continuous things never stop; the moon surely qualifies]
9. He quit the commission even though they were making progress. [get rid of unnecessary words]
10. The mayor lost a lot of support because she often depreciated minorities. [if she deprecated them—wished they'd go away—she deserved to lose more than support; let's hope this reporter meant she belittled them]
11. I hope the Giants will have a better season next year. [at least they may play more hopefully]
12. Five nations have a SEATO membership. [the acronym is pronounced like a word in this case, not like a string of letters beginning with an *es* sound]

13. Teachers who do not have their students' respect should resign and find another line of work. [not all efforts to avoid sexism are successful; the sentence sounds much better recast in the plural]
14. A good author tries, figuratively, to paint pictures in readers' minds. [a tricky one, wasn't it? It would be messy if the statement were taken literally]
15. President Kennedy was assassinated in 1963. [don't try to cast a sentence like this into the active voice; it's a simple statement of fact, and changing it will make it at best awkward and at worst perhaps libelous]

► KEY POINTS IN THIS CHAPTER

Style

- Don't impose your own style on the author's work; instead make suggestions that will enhance the work and make it more consistent and readable. Changes you make should always reflect the original style of the material. Before you make changes, ask yourself if you've changed the meaning.
- Use active voice whenever possible.
- Use positive statements.
- Use concrete language.
- Delete unnecessary words.
- String phrases together if they belong together, but don't make sentences unwieldy.
- Whenever possible, do not use indefinite words without a specific antecedent.
- Do not change from one person, gender, tense, or voice to another unless you intend a change in meaning.
- Use language properly; watch out for mixed metaphors and nonsequiturs.

Sexism, Racism, and Ageism

- Recast sentences into the plural to avoid references to *his or her*, or alternate references to *his* and *her.*
- Do not characterize professions by sex.
- Avoid, wherever practical, words that use the suffix -*man* in the traditional sense of "male."
- Never draw parallels using nonparallel words.
- Except in dialogue, query all put-downs of women.

- Do not allow any group to be left out by virtue of language or stereotyping.
- Be on the lookout for sexist, racist, and ageist references, and point them out to the publisher, but do not change them without permission.

Usage

- When an indefinite article precedes a letter, number, symbol, or acronym, first pronounce the term and then decide which article, *a* or *an*, to use.
- Become familiar with at least one usage guide and refer to it often.

Numbers and Abbreviations

So far we have looked at copyediting mostly from the point of view of how words are treated—how they're spelled, when they're hyphenated, how they should be used in context. But copyediting doesn't deal just with words. Equally important is the shorthand authors use—numbers and abbreviations. In this chapter we look at these two important elements of copyediting.

NUMBERS

We saw in Chapter 3 that numbers are sometimes spelled out, sometimes not. Now we will see when to use each style, and we will look at the ways numbers are used in writing.

Numbers are used in the following ways:

1. to count
2. in dates and time
3. with money
4. in percentages, decimals, and fractions
5. in addresses
6. with names
7. with organizations
8. with units of measure
9. as cross-references
10. in lists

In most of these cases digits are used, simply because they're easier than words to recognize quickly. There are some exceptions, which we'll cover when we discuss each situation, but first let's look at the main exception.

Counting

Did you see the movie three times or 3 times? Were there seven girls at the picnic, or were there 7? Have you received only twenty-one issues of the magazine, or 21 issues?

First you must recognize simple enumeration and its difference from the other uses of numbers just given. Times, girls, and issues are not dates, money, or units of measure; they are simply things enumerated, items you've counted. *Enumerations are spelled out* (at least up to a certain point). Most publishers have their own style; some spell out all numbers up to 100, some up to 20, some only to 10. *You must always follow the style of the company you are working for.* In the absence of such a style, however, I recommend that you spell out all numbers up to 100, using digits for 100 or more, unless, of course, your manuscript contains so many numbers as to make that practice impractical. This is the University of Chicago style (on which *Chicago Manual* is based). But remember, we are talking here only about enumeration; we will discuss all other items in that list shortly.

> At the end of the day, the thirty-eight contestants had been narrowed down to seven.
> By noon, 312 applicants were in line for the seventeen CETA jobs available.

There are a few exceptions to the rule of spelling out numbers under 100:

1. Do not begin a sentence with a digit.

   > Three hundred applicants showed up.

2. In parallel construction, generally either spell out or use digits for all numbers.

   > Of the total, 112 were white, 49 were black, and 7 were Hispanic.

Note: Many periodicals draw no distinction between parallel constructions and other numerical situations; they set their dividing line, usually at 20, and follow it rigidly.

3. Use digits with any rate, such as pages per hour, words per minute, cookies per child, or cars per millionaire.

He can type 70 words a minute.
Success is more than 5 fan letters per day.

4. If two numbers occur sequentially, spell out one and use digits for the other to make the phrase easier to follow.

    She planned to purchase eight 3-story buildings.

Of course, the number you decide to spell out may change. If one of the numbers is supposed to be written in digits—for instance, because it's over 100 or used with a unit of measure—then the other number will be spelled out.

    He bought seven 2-liter bottles of soda.
    The department ordered 250 four-part NCR memos for each employee.

5. Use digits and words for round numbers over 999,999.

    Over 1 million people were expected to attend the exhibit.
    By the end of the century, at least 6.5 billion people will inhabit the earth.
    The average novel contains about 120,000 words.

Note that in accordance with my rule of using 1 million as the cutoff point, I have chosen to use digits in this last example. Many style books tell you to spell out all round numbers, and if your publisher wishes you to, then you certainly must. I prefer digits because they are much easier to grasp and are always shorter. For a discussion of round numbers, see *Chicago Manual* or *Words into Type*.

6. When editing textbooks in foreign languages, consider the context. If the reader (the student) is expected to "translate" the number, then you'll want to use digits.

    J'ai acheté 14 croissants. [I bought 14 croissants.]

In reading aloud, the student must say,

    J'ai acheté quatorze croissants.

Units of Measure

Whether you spell out or abbreviate the unit of measure, use digits with it.

    7 grams
    31 mL
    193 miles

10-point type
4 years old

Here are a couple of rules for use with units of measure.

1. Never abbreviate a unit of measure without a number.

    The box was weighed in grams.
    The package weighed 48 g.

2. When using abbreviated units, use a singular verb.

    When 15 mL of the liquid is siphoned, proceed with the rest of the experiment.

3. In a range, normally you should repeat the unit of measure only if it is a symbol; do not repeat abbreviations.

    a 5″ × 7″ photo
    a drop of 10°–15° in temperature
    15–20 g is needed for the experiment
    35–40 degrees

4. Consider seconds, minutes, hours, days, weeks, months, and years to be units of measure, and therefore use digits.

    Call back in 5 minutes.
    The boy was 8 years old in March.

Dates and Time

Except as noted below, use digits when citing dates or times.

We eat dinner at 7:00 on weeknights.
He was born on July 7, 1948.
Smith (b.1930) [not Smith (1930-)]

Now for the exceptions:

1. Spell out centuries.

    a nineteenth-century poet

2. Spell out decades.

    There was much student unrest during the sixties.

Note that many publishers reject that style completely, preferring to use this instead:

There was much student unrest during the 1960s.

Naturally you must follow house style.

3. In dialogue, you should spell out most numbers. (It is assumed that characters cannot speak in digits!) I recommend that you discuss this point with your employer, who may prefer digits, especially for complicated numbers, such as 14.2.

> "I hope you feel differently in nineteen ninety-four," Ann said.
> "I'll catch the five-oh-two train," Jack said.
> "But I can't have it completed by the fifteenth," Laura complained.
> "I'll be there by four-thirty," she assured her mother.

There are a couple more points about time that we should look at now.

1. The abbreviation B.C. follows the year, A.D. precedes it. Both are set in small capitals with no space between them.

> A.D. 1120
> 273 B.C.

2. The abbreviations A.M. and P.M. are set in small capitals with no space between them but with space preceding.

> 2:00 A.M.
> 4:25 P.M.

3. Never use the ordinal form in a date.

> March 5, *not* March 5th

4. Military times are given without a colon.

> 0900 (9 A.M.)
> 2345 (11:45 P.M.)

5. What does 1.4.71 mean? To me it means January 4, 1971, but my British friend thinks it means April 1, 1971. Don't use any numerical conventions that can be misunderstood.

Money

The biggest question about how to express amounts of money is whether to use symbols and digits or all words. Some style manuals tell you to follow the rule of spelling out numbers under 100. I do not agree with that, for the simple reason that money is a unit of measure, and units of measure take digits. Unless you have other instructions from the publisher, I recommend that you use symbols and digits to express all amounts of money—U.S. currency or otherwise, whole numbers or fractions. The only exception is with amounts over 999,999, when digits and words should be used.

73¢	$71,000
$.73	$2 million [*note:* no hyphen]
$45.23	$4.3 million
$71	£1.95

Sometimes, as in this book, you will prefer *73 cents* to the use of any symbol. In dialogue, of course, only words will be used.

> "I paid only twelve dollars and eighteen cents for this shirt," beamed Eve.

For an excellent section on foreign currency, see the GPO Manual.

Percentages, Decimals, and Fractions

Normally you should spell out *percent* (one word, notice) and use digits with it. In tabular matter or statistical material, the symbol may be used instead.

> Only 4 percent of the audience had been to a concert before, the survey indicated.

In the United States, decimals are indicated by a period, but in Europe (except for Great Britain, which formerly used a raised dot but now follows the United States) a comma is used instead. (Instead of a comma, space is used to indicate thousands.)

> 4.15 (United States)
> 4,15 (Europe, except Great Britain)
> 4˙15 (older British usage)

For some reason, the form fractions take causes a great deal of difficulty with copyeditors. I am going to try to clear up some of the difficulty now.

1.   Hyphenate word fractions.

> a three-fourths majority
> one-fifth of the class

2.   Spell out fractions only when clear; use digits for cumbersome fractions.

> three-quarters of an inch
> 31/32 of an inch

3.   Do not use *th* with fractions expressed in digits.

> 45/100 [not 45/100ths]

4.   Where possible, change fractions to decimals.

> 3.5 million [not 3½ million]

5. Simple fractions are always less than 1; complex fractions are always more than 1. Be sure to use the correct verb—singular or plural—with a fraction or its decimal equivalent.

> 0.5 percent was found to...
> 3½ acres adjoin the house

6. There is no space between the parts of a complex fraction.

> 7½ feet

In typing, of course, only ½ and ¼ (sometimes appearing as $\frac{1}{2}$ and $\frac{1}{4}$) can be typed as fractions; all others must be made up, usually like this: 7-3/4. In copyediting, mark to delete the hyphen *and* to close up the whole number and the fraction, and mark the fraction for "case" or "piece."

78̸/4 ← ⟨ease⟩

In Chapter 11 we look at all technical marking, including how to mark fractions.

Addresses

Street numbers, house numbers, highway numbers, zip codes, and the like, are normally written in digits. Numbered streets are sometimes spelled out instead, for appearance's sake. Likewise, some building numbers, especially round ones, are given in words. Such a style is considered quite classy.

> Interstate 80
> 700 East 53rd Street, New York, NY 10093
> Two Park Avenue

Note that ordinal numbers are appropriate in street addresses.

Names

It is a matter of personal preference whether a person using II or III or any other number after his name (only men do) places a comma before it, but to omit the comma is more common. A comma is never used in a monarch's name or in the name of a spaceship or yacht.

> John R. Smith II
> John R. Smith, III
> Edward VIII
> *Mariner* IX

Roman numerals are always used.

Organizations

Almost all numbers used with organizations are spelled out in the ordinal form, unless they are over 100.

> First National Bank of Duluth
> First Church of Christ
> Eighty-fifth Congress
> Eighth Circuit Court of Appeals

Because of their narrow columns, newspapers generally use digits for ordinal numbers (85th Congress, 8th Circuit Court of Appeals). The GPO Manual also recommends digits, in most cases, for *10th* and above. Labor unions, of course, use digits after their names.

> Local 32B
> District 65

Cross-References

References to numbered parts of a book, magazine, or any other work are always given in digits, except sometimes for chapter or part numbers.

> See Table 12 on page 231.
> As Figure 14.2 indicates. . .

It is a good idea to flag for yourself references to parts of the manuscript you are copyediting so that if the style is changed from, say, *Chapter 3* to *Chapter Three* (as the designer might change it), all the cross-references can be caught. You may also need to locate all cross-references if a figure is added or dropped.

Lists

Parts of a list, whether in outline form or in running text, are given by digits, not words. Sometimes, of course, letters are used instead of or in addition to digits, and bullets or asterisks may be used to replace either of these. There is a difference in meaning, though: Bullets show *some* of the possibilities, while numbers or letters show *all* of them.

In lists, by the way, always align the periods of points 9 and 10, as is done in this book. The copyediting instruction is "clear for 10," meaning that the compositor needs to allow enough room for a two-digit number, 10.

Some Special Rules

Let's look now at some special rules for using numbers.

1. Use inclusive numbers unless otherwise directed.

> pages 232–238 [not 232–38]
> 1970–1974 [not 1970–74]

2. Except with dates, normally use a comma after every group of three digits, beginning with the right-hand group.

> 1,112
> 10,112
> 1,112,000

Often you are told not to use a comma in four-digit numbers, but that rule just gets in the way when the four-digit number appears in a list with a five-digit number. I think it's just easier to always use the comma, and it's always easier to read. Naturally, if you are given instructions to delete the comma, you will have to follow them. Large newspapers, which usually have a house style, are among those publications preferring no comma.

3. In continental Europe, as we saw earlier, space is used instead of commas.

> 3 300 000 [not 3,300,000]

That style should be changed when you copyedit, except in quoted material (unless you have been asked to restyle it).

4. Usually spell out ordinal numbers.

> the third time
> the Ninth Trust Company
> a nineteenth-century poet

5. Circling a digit tells the compositor to spell it out. Circle digits under 100 only, and only in English context.

ABBREVIATIONS

There are so many different abbreviations that whole books have been written about them! It is not my desire in this book to compete with those others, so I'm not going to give you a list at all. *Chicago Manual, Words into Type,* and the GPO Manual all explain abbreviations nicely.

As a copyeditor, you should watch for abbreviations in the material you work on, then go to one of these sources—or even the dictionary—to be sure they're being used properly. Some abbreviations take capital letters, or caps and lowercase, or lowercase, or small caps. Some take periods, some don't. Abbreviations are always set without space (MIT, M.A.), except that a person's initials do take space (R. E. Edwards).

It is not always easy to be consistent in styling abbreviations, but if you use the same source most of the time, you will do fairly well.

Periods or No Periods?

Most government and other organizations take no periods in their abbreviations (AFL-CIO, HUD). There are exceptions, of course, the most notable of which is *U.S.* itself. Others are a matter of choice, not really exceptions; *U.N.* or *UN* is equally common and correct. You will probably find in time that abbreviations currently popular with periods will lose them. Lowercase abbreviations usually take periods (Sgt., c.o.d.). Remember that some abbreviations are in small caps, notably A.M., P.M., B.C., and A.D.; these do take periods. Some abbreviations are peculiar to a particular subject, and you should check the literature for appropriate style.

Roman or Italic?

Foreign abbreviations used to be set off in italic, but current style prefers roman for all but the most bizarre or uncommon abbreviations. Thus you can assume that *ibid., e.g.,* and the rest of them are almost certainly roman. A good rule is that if an abbreviation is common enough to be in the latest edition of *Webster's Collegiate* (the main text, not the special lists of abbreviations), then it's common enough to be in roman.

Abbreviations or Words?

Abbreviations should be used sparingly; they are a shorthand form of writing and therefore informal. Latin abbreviations are often used in bibliographic citations, where they are appropriate. (They will be discussed further in Chapter 8.) Other familiar Latin abbreviations are *e.g., i.e., etc.,* and *viz.* (which stand for, respectively, *for example, that is, and so forth,* and *namely*). In running text these abbreviations are best avoided, but they can be used in parenthetical expressions, footnotes, and exercises.

Parts of a book may be abbreviated in cross-references, but be sure to be consistent in your use of the abbreviations *Chap., Sec., Fig., p.,* and so on. Note also that there is always space after the period, before the number.

Abbreviations such as *U.S.* and *U.N.* are most properly used as adjectives, not nouns.

> the U.S. government
> The issue was debated at the United Nations.

In tabular material, where space is at a premium, these and other abbreviations are appropriate, of course.

Do not begin a sentence with an abbreviation, even if that abbreviation forms a word (called an *acronym*).

Never use an abbreviation so obscure as to be unrecognizable. Do not think it acceptable to decipher it on first mention and then continue to use it; that is affectation. But of course you should identify all but the most obvious abbreviations at least the first time you use them. In material that can be divided into several parts or read out of order, such as a college textbook, it is wise to identify the abbreviation the first time it is used in each chapter (or part, if that is the way the material is to be divided). It makes little difference whether you cite the abbreviation first and then put the full name in parentheses, or whether you do it the other way around; it's largely a matter of style.

> According to NOW (the National Organization for
> Women),...
> Latest figures from the Bureau of Narcotics and
> Dangerous Drugs (BNDD) indicate...

The use of an abbreviation indicates that you plan to reuse the term and want your readers to recognize it. If you do not plan to reuse it, do not introduce the abbreviation unless it is so common that it is better known than the full name.

Postal Service Abbreviations

Along with revolutionizing how authors prepare manuscripts, the computer has changed how we address our letters and cite our bibliographic references. Gone is the abbreviation Calif.; in its place is the two-letter Postal Service code.

To be used properly, there should be no comma between the city and state; that's because the scanner reads the comma as a glitch on the end of the city's name and gets confused. (Of course, the Postal Service also requests that we type addresses in capital letters on a high-quality printer in 10-pitch sans serif type, with letters 10/1000 inch apart.) Scanning mail sends it on its way faster, and it probably won't be long before we follow the Postal Service's advice. Until then, simply use the two-digit code everywhere you used to use the old abbreviation, and use it consistently with or without the comma after the city.

Alabama	AL	Arkansas	AR
Alaska	AK	California	CA
Arizona	AZ	Colorado	CO

Connecticut	CT	New Hampshire	NH
Delaware	DE	New Jersey	NJ
District of Columbia	DC	New Mexico	NM
Florida	FL	New York	NY
Georgia	GA	North Carolina	NC
Hawaii	HI	North Dakota	ND
Idaho	ID	Ohio	OH
Illinois	IL	Oklahoma	OK
Indiana	IN	Oregon	OR
Iowa	IA	Pennsylvania	PA
Kansas	KS	Rhode Island	RI
Kentucky	KY	South Carolina	SC
Louisiana	LA	South Dakota	SD
Maine	ME	Tennessee	TN
Maryland	MD	Texas	TX
Massachusetts	MA	Utah	UT
Michigan	MI	Vermont	VT
Minnesota	MN	Virginia	VA
Mississippi	MS	Washington	WA
Missouri	MO	West Virginia	WV
Montana	MT	Wisconsin	WI
Nebraska	NE	Wyoming	WY
Nevada	NV		

Note: The correct abbreviation for Nebraska is NE, according to the Postal Service. (It is recorded differently in different style guides.)

SI Units

Most publishers of technical materials are now going over to SI (Système international) units. It is the publisher's responsibility to see that the material is written in SI, but yours to be sure the correct SI unit is used. In Chapter 11 you will find the list of SI units and the units derived from them, along with a discussion of SI.

EXERCISES

Correct the following sentences according to the rules given in this chapter. (Some sentences are correct as written.) Answers and explanations follow.

1. 17 people showed up for the concert.

2. Of the hundred and fifty students in the ninth grade, only eighty-three got better than a C on the exam.

3. I saw Star Wars 4 times.

4. Figure twelve gives an example of such a graph.

5. CORE (the Congress of Racial Equality) was formed in the 1960's.

6. Unemployment in the U.S. reached a critical level in the late seventies.

7. Helen said to Sandy, ''I'll meet you at 10 Downing Street in 45 minutes.''

8. Sharon felt that fifty thousand dollars was a reasonable salary at her age.

9. The Ides of March are on March 15th.

10. Do steps 1 and 2 before reading on.

11. She asked him to pick up 20 15-cent stamps when he went to the Post Office.

12. The six-member commission was appointed Monday.

13. At last count, four million dollars had been spent on the project.

14. I met him at 3 PM.

15. I had decided that we could go to the beach if it got to be 75 or 80 degrees.

16. VISTA volunteers now number in the thousands.

17. The vote was one hundred twelve for, seventeen opposed, and two abstentions.

18. At least three-fourths of the class is unprepared.

19. Whatever happened to $16\frac{1}{4}$-rpm recordings?

20. She was charged with S.E.C. (Securities and Exchange Commission) violations.

21. The company's hiring practices were being investigated by the EEOC (Equal Employment Opportunity Committee).

22. I sent the letter to 55 7th Street, Urbana, IL.

23. Write your answer to the nearest cm.

24. Type the manuscript on 8½ x 11" paper.

25. The hegira occurred in 622 A.D.

Answers

1. Seventeen people showed up for the concert. [Don't begin a sentence with a number; furthermore, spell out numbers under 100.]
2. Of the 150 students in the ninth grade, only 83 got better than a C on the exam. [One of the numbers is over 100, one under, but both should be treated the same, for parallelism. In the exercise they *were* treated the same, but they were difficult to comprehend quickly; digits are better in this case.]
3. I saw *Star Wars* four times. [There's no unit of measure, so spell out numbers under 100]
4. Figure 12 gives an example of such a graph. [Always use digits with cross-references.]
5. The Congress of Racial Equality (CORE) was formed in the 1960s. [It is preferable not to start a sentence with an abbreviation; don't use an apostrophe in years.]
6. Unemployment in the United States reached a critical level in the late seventies. [U.S. is only used as an adjective. You might also question "seventies" here and change it to "1970s," depending on how formal you thought the material was. The shorthand form "seventies" is more suited to informal style.]
7. Helen said to Sandy, "I'll meet you at Ten Downing Street in forty-five minutes." [In dialogue, there are no digits.]
8. Sharon felt that $50,000 was a reasonable salary at her age. [Don't start using words until the millions; there's no reason, either, to avoid a dollar sign.]
9. The Ides of March are on March 15. [Don't use *d*, *st*, or *th* with digits.]
10. Do steps 1 and 2 before reading on. [Fine as is; always use digits in lists.]
11. She asked him to pick up twenty 15-cent stamps when he went to the Post Office. [When two numbers occur together, spell one out. I chose the first one because I'm considering "15-cent stamp" to be a unit of measure. In

this example, both numbers are easy to follow. If she had wanted 37 stamps, however, it might have been preferable to say, "She asked him to pick up 37 fifteen-cent stamps."]

12. The six-member commission was appointed Monday. [Fine as is; there's no unit of measure here.]

13. At last count, $4 million had been spent on the project. [There's no dialogue here, so the dollar sign and digit are appropriate; over 999,999 we use words and digits in combination.]

14. I met him at 3 P.M. [Make the abbreviation small caps. Note that 3 is as good as 3:00; there's no need to change it.]

15. I had decided that we could go to the beach if it got to be 75 or 80°. [This is a tricky sentence. It could probably have been left as it was, but I changed the word "degrees" to the symbol. I didn't add the degree sign after 75 because I felt that would have been overkill. (If I had said, "when the temperature reaches 75°–80°," I would have repeated the symbol.) This sentence proves that a style sheet is necessary; you'll want to be sure you remember to treat similar sentences the same way always]

16. Volunteers in Service to America (VISTA workers) now number in the thousands. [Another tricky sentence. Technically you can't say "VISTA volunteers," because the abbreviation contains the word "volunteers," but it *is* said frequently. Furthermore, I said you should avoid starting a sentence with an abbreviation. I'd be tempted to leave this sentence alone in informal writing.]

17. The vote was 112 for, 17 opposed, and 2 abstentions. [The numbers are important here, so digits are better.]

18. At least three-fourths of the class is unprepared. [Fine as is.]

19. Whatever happened to 16¼-rpm recordings? [I don't know, but I know the sentence is OK as is.]

20. She was charged with SEC (Securities and Exchange Commission) violations. [There are no periods in most government abbreviations.]

21. The company's hiring practices were being investigated by the EEOC (Equal Employment Opportunity Commission). [Did you get this one right? Don't let an author fool you; remember that it isn't right just because it's in print.]

22. I sent the letter to 55 Seventh Street, Urbana, IL. [To avoid confusion, spell out ordinal street numbers.]
23. Write your answer to the nearest centimeter. [Don't abbreviate units of measure that stand alone.]
24. Type the manuscript on 8½″ × 11″ paper. [Repeat the symbol on adjacent digits, and remember to mark for a multiplication sign.]
25. The hegira occurred in A.D. 622. [Put A.D. before the year, and remember the small caps.]

► **KEY POINTS IN THIS CHAPTER**

Numbers

- Spell out numbers below 100 if they are used for counting or enumerating.
- Do not begin a sentence with a digit.
- To be parallel, generally either spell out or use digits for all numbers; however, if two numbers occur together, spell out one and use digits for the other.
- Use digits with rates and with units of measure.
- Use digits and words for round numbers over 999,999.
- Spell out centuries and decades.
- Spell out numbers in dialogue.
- Do not use ordinal forms in dates.
- Use a digit with the word *percent.*
- Use digits in references to numbered parts of a book or magazine.
- Use inclusive page numbers.
- Use commas to separate every group of three digits, starting from the right.
- Usually spell out ordinal numbers.
- Spell out fractions only when clear; use digits for cumbersome fractions. Hyphenate word fractions.
- Simple fractions and decimal equivalents take a singular verb.

Abbreviations

- Never abbreviate a unit of measure without a number.
- Use a singular verb with an abbreviated unit of measure.
- In a range, repeat the unit of measure only if it is a symbol; do not repeat abbreviations.
- Use the abbreviations *U.S.* and *U.N.* as adjectives; spell out as nouns.

- Use Postal Service abbreviations in references.
- Abbreviations common enough to appear in *Webster's Collegiate Dictionary* should be roman.
- Use abbreviations only within parentheses, footnotes and bibliographies, and exercises; within running text, spell out the correct term.
- When using acronyms, spell out the term at the first usage.

Notes and Bibliographies

If you work in any field other than general trade, you will almost certainly run into footnotes and bibliographies. Scholarly materials rely heavily on other people's research and are laden with notes. Even nonfiction for general audiences often has footnotes and reading lists. In this chapter, first we look at the different kinds of notes and reference lists there are and how to treat their in-text references; then we discuss how to style bibliographic references.

NOTES AND BIBLIOGRAPHIC INFORMATION

Footnotes

Footnotes contain material not completely relevant to the discussion in the text, so they are dropped to the foot of the page. They may contain substantive or bibliographic material. Even in novels you may come across substantive footnotes; sometimes the editor will explain a term in a footnote, or sometimes the author will slip in an aside. Bibliographic footnotes may refer the reader to additional material on the subject, or they may contain complete publishing information about something that appears in the text.

Isolated footnotes, whether substantive or bibliographic, are usually cited with an asterisk. If two footnotes appear in the same column or on the same page, a dagger is used for the second one. For the third footnote, a double dagger is used. If you are likely to have more than three footnotes falling together, you should use sequential numbers instead of asterisks and daggers (although other symbols *are* available to you; the sequence is *†‡§ ‖ ¶). Of course, if you do number footnotes consecutively, you run the risk of having to change all the numbers if the author deletes or adds a footnote. Monographs and other technical materials often contain over 100 footnotes, even in one chapter; renumbering—not only the footnotes but the text references as well—can be quite a chore. On the other hand, with so many footnotes, where several are sure to come on the same page, symbols become cumbersome. Discuss with the publisher which style is preferable.

Footnote numbers are usually small and are placed in the superscript position preceding the footnote, with no space following. But they may also be full size, on the line, with a period and space after, as in a list.

In-text references use the same symbol as the footnote itself, with the exception that in a numbering system, superscript numbers are always used, regardless of whether on-line numbers precede the footnote itself. Always mark in-text footnote references with a superscript mark, and in the left margin of the manuscript write "ftn" and circle it. The compositor can then repeat the callout in proof, and the makeup person will be able to spot it easily. Why is that important? Well, a footnote always appears in the same column or on the same page as its reference, and if a footnote is left out in makeup, considerable remake may be necessary. (By the way, only the beginning of the footnote need appear in position; if it's a very long footnote that won't fit, the rest may move to the bottom of the next column or page, where it will be preceded by a horizontal rule.)

Here's how a manuscript page with a footnote looks when properly marked:

```
According to Howe, ''There is no certain method for

learning French, although I have had the best luck with the

videolingual approach.''  She went on to describe that

method in detail.

    ¹Virginia Howe, Learning French (New York: Paris Press,

    1988), p. 17.
```

The footnote itself is keyed so that the compositor will follow the designer's specifications for footnotes (see Chapter 9).

Substantive footnotes should not replace text. If the material in the footnote is important, perhaps it should be made into a new text sentence or a parenthetical phrase following the previous text sentence. If you feel strongly that a footnote is inappropriate, make your case with the author. Likewise, if you think some material works better as a footnote than as text, tell the author. And be sure to renumber footnotes properly after making all the changes. Within each chapter in a book, or article in a magazine, footnotes run from 1 on, starting again from 1 in the next chapter or article. (Asterisks, of course, repeat on each page.)

Endnotes

If a book or article has a lot of footnotes, the makeup person may have difficulties positioning them all; for that reason, sometimes footnotes are grouped at the end of the book (or chapter or article) under the heading "Notes." Endnotes are simply footnotes in a different location. They may be substantive or bibliographic or a combination of the two. Some publishers require authors to place substantive notes at the end of the chapter, as endnotes. Like footnotes, all endnotes are called out in text with superscript numbers (beginning from 1 in each chapter), but in the endnotes section they are preceded by on-line, full-size numbers followed by a period.

What happens if the author groups the notes at the end of the chapter (or book!) in manuscript and the publisher wants them at the foot of the page? Well, on each page where a callout appears you write, at the foot, "Footnote appears on msp. x," filling in the appropriate manuscript page number on which the compositor will find the note. Likewise, if the author types the footnotes at the bottom of the manuscript page and the publisher wants them at the end of the book or chapter, write, at the bottom of the page, "Set footnotes together at the end of the book [chapter]." Then at the end of the book or chapter, you will write the head "Notes," give it the proper key (see Chapter 9), and say, "Insert footnotes 1-x here," where x is the number of the last footnote in the chapter. Of course, all this writing is quite a lot of work; a good compositor will get the picture from the start or from a covering memo, so always check with the publisher to see how much the compositor needs to be told.

Remember, if you are separating substantive footnotes from bibliographic ones, you will have to renumber carefully.

Source Notes

Some books and magazines are nothing more than compilations of reprinted material, often with a few paragraphs introducing each reading. Anthologies are collections of poems, plays, stories, or all of these and more, sometimes with original material describing what's to come or relating one item to a previous one. Trade magazines sometimes reprint articles from a variety of sources. And supplementary readings books do the same; they have such titles as *Readings in Ecology* or *Case Studies in Marketing Research*. Each item from another source must get a source note. Sometimes the source note appears at the foot of the page on which the item begins, sometimes it goes at the very end. It is usually unnumbered but is otherwise treated like other footnotes in the work. It contains complete bibliographic information along with a permission line specified by the copyright holder.

Source notes are often the one inconsistent item in a book or magazine. You should always use the source note requested by whoever grants permission to use the material, even though it may be inconsistent with one or several other source notes in the work. To a certain degree you may impose consistency, but not at the expense of altering the sequence in which the information is given.

Here is a typical source note.

> From *Learning French*, by Virgina Howe. Copyright © 1988 by Paris Press. Used by permission of the publisher.

That little *c* in a circle is the international copyright symbol and was adopted in 1955. It does not replace the word *copyright*. Even though you will see copyright lines treated in many ways, do not attempt to make them consistent. In any one book, you may see all of the following in source notes:

> Copyright © 1988
> © 1988
> Copyright 1988

(The one thing you can correct is if the letter granting permission leaves off the circle around the *c*. My Macintosh prints the symbol, but not all computers and typewriters can, and some people forget to draw the circle after they've typed the *c*. If the *c* is there, the circle belongs there, and you should add it. If there is no *c*, do not add one; it is the original publisher's prerogative whether to include it.)

Descriptive Notes

Magazines, in particular, often include original work by a number of different contributors. An editor who wants to describe the author's background may place a note either at the bottom of the first page of the article or at the bottom of the last column of the last page. The note will say something along these lines:

Michael Street is a freelance writer working in Nome, Alaska, and is a frequent contributor to *Alaska Today.*

Such notes should be made consistent, as much as possible, throughout the magazine: Treat credit lines similarly, give the same kind of background information, and keep the length about the same.

References and Readings

Some books or articles refer the reader to other materials on the same subject; such materials appear in the reference or reading lists at the end of each chapter or article. Sometimes reading lists are annotated; that is, in addition to the bibliographic information there is a short description of the material. At the end of this book you will find an annotated bibliography.

Reading lists rarely serve the purpose for which they were intended. The longer the list, the more it tends to intimidate the average reader. Clever copyeditors can help, however, by changing the inevitable heading "Suggested Further Reading" to something more inviting. One copyeditor I know *never* leaves such headings alone. With the author's permission he changed one series to "One Step Beyond," another to "Looking Further...," and a third to "For More Information." Almost anything except "Suggested Further Reading" will help stimulate interest, and it's especially important to be creative with annotated references, which the author clearly considers worth looking into.

Bibliographies

Strictly speaking, there is only one bibliography per book or article, and it falls at the very end. Unlike references, which are works that have been cited in the manuscript, the bibliography lists all materials used by the author in preparation for writing the manuscript. Readers are not necessarily encouraged to go to those sources for more information; rather the bibliography is a way of giving credit where it's due. Of course, some authors include in the bibliography those works actually cited in their material. In that case you should consider asking the author to separate such references into a "Works Cited" section, to make it easier for the reader to find when faced with a short citation in the text. If your author agrees, then the references remaining will be a true bibliography, and the author may be able to introduce it with a short note explaining how readers can do their own research.

Occasionally the bibliography will contain permission information, but normally it should not. Permissions statements should be made as source notes or footnotes or in a separate paragraph on the copyright page. (For a discussion of credit lines on the copyright page, refer to Frontmatter in Chapter 10.)

IN-TEXT REFERENCES TO SOURCES

There are many ways to refer the reader to notes and bibliographies. Let's first take the case where the sources are footnotes. We've already discussed the use of superscript numbers or asterisks for footnotes, but we haven't looked at where the number or asterisk should go in the text. Normally, place the footnote at the end of a sentence, not after the word to which the footnote refers. Thus you would have

Frost says that intelligence is inherited, not learned.[3]

and not

Frost[3] says that intelligence is inherited, not learned.

In mathematical copy, however, a superscript number—or even an asterisk—on mathematical expressions at the end of a sentence may be totally misunderstood. If you cannot rewrite the sentence easily, move the reference to somewhere else, where it will not be lost. Thus,

To 1 L of CCl_4 add 1 L of H_2O.[1]

is going to be confusing at best. Rewriting doesn't help, because instead of H_2O at the end of the sentence you'll have CCl_4. It is far better in this case to ignore the rule of footnote referencing and say

To 1 L of CCl_4 add[1] 1 L of H_2O.

And even in this sentence, perhaps an asterisk would be better still. (By the way, some technical authors mix the use of numbers and asterisks in footnotes for just that reason; sometimes an asterisk just works better.)

In-text references to bibliographies are even more complicated than footnote references. If the bibliography is numbered by item (in which case it is a combined list of works cited and works used in writing the material), then often just a number is used to refer you to a work. The number is full size, on the line (i.e., not superscript), and within brackets.

This is called the *videolingual approach* [23].

Here the bracketed number refers to a numbered list of references at the end of the book or chapter; you've probably guessed that the twenty-third reference is to Virginia Howe's book *Learning French* and that in that book the term *videolingual approach* is coined.

But if possible, avoid an in-text reference system that's based on numbers: If the alphabetized sources are numbered for reference and one is deleted, they're all wrong after that number. (If you do get stuck with a manuscript of numbered references, copyedit them first. Sometimes you'll find errors, such as two works covered by one number, and you'll want everything straightened out before you have to renumber the text references.) A far better referencing system is the author-date system.

> This is called the *videolingual approach* (Howe 1988).

Chicago Manual calls it the most practical system. If the author's name is already part of the sentence, you can say,

> Howe (1988: 33) says . . . ,

where 33 is the page reference. When there are several Howe articles, use an op. cit. citation or a short-form citation (we'll discuss these shortly).

> Smith, op. cit. (see note 13), p. 33.

Or even easier, append *a, b, c,* and so on, to the year to indicate which of several works by the same author you are referring to; add the same letter in the bibliography. Be sure to check that the years are the same in the text as in the bibliography.

Like bracketed reference numbers, author-date references come at the end of the text sentence, before the period.

> This situation is sometimes referred to as "ecological warfare" (Frost 1971*a*).

If the quotation is displayed, the reference (if it's appropriate at all) follows the period. Anthropology materials often use this style.

> One reporter found almost inconceivable brutality.
>
>> Over 10,000 tribespeople were murdered and 23,000 maimed following the uprising. The soldiers claimed no responsibility for the "incident." (Frost 1971*a*)

Try to be consistent about how you introduce long quotations. Do you end the introduction with a colon? Or does the thought of the sentence run into the displayed quotation? You decide. If the quotation runs logically from the introductory phrase, you can begin it with a lowercase letter, but it is easier, *if what follows is a complete sentence,* to make it a capital regardless of the style in the original.

> Martinez complained that
>
>> Thousands of people are starving to death, and no major government has volunteered to send food. Why must the smaller nations bear the brunt of this deplorable situation?

FOOTNOTE FORM

Substantive footnotes, obviously, take the form of text, from which they differ only in location. Bibliographic footnotes have a special form, as follows:

> ³John R. Author, *Book Title* (Indianapolis, IN: Bobbs-Merrill, 1980), chap. 2.
> ⁴Mary K. Writer, "Article Title," *J. Educ. Soc.* 8 (1970): 421–425.

I want to emphasize that this is *one*—not the only—acceptable method for writing footnotes. If the author has consistently used another method, *do not change it;* just be sure to have all notes conform to that style.

Let's look at the individual points in these notes and formulate some rules, however arbitrary.

► DID YOU NOTICE?

1. The first name goes first.
2. Main items are separated by commas.
3. Publication information for books appears within parentheses.

Note that *in this system of referencing,* the article title appears in capital and lowercase letters within quotation marks, and the book and journal title appear in capital and lowercase letters in italic type; the journal number is in roman type (not italic). That is *one* way of treating the information—not *the* way.

BIBLIOGRAPHIC FORM

Within a bibliography or reference list, entries take a different form from footnotes. One such form is as follows:

> Author, John R. *Book Title,* 2nd ed. Indianapolis, IN: Bobbs-Merrill, 1980, chap 2.
> Writer, Mary K., and John Q. Public. "Article Title." *J. Educ. Soc.* 8 (1970): 421–425.
> Writer, Sally. "Article Title." *Daily Newspaper,* 7 May 1977, p. 20.

What differences do you see between footnotes and bibliographies?

► DID YOU NOTICE?

1. The last name goes first.
2. When there is more than one author, the first author's name is

inverted but the second author's name appears in regular order.
3. There is a comma after an inverted name preceding another name.
4. Main items are separated by periods.

That was easy enough, wasn't it? Of course, there's a lot more to it than that, mostly because few references actually conform to these simple patterns. Before we look at some of the exceptions, though, let's look at more rules. These rules apply to bibliographic references of all types.

Rules for Notes and Bibliographies

1. Place a space between the initials of a person's name.

   G. K. Smith

2. Use Postal Service abbreviations if possible. If you use traditional abbreviations, do not use space in the abbreviation of a state.

   Minot, ND

   or

   Minot, N.D.

3. Use the publisher's name and location as they appear on the title page of the book or the periodical's masthead. Naturally, you personally are not expected to check out books from the library to verify the author's information; just be aware that most authorities agree that publisher names and locations should not be updated. I used to be one of the dissenters. My theory was that if you are reading something and find a reference to a book you want to buy, you will not be able to locate it if the publisher has moved or been bought by another publisher. The trouble is, there are so many mergers these days that no publisher is safe. There's no way to know which imprints the new owner is retaining and which are being sacrificed in favor of the new owner's name. So the reader who can't find Row, Peterson in Evanston, Illinois (because that's long since been Harper & Row in New York—and owned by Rupert Murdoch's huge British conglomerate), will just have to go to the library or bookstore and track down the publisher through *Books in Print* (see the bibliography).

4. Include the state for all cities except New York, Boston, Philadelphia, Chicago, San Francisco, and Los Angeles.

Columbus, OH
Indianapolis, Ind.

5. Repeat the state for university presses.

University of California Press, Berkeley, CA

6. Use short forms for publishers unless otherwise directed. But be sure the short form is appropriate. The short form for Harcourt Brace Jovanovich, for example, is Harcourt Brace Jovanovich. Usually a short form is made by getting rid of "Publishers," "Publishing Company," and first names. Retain "Books" and "Press" as part of the short form. (Always delete "Co.," "Inc.," and "Ltd.")

Long Form	*Short Form*
John Wiley & Sons	Wiley
Harper & Row, Publishers	Harper & Row
The Benjamin/Cummings Publishing Company	Benjamin/Cummings
Beacon Press	Beacon Press
University of Chicago Press	University of Chicago Press

Note: Magazines have short forms, too, gleaned mostly from tradition and common sense. Major magazines (*House Beautiful, New Yorker,* etc.) should not be shortened, and indeed there is little need to. But professional journals often have very long titles and fairly standard, accepted abbreviations. They use *J.* for *Journal* and get rid of most articles and conjunctions, leaving, for example, *J. Soc. Research* (*Research* isn't abbreviated because *Res.* could stand for too many terms) or *Sci. Amer.,* for *Journal of Sociological Research* and *Scientific American,* respectively. Be consistent in abbreviating journal titles (but you'll find the task fairly simple).

7. Use inclusive page numbers.

pp. 236–238

Some magazines, such as *Consumer Reports,* number their pages consecutively for the entire year. Most, however, begin from page 1 each month. Thus, to provide a proper reference, you need to include both the volume number (which tells which year it is) and either the month or the issue number (the issue number tells which month it is).

REFERENCES TO PREVIOUSLY CITED WORKS

You've seen those strange words *ibid., op. cit.,* and *loc. cit.,* right? Do you know what they mean? Well, they're Latin, of course, and they mean, respectively, "in the same place," "in the work cited," and "in the place cited." Simply knowing what they mean should help you figure out why and how they're used. Let's look at each briefly.

Ibid.

We said that *ibid.* means "in the same place." Thus *ibid.* (which should be set roman, as should all the rest) is used to refer back to the *last* reference. It replaces the author and work, although a volume or page number can differ. A reference to page 433 of volume 9 of a particular journal of the same name as the previous reference may therefore read, "Ibid. 9: 433."

Op. Cit. and Loc. Cit.

If you're referring to a work other than the immediately preceding one, *loc. cit.* takes you to the exact same usage given previously (the same page) and *op. cit.* to the same work but a different page. With either abbreviation you must repeat as much of the bibliographic information as needed to distinguish one work from another. For example, let's say that these footnotes have already shown up in Chapters 1 and 2:

> [2]Virginia Howe, *Learning French* (New York: Paris Press, 1988).
> [3]Mildred Tobias, "Franglais: Enemy of the People," *J. Educ. Research* 20 (1988): 79–83.

When you refer back to these sources when you edit Chapter 3, here's how your references may read:

> [4]Howe, op. cit., p. 33. [This refers to the only work by Howe; the material cited appears on page 33.]

> [5]Tobias, op. cit., p. 80. [This is Tobias's only work, and the material cited is on page 80.]

> [6]Howe, loc. cit. [Now we're referring once again to page 33 of Howe.]

> [7]Ibid., p. 39. [This refers to page 39 of the immediately preceding work cited, that is, *Learning French.*]

Now it's time to tell you that *Chicago Manual* (and let's face it, they *are* the experts) does not use these abbreviations. Instead they shorten the title of the work on the assumption that even a short title has more meaning than an obscure Latin abbreviation. In that system we would say

> [5]Tobias, "Franglais," p. 80.

EXERCISES

If you are a good copyeditor, you try to be consistent, right? Then it should be easy for you to put all sorts of information into consistent bibliographic style. Let's look at a few common types of bibliographic references and try to make them consistent with the forms given earlier. Punctuation has been deliberately altered.

1. Paul Smith, Darcy R. Conrad, and Jan Connors, Deviant Behaviour in Adolescents, in Adolescent Sex, edited by Theresa Lake (Chicago, Illinois: Fast Publishing Company, 1973).

2. Michael Dekker, Sociology: A Modern Approach, revised edition (New York: Blankman Press, 1979).

3. Judith Weidner, Being a Whole Person Requires Patience, Living Magazine, October 8, 1979, p. 27.

4. Robin Small, Financing a New Car Doesn't Have to Put You into Debtor's Prison, New York Daily Press, March 5, 1980.

5. How to Be a Winner, Los Angeles Tribune, March 13, 1969.

6. David S. Tynan, The Voice of the Turtle: American Literature in the Twentieth Century, unpublished dissertation.

7. Page Turner, Life After Death, translated by Derek Jones (Pittsburgh, PA: Clarkson Book Company, 1975).

8. Clayton and Susan Walden, Writing Your Own Ticket, Social Animals, volume 7, December 1977.

Answers

Now, how would you make these consistent with the bibliographic form we've already seen? Remember, if they were footnotes, they'd be treated almost the same way, with just minor changes.

1. Smith, Paul, Darcy R. Conrad, and Jan Conners. "Deviant Behaviour in Adolescents." In *Adolescent Sex*, Theresa Lake, ed. Chicago: Fast, 1973.

What have I done here? First I inverted the first author's name; the others stay in proper order in a bibliography. Then I ended the first major item—the authors' names—with a period. I determined that the first title was a chapter within a book (and note that I didn't change the spelling of "Behaviour"; if that's the way the chapter title appeared, that's what I leave, although I may query the author), so I punctuated accordingly, using quotation marks for the chapter, italic for the book. The second piece of information, the chapter title, ended with a period, so "In" begins with a capital letter. Why did I put a comma and not a period after the book title? Well, that piece of information wasn't complete; if the editor's name were not part of the information, what would that name connect to? And notice that I changed "edited by Theresa Lake" to "Theresa Lake, ed."—which can be "Theresa Lake (ed.)," if you prefer. That's consistent with the effort to keep entries short, and it also fits in with the use of "2nd ed." in the basic bibliographic form. (It would not have been incorrect to leave it alone, however.) Then I got rid of "Illinois" (Chicago doesn't need further identification, I decided), got rid of the long form of the publisher's name, and took the publication information out of parentheses.

That was simple enough, wasn't it? Let's look at number 2.

 2. Dekker, Michael. *Sociology: A Modern Approach*, rev. ed. New York: Blankman Press, 1979.

This time I didn't delete "Press" because that's part of the short form. But the other changes are straightforward.

 3. Weidner, Judith. "Being a Whole Person Requires Patience." *Living Magazine*, 8 October 1979, p. 27.

Note how the date was changed to fit the bibliographic form for weekly magazines and daily newspapers. Also query the author (unless you know for sure) about the magazine title: Is it *Living Magazine* or just *Living*?

 4. Small, Robin. "Financing a New Car Doesn't Have to Put You into Debtor's Prison." *New York Daily Press*, 5 March 1980.
 5. "How to Be a Winner." *Los Angeles Tribune*, 13 March 1969.

No author known? No problem. Just put the title first and put the reference into alphabetical order with the rest.

 6. Tynan, David S. "The Voice of the Turtle: American Literature in the Twentieth Century." Unpublished dissertation.

Dissertations are treated like articles, not books. If you know what school the dissertation was given at, include it: "Unpublished dissertation, University of California at Irvine, 1979." You might ask the author to supply that missing information.

> **7.** Turner, Page. *Life After Death,* Derek Jones, trans. Pittsburgh, PA: Clarkson, 1975.

A translator is treated the way an editor is. If you choose the form "Theresa Lake (ed.)," then make this "Derek Jones (trans.)." Note that the state abbreviation is used because Pittsburgh, while familiar, is not one of the six cities named earlier.

> **8.** Walden, Clayton, and Susan Walden. "Writing Your Own Ticket." *Social Animals* 7 (1977): 81–98.

When two people with the same last name are the authors of the work, repeat the last name. And did you notice that this is an article in a magazine? Then put it into journal format. Don't be misled by extra information, such as the word "volume" or the month (or even, sometimes, the city where the magazine is published). The page numbers came from querying the author; in this bibliographic form, they're really necessary. And surely you remembered to put the comma after "Clayton" when you inverted the name!

Of course, many references and footnotes you see will be more complicated than these examples, but you should be able to see a pattern emerging from them. If you edit all bibliographic information together, you'll have no trouble maintaining consistency. By all means, feel free to follow *Chicago Manual* or *Words into Type,* as long as you note how they differ from my form and as long as you can adapt similar forms to be consistent. But most of all, follow the author's style. The author may be following Modern Language Association style, or National Education Association style, or a style laid down by the American Institute of Biological Sciences, the American Chemical Society, or even a particular publishing house. Don't be alarmed if you see the date first, or right after the author's name: Many styles use that system. Never change a good style to another good style without the author's permission; the author has a perfect right to ask, "What was wrong with the way *I* did it?"

► KEY POINTS IN THIS CHAPTER

- The sequence of footnote symbols is *†‡§‖¶. Use symbols when there are few footnotes per chapter or in mathematical copy, where numbers may be confusing.

- In-text references use the same symbol as the footnote; but when numbers are used, superscript numbers are always used for the in-text reference, even if an on-line number precedes the footnote itself. On-line numbers appear in the note in an endnotes section; superscript numbers appear in footnotes.
- Always mark in-text footnote references with a superscript mark, and in the left margin of the manuscript write "ftn" and circle it.
- Use the source note requested by whoever grants permission to use the material; do not add the copyright symbol or the word *copyright.*
- Make descriptive notes consistent.
- An in-text referencing system based on short forms rather than numbers is preferable. If numbers are used, they go in brackets before the period; if short forms are used, they go within parens— before the period in text, after in display.
- Be consistent about how you introduce long quotations, whether with a colon or running into the displayed quotation. Begin a long (displayed) quotation with a capital letter if what follows is a complete sentence, regardless of the style in the original.
- Use short titles or Latin abbreviations to refer back to sources already cited.

CHAPTER 9

Typemarking and Keying

When you write a letter to a friend, you treat everything the same and just indent or add space for paragraphs; you don't write different sections in different styles. But when a newspaper or magazine prints an article, it includes paragraph headings, footnotes, headlines or titles, bylines, and many other elements. And in a college textbook there may be exercises and headings of various levels and boxed cases and case study titles and tables and captions and just about anything else you can think of. Merely providing the compositor with manuscript for all these elements is not enough; you have to explain how the elements should be differentiated typographically.

In Chapter 2 we saw that copyediting has its own set of symbols, just as dance has choreographic symbols and football has x's and o's. Anything can be explained typographically using these symbols. But to describe all the elements that may appear in a book or magazine or newspaper, you need another set of marking instructions, instructions to show the compositor how large to set a particular piece of copy, and where on the page it should go, and how much space to put around it, and how flowery or sedate the type should appear. Such instructions pertain to the *design*, and they are translated by *type specifications,* or *specs.* The compositor understands what type specifications to follow by reading *keying* instructions that the copyeditor puts on the manuscript.

Typemarking consists of writing the actual specs for each element directly on the manuscript. In keying, however, a symbol is used to stand for the specs for the element. For example, a circled 1 immediately to the left of a first-level heading (keys are normally written on the left) may mean, "Set this heading in 12-point Helvetica bold, initial cap, flush left, 36 points space base to base above, 18 points base to base below." How much easier it is to just use the key! (In the next several pages we'll see what those specs mean.)

Most freelance copyeditors are not asked to understand typemarking, but they need to know enough to key elements properly. And if you work in a publishing office, you almost certainly will be exposed to the technical language of typographical design instructions. These specs are often written on a *composition* (or *comp*) *order.* In this chapter we will look at some of the instructions given in a comp order and what they mean. Then we will see how easily these instructions can be applied to straight copy that you wish to differentiate typographically.

We begin our discussion of design specs by defining the terms you will need to understand.

TYPEFACE

The most important element in a design is the typeface, or appearance of the type. Following are several samples of six divergent typefaces, including a couple of weird ones.

Garamond	**Eras Bold**
Helvetica	*Lubalin Demi Oblique*
BROADWAY	**Harry Obese**

Can you imagine what it would be like to read a whole book printed in Eras Bold? Clearly, that face is used sparingly—for headlines, perhaps, or for advertising. Garamond, on the other hand, is frequently used for entire books and articles. And Helvetica could be used in large amounts but is more frequently used only for small passages, areas of type that a designer wishes to distinguish from the rest, such as captions and tables.

TYPE SIZE

The size of a typeface is measured in *points.* The examples just shown are all in 10-point type; and although the lowercase letters vary a lot, the capital letters appear to be approximately the same size. Type can also be measured in *picas*, which are larger than points. An inch is approximately 6 picas; a pica has 12 points (Figure 9.1). This book was designed in 10-point type. In fact, most books and magazines are designed in 10-point type, with a few in 9- or 11-point. Children's books, of course, use much larger type, and newspapers smaller.

Why is a particular point size used? In most cases it is easiest to read 10-point type. But what would happen if newspapers set everything in 10-point type? The columns would have awfully few characters! It is not always practical, for reasons of space, to use a standard-size type. Furthermore, as you can see from the examples given earlier, some 10-point type looks bigger than others. That's because it has a lower *character count*—that is, fewer characters to a pica. Character count tells the designer how many characters, on the average, will fit in 1 pica. If a designer has a lot of space to play around with, it will be OK to use a typeface with a poor character count.

All compositors can supply lists of their typefaces and the character counts of those typefaces. The major compositors print these lists very neatly in *type books.* In these books each page shows the typeface in many different sizes and in italic, boldface, and whatever else may be available. Thus the designer can see at a glance whether 10-point Baskerville will look too small or whether 10-point Lubalin will be too hard to read. After choosing a suitable typeface and size, the designer can test the character count against the amount of material she or he must fit and see whether the typeface will work. Doing these calculations is called *casting off.*

Simple arithmetic shows how a castoff works. Suppose you have a page of manuscript that contains 1,600 characters. The designer wants to use a typeface with a character count of 2.8 characters per

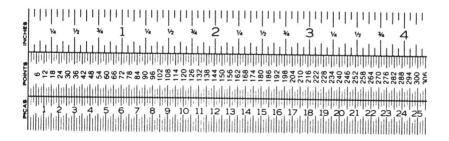

Figure 9.1. The standard ruler and the pica ruler (or pica stick).

pica, and she or he wishes to work with a 28-pica line. How many lines will the manuscript page take up?

$$2.8 \text{ char.} \times 28 \text{ picas} = 78.4 \text{ char. per line}$$
$$1,600 \text{ char.} \div 78.4 \text{ char. per line} = 20.408 \text{ lines}$$

Well, you can't have 20.408 lines; you have to have 20 lines plus part of another, or 21 in all; the manuscript page will take 21 lines. If the designer doesn't have room for 21 lines, such as in a page of advertising copy, then either the line length will have to be increased (from 28 to, say, 29 picas) or a typeface with a better character count will have to be chosen. That may mean going to a smaller-size type.

Naturally, castoffs are not completely accurate. No two manuscript pages will have the same number of characters, and some characters are smaller than others; an *i* takes up less space than an *M*, for example. Then, too, how can you put, say, 78.4 characters on a line? You can't put 0.4 of a character on one line and 0.6 on the next! But designers allow for differences and thus can cast off manuscripts fairly accurately.

If you have the opportunity, take a look at a compositor's type book; it's fascinating. And if you have a real interest in the material in this chapter, get hold of a copy of James Craig's superb book *Production for the Graphic Designer*, described in the bibliography.

Now on to the other elements of design.

LEADING

Leading (pronounced "ledding") is the amount of space between lines, and it, too, is measured in points or picas. (Leading takes its name from the slug of lead used in hot-metal composition. Although hot metal is rarely used now, its language lingers.) If something has 3-point leading, there is more space between lines than if it had 2-point leading. Normally, the larger the point size of the type, the more leading will be needed between lines to keep the material readable. Point size and leading are usually read together, for example, 10/12 (read "ten on twelve"). This means 10-point type on a 12-point line depth, or, in other words, 2 points of leading. Can you see that 9/11 also has 2 points of leading? And 10/13 has 3 points of leading. Here are some examples of Garamond with different point sizes and different leading.

This is set in 9/11.	This is set in 9/12.
This is set in 10/11.	This is set in 10/12.

You might get the impression from these examples that items get only 1, 2, or 3 points of leading. Most straight reading material, it is true, is fairly tightly leaded. Some material is not leaded at all (for example, 7/7 indicates 7-point type on a 7-point line, with no leading). But that is not to say that one line runs right in with the next. Remember from the examples of 10-point type shown earlier that not all 10-point type looks the same size. By the same token, some 7-point typefaces appear to be more open than others. Those faces don't look crammed on 7-point lead, whereas other faces do. The designer must decide just how much leading is readable. Too much can be just as bad as too little. Imagine how difficult it would be to read this book if there were an inch of space between the lines—to say nothing of how long the book would be! There is obviously a happy medium, one the designer strives to reach.

In most cases, if a line of type is to be leaded out greatly, the instructions are given as a typeface and the amount of space below, rather than in the form of a certain point-size type on a certain point-size line. For a particular heading a designer may specify, "10-point Garamond with 18 points space base to base below." This means that whatever copy is to fall below the heading has to fit into the 18 points left for it. Any extra space is simply visual space below the Garamond head. You can draw this to see how it would look (Figure 9.2). Can you see in the figure that if the line below the head is 10/12, there will be 6 points of visual space below the head, and if the line is 10/11, there will be 7 points of space? What determines visual space is the specified line depth (the vertical distance from the base of one line to the base of the next one, indicated by the number following the slash).

Figure 9.2. A thumbnail sketch showing visual space below a head.

As mentioned in Chapter 2, compositors can figure out all sorts of shorthand notation. One quick way some designers might write the spec for the head shown in Figure 9.2 is "10-pt Garamond, 18 pts b/b below." They may also stipulate this by saying "10/18 Garamond." That means that if you subtract the 12-point line depth below the head, you're left with 6 points of space below the head. Let's see how that works (Figure 9.3). If they want to spec space above a head at the

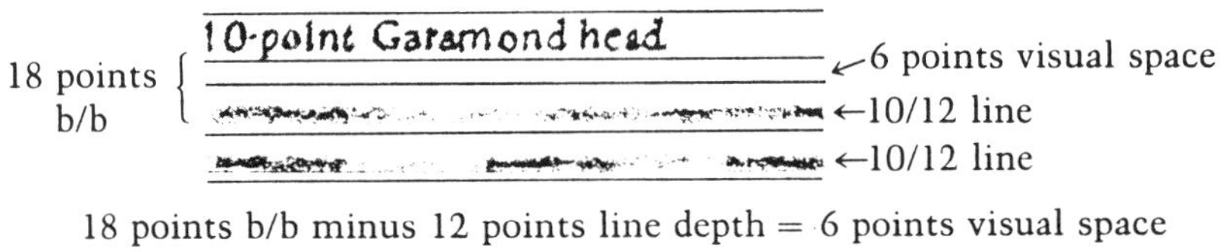

18 points b/b minus 12 points line depth = 6 points visual space

Figure 9.3. A thumbnail sketch showing lines of type below a head.

same time, designers may write "10-pt Garamond, 48 pts/18 pts," meaning 48 points of space baseline to baseline (or "base to base") above the head, 18 below. To tell the compositor to put equal space above and below a head, some designers will say, "Eq. # above and below." But no designer will get carried away with shorthand notation without being sure of the compositor and of what the compositor is likely to do.

POSITIONING

Every item on a printed page has a position relative both to the margins on that page and to everything else on it. The block of type you're reading now has a position on the piece of paper it appears on; everything that is not type area is margin. The designer must spec both type area (i.e., how much margin to allow) and positioning of each element within the type area.

The size of the piece of paper in a finished book, article, or newspaper is called the *trim size.* The trim size you are most familiar with is 8½ × 11, which is the size of notebook paper. Some books and magazines are this size, but there are many other standard trim sizes as well. The designer is usually told what trim size the publisher is willing to use and then must work with that size.

For the rest of this discussion, let's look at a simple example. A popular trim size in book publishing is 6 × 9; that means that the finished paper size (disregard the cover) is 6 inches wide and 9 inches high (the width always comes first). Knowing this, the designer must now spec the *type page* or *type area,* or how much of the trim size will be taken up by type. Designers know that there is a certain comfortable reading length for a line of type, so even if there's room for more words on a page, a designer will avoid trying to cram them in. In our example let's pick a reading length of 27 picas. (Notice that although the trim size is given in inches, the line length is in picas. In fact, *only* the nontype areas—trim size and margins—are given in inches; everything else is given in picas and points or, occasionally, as we saw in Chapter 2, in ems and ens.) If we translate the 6-inch width into picas (remember, there are about 6 picas to an inch), we get a total of 36 picas, 27 of which are taken up as the line length. That leaves 9 picas for the inside and outside margins. Margins, remember, are given in inches, so we have 1½ inches total for the two margins. It is common for the outside margin to be slightly wider than the *gutter*, as the inside margin is called, although, of course, there must be enough of a gutter so that the book can be laid open flat enough to read. In this example, our designer chooses to have a $^{13}\!/_{16}$-inch outside margin and an $^{11}\!/_{16}$-inch gutter, totaling 1½ inches.

The designer then decides how much of the depth of the page can be taken up with type. Top and bottom margins usually relate to the outside and gutter margins, with the top normally bigger than the bottom. Let's say the designer decides on a 1-inch top and $^{11}\!/_{16}$-inch bottom for a total of $1^{11}\!/_{16}$ inches out of the 9 inches of trim size. That leaves $7^{5}\!/_{16}$ inches for type, which equals 44 picas. Now remember, there are 12 points in a pica, so there are 528 points on the page. The designer may choose to set this book in 9/11, meaning there can be 48 lines of type (528 divided by 11) on the page. Or if the designer adjusts the top and bottom margins a bit, there can be 53 lines of 8/10 or 9/10 type on the page (528 divided by 10). But to make everything easier, we're going to assume that there are 44 lines of type (528 divided by 12) on the page. It can be 8/12, 9/12, 10/12, or even 11/12; the number of lines on the page says nothing about the size of the typeface, only the size of the line depth.

Let's say, again because it's the most common type size for a book, that the designer chooses 10/12, and we'll pick a typeface, say, Garamond. What do we know so far? We know that the trim size is 6 × 9, we know the margins, and we know that the book is being set in 10/12 Garamond 27 picas wide (written "10/12 Garamond × 27 pi") with 44 lines to a page. So we know the position. We could draw an exact layout by first drawing a rectangle 6 inches by 9 inches and then by measuring off the margins. The rectangle inside the 6 × 9 rectangle will be our type area. Figure 9.4 shows a scale drawing of how this layout would look; the figure is drawn to 50 percent of size.

Every other instruction the designer gives will relate to that type area. If the spec says "flush left," it means on the type area, not on the trim size. If the spec says "indent 3 pi," it means that 3 picas of the 27-pica line will be taken up by the indent.

Let's look at a couple of simple instructions. Let's say that a book has two types of headings. The primary head is going to be set in 12-point Helvetica with 4 lines of space above it and 18 points of space below it. (Remember that only 6 of those 18 points are visual space; the rest is the leading of the 10/12 type line that falls below the head.)

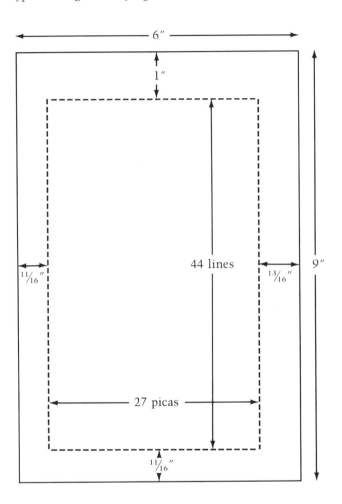

Figure 9.4. A possible layout for a 6 × 9 book. The figure is drawn to 50 percent of actual size.

The secondary head is to be in 10-point Helvetica with 2 lines of space above and 18 points of space below. Both will be flush left. The primary head is going to be set in capital letters, the other one in capital and lowercase letters. How might these instructions look? (By the way, there are various conventions, but no rules, for describing type and position; the main rule the designer follows is to make it clear to the compositor.) The first head, which we'll call #1, might be specified thus: 12 pt. Helv. caps, fl.l., 48 pts b/b above, 18 pts below. Specs for the second head, or #2, might read: 10 pt Helv. clc, fl.l., 24 pts b/b above, 18 pts b/b below. You can probably guess what some of the shorthand means:

pts	points
caps	capital letters
fl.l.	flush left
b/b	base to base
clc	capital and lowercase letters (i.e., initial cap all important words)

What would these heads look like if we tried to draw them? A thumbnail sketch is shown in Figure 9.5.

Now that you know what a designer does in preparing a composition order, you're probably saying, "So what? I don't want to be a designer." That may be true, but as a copyeditor you must be able to see design patterns arising. It will often be your job to determine what bodies of copy merit particular treatment. Every element in a book, magazine, newspaper, advertisement, or brochure must be identified with its size, typeface, and position on the page. To make it simple for you, the copyeditor, the designer will assign a keymarking symbol for each element for which there are instructions for the compositor: #1 heads set this way, #2 heads set that way, footnotes set some other way. All *you* have to do is tell the compositor what's a #1 head, a #2 head, and a footnote! This identification process is called *keying* or *coding*.

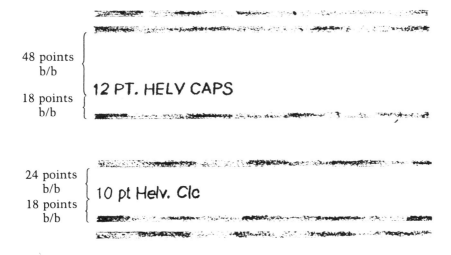

Figure 9.5. A thumbnail sketch showing how a designer might draw heads within a page. In this figure there are 48 points of space above and 18 points of space below the #1 head, and 24 points above and 18 points below the #2 head.

KEYING

Most newspapers and magazines follow *standard specs;* that is, every issue looks pretty much the same. Books, brochures, and ads, on the other hand, are designed from scratch each time. But because the compositor has a legend to follow—the composition order—the manuscripts for these newly designed materials can simply be keyed, or coded. If you are a staff copyeditor, you may be the one asked to come up with the codes, although sometimes coding is done by an editor or designer. If you freelance, the publisher may supply the codes and ask you to mark the manuscript accordingly.

Remember from our example in the previous section that the only standard instruction is where the type area fits onto the trim size. *Every variation must be keyed into the composition order.* As a copyeditor you may be told to use the keys 1, 2, 3, and so on, for head levels, FN for footnote, TC for table column head, TB for table body, and so forth. You must decide, therefore, what head should be level 3, where the table column head leaves off and the table body begins, and all other typographic distinctions. Do not assume that the author has typed the manuscript properly. You must be able to improve the organization of the manuscript by giving elements design emphasis. With each element other than straight text, ask yourself, "What is this? Does it resemble anything I've seen earlier or am likely to see again? If I designate it as a certain design element, am I likely to give it too much importance? Does it fit the design keys, or should it perhaps be treated specially? Or, could I typemark it myself and not give it a special design treatment?" Bear in mind, you may never see the composition (or comp) order, just the codes, so you won't know how the designer has chosen to treat something. If no suitable key exists, it's possible that the designer has not accounted for the element, and *you* will have to decide how to treat it. Remember, the compositor can only follow the comp order; the compositor will never (under ordinary circumstances) try to design special elements for the publisher.

If you decide to typemark the element yourself, you are limited to certain simple choices; after all, you may not even know what typeface and size have been selected. You can choose between roman and italic and boldface type, between caps and lowercase and small caps and their combinations (initial cap only, caps and small caps, etc.), space above and below, and position on the page (indent, flush left, flush right, center, or run in). If the element is complicated, naturally you should call it to the publisher's attention.

Let's look at some simple typemarking instructions. Suppose a section of manuscript is typed like this:

```
Now take 1 liter of hydrogen sulfide from the shelf.

    WARNING!

Do this experiment under the hood.
```

You decide that the warning should be treated differently, so you want to typemark it. Here are some possibilities—not the only ones, but sufficient as examples of how to typemark. Please realize that this is the simplest case of typemarking. Following each numbered example is the way it will appear in type.

1.

```
Now take 1 liter of hydrogen sulfide from the shelf.
    (WARNING:
Do this experiment under the hood.)
```

Now take 1 liter of hydrogen sulfide from the shelf. (WARNING: Do this experiment under the hood.)

2.

```
Now take 1 liter of hydrogen sulfide from the shelf.
    WARNING!
Do this experiment under the hood.
```

Now take 1 liter of hydrogen sulfide from the shelf. **WARNING!** *Do this experiment under the hood.*

3.

```
Now take 1 liter of hydrogen sulfide from the shelf.
    (WARNING!)
Do this experiment under the hood.)
```

Now take 1 liter of hydrogen sulfide from the shelf. (*WARNING!* Do this experiment under the hood.)

4.

```
Now take 1 liter of hydrogen sulfide from the shelf.
    ¶ WARNING! □
Do this experiment under the hood.
```

Now take 1 liter of hydrogen sulfide from the shelf.
WARNING! *Do this experiment under the hood.*

Sometimes you will have to use typemarking in conjunction with keying to change solid text material into displayed text material, or vice versa. Maybe you want to make a paragraph into a list, or a sentence into a heading, or a long quotation into a set-off extract. You will need to use the symbols you learned from Chapter 2 along with the keys provided by the publisher (or that you invented). The following are some examples of common typemarking situations. Each shows the typed manuscript and the copyeditor's marking, followed by the typeset version. See if you can follow how the copyeditor's marking showed the compositor what to do. Remember that the compositor has a comp order specifying how each key—EXT (extracts), L (lists), the various heads, and so on—is to be set. If you forget what the symbols mean, go back to Chapter 2 and find them in the headings.

In this chapter we will investigate the reasons students have difficulty in studying: (1) lack of concentration (2) distractions from outside (3) laziness (4) the feeling of hopelessness and (5) psychosomatic illness. Then we will look at ways to overcome these difficulties.

In this chapter we will investigate the reasons students have difficulty in studying:

1. lack of concentration
2. distractions from outside
3. laziness
4. the feeling of hopelessness
5. psychosomatic illness

Then we will look at ways to overcome these difficulties.

► **DID YOU NOTICE?**

1. When (as in the example just given) you turn a run-in series of numbered items into a displayed list, the connective *and* before the last item becomes unnecessary. Always reread your changes as they appear so that you can determine if extra words are needed or certain words can be dropped.

2. After the last entry in the list we had a choice between beginning a new paragraph and having the discussion continue flush left. A paragraph is used if a new thought begins. In this case there was no new thought, so I marked for flush left. In either case you *must* decide and then mark accordingly.

Here's another example of a common situation.

According to Howe, there is no certain method for learning French. Many students have found over the years that the audiovisual method gives the longest-lasting results, but I have also had good luck with what I like to call the 'videolingual' approach. Under this system the students listen to the instructor, see slides to help them connect what they hear with the real world, and then repeat what they have learned.

EXT

According to Howe, there is
no certain method for learning French. Many students have found over the years that the audiovisual method gives the longest-lasting results, but I have also had good luck with what I like to call the "videolingual" approach. Under this system the students listen to the instructor, see slides to help them connect what they hear with the real world, and then repeat what they have learned.

► DID YOU NOTICE?

1. To make an extract out of this quote, I had to do something about the incomplete sentence. I had several options, of which I chose the simplest. This solution, however, is not really the best one. The others are (a) to begin with a capital letter and "invent" the missing verb by enclosing one within brackets (see Chapter 4) or (b) to use part of the quotation to complete the sentence. Here is how these choices would look in type. Can you see how you would mark them to get them this way?

According to Howe,
No certain method [exists] for learning

or

> According to Howe, there is "no certain method for learning French."
> Many students...

Notice in the first example that we made a capital N out of a lowercase letter; that is perfectly acceptable. What we cannot do is put words into Howe's mouth. If she did not say "there is," we cannot have her say it, unless, of course, we enclose it in brackets.

2. When the quotation became extracted and set off typographically, the quotation marks became redundant. However, because the speaker herself used a quoted term, we had to change those single quotation marks (which were originally needed in the double-quoted passage) to double quotation marks, which are now the only ones we're using.

3. By the way, and we'll discuss this point in more detail later, you may not change any word within a quotation unless you bracket your change. You *may* make typographic changes. Thus Howe's hyphens remain or go, depending on her original quote.

Now here's an example of making a sentence into a footnote.

Cullen discussed this topic more fully in several fine books. (One of my favorites is The Pregnant Ballerina and Other Atrocities, published by Clandestine Press in 1969.)

Cullen discussed this topic more fully in several fine books.[1]

[1]One of my favorites is *The Pregnant Ballerina and Other Atrocities,* published by Clandestine Press in 1969.

► **DID YOU NOTICE?**

1. As a footnote, the second sentence no longer needs parentheses, but now a footnote reference is needed, both on the note and in the text.

2. Footnotes often contain complete bibliographic information, so although the informality of this note is basically acceptable, it would have been better done in note style, with the place of publication added.

By now you should have the hang of how to make typographic changes in running text. Remember the following points:

1. Key the new element so that the compositor knows its exact boundaries and will set just that material, according to the specifications for that key.
2. Delete old punctuation that becomes unnecessary when a new typographic element is created.
3. Add any punctuation that may be needed once the change has been made.
4. Determine whether single or double quotation marks are needed internally if you display a quotation.
5. Mark for paragraph or flush left where appropriate.
6. Mark the text following an illustration or table with either a run-in mark or a paragraph indent; it cannot go flush left.
7. Reread your proposed change *mark for mark* to determine whether it is accurate. If necessary, diagram the change as you have marked it to see if the compositor will be able to follow your instructions.

If you work for a magazine or newspaper, you may be asked to type-mark rather than key. To do so you'll need to know the designer's specs for each element or have access to the publisher's standard specs.

Although on complex projects it can be quite a lot of additional work, typemarking itself is very simple. To take just one example, let's see how we would typemark Howe's quotation. We will assume that an extract (which we keyed EXT earlier) is to appear as 9/11 Garamond italic with a 2-em indent, ragged right (that means that the right ends of lines don't align), with ½-line space above and below. You would typemark the quote this way.

What could be easier?

EXERCISES

Following is an exercise to test your typemarking and keying abilities. You will see a typeset passage followed by a typewritten manuscript. To get to the typeset version, the compositor had to follow the copyeditor's marks on the typed manuscript; that is, the manuscript was marked up by the copyeditor (me) in such a way that a compositor was able to read and understand it well enough to produce the typeset version. See if you can do the same. Notice that I said "understand it well enough." I meant just that. You can invent your own symbols if necessary—compositors are used to that—if you can't find anything suitable from your repertoire; just make your intentions clear and unambiguous. After you do the exercise, see how close your marks were to mine. Would you do anything differently next time, or do you think your marks were readable to the compositor? Be sure you look for *all* manuscript changes, not just the ones dealing with typemarking.

As far as style is concerned, this play makes use of one comic device in particular—having the characters narrate their own dreams, personalities, and appearances. One such situation goes like this:

> FIRST VOICE: . . . but deep in the backyard lockup of his sleep a mean voice murmurs
> A VOICE [*murmuring*]: You'll be sorry for this in the morning,
> FIRST VOICE: and he heave-ho's back to bed.

It would be much less effective to have the two main voices narrating all the short lines, leaving only scenes to their characters.

The style is what particularly characterizes the play. According to Richard Hayes,

> Its poetic form is one which has been manipulated with conspicuous success by Browning, by Eliot, and in our time, Robert Lowell: that of the dramatic landscape with figures . . . What distinguishes it in the contemporary vogue of "readings" . . . is the sureness and certainty of its dramatic shape, the very real, legitimate theatrical springs from which it proceeds.[2]

The people who live in Thomas's town are much like a cross-section of any other town. There is the blind seacaptain, the postman and his wife who steam open all the letters, the prim mistress of a tourist home, and the young dressmaker in love with the slightly foppish Mog Edwards. In the town are also the drunkards, gossips, henpecked husbands—and perhaps would-be murderers?—of Anywhere, U.S.A. The one supernatural effect is the coming to life of five drowned members of one of Captain Cat's sea voyages.

[2]Richard Hayes, *Commonweal,* June 26, 1953, p. 297.

Here is the unmarked manuscript for this essay fragment. Can you mark it so that what the compositor will set is like what you've just seen? Be careful! Remember that there are copyediting changes here.

As far as style is concerned, this play makes use of one comic device in particular: having the characters narrate their own dreams, personalities, and appearances. One such situation goes like this. First voice: . . . But deep in the backyard lockup of his sleep a mean voice murmurs, ''You'll be sorry for this in the morning,'' and he heave-ho's back to bed. It would be much less effective to have the two main voices narrating all the short lines, leaving only scenes to their characters. The style is what particularly characterizes the play, as Richard Hayes describes in Commonweal, published by the Commonweal Publishing Co. on June 26, 1953 (page 297): ''Its poetic form is one which has been manipulated with conspicuous success by Browning, by Eliot, and in our time, Robert Lowell: that of the dramatic landscape with figures. . . what distinguishes it in the contemporary vogue of 'readings'. . .is the sureness and certainty of its dramatic shape, the very real, legitimate theatrical springs from which it proceeds.
The people who live in Thomas' town are much like a cross section of any other town. There is the blind sea captain, the postman and his wife who steam open all the letters, the prim mistress of a tourist home, and the young dressmaker in love with the slightly foppish Mog Edwards.

In the town are also the gossips henpecked husbands, and
drunks--and perhaps the would-be murderers?--of Anytown
U.S.A.

The one supernatural effect is the coming to life of
five drowned members of one of Captain Cat's sea voyages.

Answers

Now look at the answers. How close did you come to marking the
manuscript the way I did? Did you find all the changes? *A VOICE*
[murmuring]:

As far as style is concerned, this play makes use of one
comic device in particular having the characters narrate
their own dreams, appearances and personalities One such
situation goes like this First voice: . . . But deep in the *Com set like DIA*
backyard lockup of his sleep a mean voice murmurs You'll
be sorry for this in the morning, and he heave-ho's back *FIRST VOICE:*
to bed. It would be much less effective to have the two main
voices narrating all the short lines, leaving only scenes
to their characters. The style is what particularly

FN characterizes the play as Richard Hayes describes in *According to Richard Hayes?*
Commonweal, published by the Commonweal Publishing Co. on

EXT June 26, 1953, (page 297) Its poetic form is one which has
been manipulated with conspicuous success by Browning, by
Eliot, and in our time, Robert Lowell: that of the dramatic
landscape with figures. . . what distinguishes it in the
contemporary vogue of readings. . .is the sureness and
certainty of its dramatic shape, the very real, legitimate
theatrical springs from which it proceeds.

The people who live in Thomas's town are much like a cross
section of any other town. There is the blind sea captain,
the postman and his wife who steam open all the letters,

the prim mistress of a tourist home, and the young

dressmaker in love with the slightly foppish Mog Edwards.

In the town are also the~~ ~~gossips,~~ ~~henpecked husbands, ~~and~~ *drunkards;* ^

~~drunks~~-¦-and perhaps ~~the~~ would-be murderers?-¦-of Any~~towne~~ *where;*

U.S.A.⌐

⌐The one supernatural effect is the coming to life of five

drowned members of one of Captain Cat's sea voyages.

► KEY POINTS IN THIS CHAPTER

Definitions of Terms

- Pica: unit of measure containing 12 points; there are approximately 6 picas to an inch.
- Point: $1/12$ of a pica; there are 72 points to an inch.
- Typeface: appearance of the type.
- Type size: nonmeasurable height of the body of type in the typeface in question.
- Character count: number of characters in 1 pica of a typeface.
- Leading: amount of space between lines, measured from the base of one line to the base of the next.
- Trim size: size of each page in the finished book, minus the cover.
- Type page (type area): that portion of each page in the finished book taken up by type.
- Gutter: inside margin.

Keying

- Key every variation from straight text using codes provided by the publisher or those you invent.
- Delete old punctuation that becomes unnecessary when you create a new typographic element; likewise add punctuation that becomes necessary.
- If you make a run-in quotation into display, do not put words into the speaker's mouth; use brackets to indicate alterations in the quotation. It is acceptable to change from a lowercase to a capital letter, however.
- Determine whether single or double quotation marks are needed once a quotation has been marked for display.
- Mark for paragraph or flush left after creating new display.

- Mark the text following an illustration or table either to run in or to begin a new paragraph (flush left is unacceptable).
- Reread your proposed change (diagram it if necessary) to determine whether it is complete and accurate.

Other Aspects of Copyediting

If you already know the copyediting marks, have excellent grammar, and know where to look up style points, you may be wondering why you've been reading this book. Well, this chapter is the reason. It contains information you *must* have to copyedit and can't get elsewhere. In this chapter I tell you how to write queries, whether to use pen for copyediting, how to handle art, what material you need permission to use, and lots of other hints about copyediting. At the end of the chapter I summarize all the key points for easy reference.

Let's begin with the most basic question.

COPYEDITING: PEN OR PENCIL?

If you work on staff, you may have staff rules about copyediting in pencil, and in a particular color at that. Some companies have the editors work, for example, in green, copyeditors in purple, and authors in red. Different colors are necessary so that everyone knows who has made which change. Unless you have been given such instructions, however, I recommend that you work in a brightly colored pen, using one color for copyediting and another for typemarking and coding. Working in pen may seem like a risky venture, but it encourages you to be neat and careful, and it is easy for the compositor to read. Furthermore, pen does not smudge the way pencil does, and the point always stays sharp. Use the finest point you can find, such as Uni-Ball Micro or Pentel. Do not use felt-tip pens, which dull quickly and begin to bleed. Use green or violet so that your work stands out at a glance; red tends to vibrate and is difficult to read for long stretches of time (and reminds some authors of having their college papers marked up!), and brown and black don't stand out. Blue does not duplicate well.

Regardless of what color you use normally, I recommend that you use red or pink if you work on manuscript for which the disk will later be used, whether by the compositor or the author. Remember when I told you that copyeditors make their marks in the body of the manuscript because the compositor is going to set every character in order? Well, that's not true when the disk is being used. In that case the "composition" already exists, and only the changes are going to be input. So you need to make your changes obvious, and nothing stands out like red or pink pen!

Naturally, all your work should be in your best handwriting or printed neatly. Although *you* may know what is intended, ask yourself whether the compositor will. If not, write it over. Especially when you are dealing with foreign language or mathematical or chemical copy, print changes neatly; the compositor will not be able to guess from context what you mean. Do not cross out material you've written in pen; use an ink eradicator (such as Clorox) or white it out with Liquid Paper or Sno-Pake. When it's thoroughly dry, write your change in again. For heavy changes, use strips of white tape. In copyediting, neatness counts.

MARGINAL NOTES AND QUERIES

Queries to the author should be written on *query slips,* usually called *flags* or *flyers,* that you will attach to the page. Flags are small strips of colored paper with gum on one end; you lick that end, stick it to the back of the manuscript page, and write your query. Some copyeditors use one color for the author and another for the editor; that way the editor can easily deal with and remove some queries before the author sees them. Other copyeditors put all author queries on the right-hand side of the manuscript and all editor queries on the left. If an editor will be looking at the manuscript again before the author sees it, you should choose one of these methods and tell the editor which. If, however, you are the person who sends the manuscript directly to the author, you can of course tell her or him to "ignore the pink flags" or something of that sort. But one word of warning here: Be sure that any flags or memos the author will see, by design or inadvertently, are tactful and in good taste. There is nothing wrong in saying, "Au: This section is not clear," but there is in saying, "Au: Can't you write any more clearly than this?" I hope you can see the difference! One of the Bay Area's premier copyeditors looks at querying this way: "After you write your query, turn the manuscript page over. Now you're the author. You've spent two years writing this manuscript and it's in its tenth draft. You think it's finally perfect. Now turn over the page and read the query." Reread your flags before releasing the manuscript to make sure your exasperation does not show.

Do not query every comma change or replaced word, and do not explain your changes unless you think the author will misunderstand and ask to have your change dropped. Flags should be used to ask the author to clarify, to supply missing information, and to verify that you have not changed the meaning. To draw attention to a word or phrase, simply write a lightly penciled checkmark above the questioned passage. The compositor will know to ignore the checkmarks should someone forget to erase them.

The question often arises whether the query should be written on the front or the back of the flag. I prefer the front—the side visible when the flag sticks out from the manuscript—because if the editor wants to tape the flag back after it's been seen, the query is still readable. Other people argue that they don't tape down the flags, so it doesn't matter which side they write on. I disagree with people who tear off the flags; I feel that answered queries are part of the manuscript and should be retained.

Because the gum on flags is not of very high quality, sometimes flags drop off as pages are turned. For that reason, I recommend that you write the manuscript page number on each flag; then if you end up with a pile of partially gummed flags, you'll know where they were supposed to go. Alternatively, you could tape them onto the manuscript pages in the first place, but that can be a lot of extra work. Some publishers ask you to supply a typed list of queries in addition to flagging troublesome passages. Although that chore helps ensure that you keep your queries to a minimum, I see no other reason for it. But you must work that out with the publisher.

What about Post-Its? They adhere beautifully and come in many sizes and colors. You can put them anywhere on the page and indicate with an arrow on the Post-It exactly what term you're calling attention to. Their disadvantage, of course, is that the reader (whether the editor or author) must remove them (or at least lift them partially off the page) to read what changes you've made underneath them; then there's the danger that the reader will put them back in a different place. If you do use Post-Its, be sure you make clear what your query refers to; then if the Post-It gets moved, whoever is doing final cleanup (inputting the author's final changes and responses to queries)—even if it's you—will know what's what.

Do not write author queries in the margins of the manuscript page; instead save that area for notes to the compositor. Do not write too close to the edge; if the manuscript is duplicated, the edges may be lost during copying. Always write your note first, then circle it; don't first draw a circle and try to cram into it everything you need to say. And I use the term "circle" loosely. All you really have to do is set off your comment from text by using a line of whatever shape you need. Most copyeditors write comments in the right-hand margin, using the left margin for figure, table, and footnote callouts. Always address comments to the compositor as "Comp:" so that they're clearly distinguished from author or editor queries.

Should the manuscript be duplicated before it goes to the author? I do not believe it should. Yes, it's possible that the Postal Service will lose it, but I have never had that happen. Always insure or register the package so that you have some way to trace it. To get insurance you will have to pack the manuscript in a box; a padded envelope cannot be insured, but it *can* be certified (you will get a receipt). Duplicating a manuscript being sent to the author is a waste of money; any changes the author makes on the manuscript will not be on your copy, so it serves no purpose other than the temporary one of keeping it safe from the Postal Service. And what are you going to do with all those flags? No copying service will accept them, and you are certainly not going to want to be bothered copying them yourself! (If you've used Post-Its, of course, the manuscript *can't* be photocopied.) Once the manuscript comes back from the author and all changes have been integrated into it, you may wish to make a copy, not to avoid the possibility of loss in the mail but as a proofreading copy if more than one person will be reading proof at the same time.

Compositors prefer that no flags be left on the manuscript when it goes for composition (other than the author flags that have been pasted to the back of the page), but occasional flags to the compositor are acceptable. If possible, however, group any notes to the compositor in a separate memo.

OTHER PHYSICAL ASPECTS OF COPYEDITING

Manuscript pages should be numbered consecutively in the upper right-hand corner. Before you begin work, check that no pages are missing. If you need to add a page, or if the author includes some interpolated pages, they should be identified with *a* and *b* numbers. On the bottom of the last page before an *a* page, direct the compositor to that page and continue giving such directions until the next true page number. On the top of each interpolated page, tell the compositor what page precedes. Thus, if page 12a comes between pages 12 and 13, you will have the following instructions for the compositor:

On page 12	*On page 12a*	*On page 13*
top: nothing	top: "page 12 precedes"	top: "page 12a precedes"
bottom: "page 12a follows"	bottom: "page 13 follows"	bottom: nothing

Thus the compositor will not misplace any pages without knowing it.

Likewise, if you add an extra page that is meant to be inserted in the middle of an existing page, be certain to identify both the added page and its new context.

On the existing page	*On page 12*a
"Page 12*a* here; run in to previous sentence."	"Insert on page 12 as shown; run in."

It is much better to interpolate a new page than to make an existing one overlong by taping material to the bottom of it so that it has to be turned up. Compositors like to work with same-size pages, and having to stop work to turn ends of pages down is a problem for them. If you wish to avoid making the added pages refer to material that falls midpage, cut and paste instead, and put the runover on the interpolated page. That way all material will fall in sequence. If you have more than twenty interpolated pages, you should probably renumber the manuscript. But remember, if you renumber, to take out references to interpolated pages; if all material is in sequence, there are no longer any interpolations.

If you delete a manuscript page for some reason, the solution is much simpler. (Unless you delete twenty or more pages, you don't have to renumber.) In place of the single manuscript page number, simply write inclusive page numbers in the upper right-hand corner. For example, if you delete page 17, write "16–17" on page 16 or "17–18" on page 18. Sometimes frontmatter is incorrectly numbered in with manuscript. When you remove it, you can simply write on the first actual page of the manuscript "1–11" or whatever the first page number is. Of course, if you have been directed to number the frontmatter in with the manuscript, cite its boundaries in any memos you write ("Herewith copyedited manuscript 1–300, including frontmatter 1–10.").

When cross-references to other material in the manuscript appear, delete any page number; it will not appear on the same magazine or book page in print. In place of the number, draw three solid boxes (■ ■ ■) so that the reference will be easy to spot in page proof.

LIBEL

The libel laws are so complex that even lawyers—and I am no lawyer—cannot explain them fully. The large trade houses have their lawyers read all problem manuscripts—but even so, at least once a month I read in *Publishers Weekly* about someone suing a publisher and author for libel. It is libel to publish a false statement that diminishes someone's reputation; that is about as simply as I can state the law. It is said that the best defense against a libel suit is the truth; that is, if what you have printed is true, then you cannot be said to have committed libel. Then, too, in certain instances, if the subject of the libel is a public figure, there can be no recovery for a libelous statement unless the subject can show that the statement was made with knowledge of its falsity or with malice—reckless disregard of truth. Of course, what you think you intended and what your subject felt—to say nothing of what the judge decides—may be two different things. Bear in mind, an awful lot of people like to use libel suits to win court decisions and make some money; they are the whiplash artists of publishing. So you must be very careful to point out any material you think may be libelous. It is then up to the publishing house and its counsel to decide what to do.

If you can recognize a public figure in a supposed work of fiction, tell the editor. If you come across an unflattering statement about a real person, point it out. If you feel a photograph puts its subject in an unfavorable light, say so. You cannot be held responsible for an author's libelous statements, but the publisher can be and will surely appreciate your thoughtful views.

The right of privacy is guaranteed to all persons, living or dead, public figures or private citizens. You can take a picture of, say, someone on the street but not in her or his doctor's office. (Guidelines for photographic situations are given later in this chapter.) If the subject of the work of art or prose is deceased, the right of privacy, or, as it is properly called, the right of publicity, extends to the estate.

PLAGIARISM

When you were in school, did you ever copy a book report out of the encyclopedia or abridge one from a college outline series? In fact, you were plagiarizing, as you probably knew at the time. Well, some authors still do that, maybe not because they need to copy the material, but because they like the way the material has been laid out. Clever copyeditors can catch them at it. A dead giveaway is tearsheet material for which no credit line exists. (Tearsheet, you will recall, is printed material from some published source, used as manuscript by the current author.) Even if the tearsheet came from another book or article by the current author, permission must be granted by its publisher. Only tearsheet from a previous edition of *the same work* is exempt.

Another indication of plagiarism is a variety of writing styles. In a textbook or other educational work, several distinct styles indicate material from a variety of sources; if the writing style is uniform, the author has at the very least rewritten published material.

If you read something that sounds familiar, look it up. If you find that it resembles a published piece in expression or form, alert the editor. The copyright law covers the *expression* of ideas, not the ideas themselves.

Be careful not to accuse the author of plagiarizing. Instead, write tactful comments on flags: "Au: Please supply source for this tearsheet material," or "Au: Please give a credit line for this material if it is not original." Once again, you are not to blame if the author chooses not to comply, but at least you have alerted the publisher to a possible problem. (If you suspect rampant theft, write a separate memo to the editor, outlining your concerns.)

An author who plagiarizes her or his own work is sometimes guilty of violation of contract. The contract signed with the publisher states that the author will publish no material that could diminish the value of the work in question. If an author has signed a contract to write a book on introductory psychology, for example, and then uses some of that same material in a book on developmental psychology, the introductory book may suffer. Whenever you come across suspected instances of self-plagiarism, tell the editor. Perhaps nothing will come of it, but the publisher will want to know.

PERMISSIONS

If you copyedit scholarly materials or anthologies, you will almost certainly have to deal with permissions. Most publishers require the author to supply all permissions with the manuscript upon submission, and they ask the copyeditor to verify that complete permissions are on hand. If the publisher does not supply a permissions chart, I recommend that you make up your own, with these heads:

> Msp. or fig. no.
> Selection author and title
> Year
> Pages
> Publisher

Rights owned by
Fee: U.S. & Can.
Fee: World
No. of copies
Permission cleared?

These heads will fit along the top of an 8½ × 11 page turned sideways, and you can make several entries on one page if you write small.

Under the first head list every item you come across in the manuscript for which you believe permission is necessary (we'll get to the guidelines in a minute), and under the next four (which can be combined on the chart if you wish) give all publication information for that material. For the rights, fee, and copies you'll have to read the permission letter received: Does the publisher own the rights, or have they given you another source to contact? (Often the publisher will be able to grant U.S. rights but will name someone else to write to for world rights.) The letter will also state the fee and any other requirements (such as two copies of the book). On the letter circle any restrictions—fee, number of copies, limited permission, credit line, and so forth—in red so that the publisher can find them easily without wading through a lot of legal jargon. Then write "OK" under "Permission cleared?" on the chart. If no permission letters exist for material for which you believe permission is required (including material you've asked the author to supply sources for), make a list for the publisher to research. Unless you are being paid for it or have agreed to take it on, getting permissions is not part of your responsibility; you need only prepare the chart.

Identify each permission letter by noting, in its upper right-hand corner, the material to which it refers. You may even wish to work out a code system to make the publisher's job easier (or your own, if you are a staff copyeditor). Thus you can number each item listed on the chart and then number the permission letters correspondingly; then you'll be able to add new letters as they are received and keep track of which items are still missing. Most publishers refuse to have the compositor make up pages until all permissions have been cleared.

Clearing permissions is laborious and tedious work. If you freelance, you could, under extreme circumstances, be held liable for overlooking something, so always make it clear, when you turn in the chart, that you are advising only.

Permission Guidelines

What material needs permission? That's a difficult question to answer. Most people follow the "fair use" doctrine: How much will your use of the material hurt the author of or market for the original material? Obviously, an author who has spent a lifetime doing research doesn't want someone to rip off her or his material without paying for it. The following guidelines, while very rough, can help you determine whether the material falls under the fair use doctrine. In general, permission is needed for:

> 400 words (total) from one book, all of whose material is by the same author or team
> 50 words (total) from an article or a chapter in an anthology
> 2 lines of poetry or a song
> any table, chart, or figure

The number of words used from any one source is *cumulative.* If the author quotes 200 words from a single source in one section and 250 words from the same source elsewhere, that makes 450 *cumulative* words—and that means permission is necessary.

These guidelines are very broad and should not be taken too literally; and of course they do not apply to material in the public domain. Always ask yourself, Is this fair use? If a 600-page book can be summed up in a few sentences, it would not be fair to use them without permission, no matter how short they are. On the other hand, poetry used for purposes of an exercise and not for poetry's sake does not need permission. A credit line, however, is always in order.

Material prepared by the U.S. Government Printing Office does not require permission, because it is paid for with taxpayers' money, but again, it should be credited. Any copyrighted material introduced into GPO publications must be credited as well, and permission gotten. For example, if a copyrighted poem was read into the *Congressional Record,* you need to get *permission* for (and credit) the poem but need only give *credit* to the GPO for their part in publishing the *Congressional Record.* Likewise, the information in maps is in the public domain, but the rendition of the map is protected by copyright. Thus a map of the parks in Utah is no secret, but if the parks are indicated by brown bears because that's the way the author's source depicted them, well, that's no longer public domain.

Where else does public domain come into the picture? The following list will help explain the terms of copyright:

Material Published	*Copyright Status*
before 1906	public domain
1906–1977	protected for 75 years if copyright was renewed properly
January 1978 or after	life of the author plus 50 years

Credit is always required, of course, even for material in the public domain; without credit, remember, you are plagiarizing.

Permissions questions create a big nuisance, but if you realize that good judgment can answer a lot of them, you'll do fine. My judgment, based on years of experience, may be better than that of a new copyeditor, and a lawyer's judgment may be better than mine. But it really all comes down to what the judge decides, should the case go to court. That's why common sense is so important. If you deliberately avoid requesting permission for certain material, you can expect some problems. But if you've done your best and have simply overlooked an item, most copyright holders will understand.

Don't call attention to your possible errors, however. I once saw a book with this notice: "We've tried our best to get permission for everything, but if we have inadvertently omitted anyone, we apologize." Wrong! A notice such as this one means nothing in a court of law. If I run a restaurant, I can post a sign saying, "We reserve the right to refuse service to anyone," but that doesn't mean the court will see it my way. If my best sweater burns up in a dryer, I don't care a fig about the laundromat's sign saying, "Management is not responsible for damage." You can bet I'm going to court! Do your best to get all permissions, but don't then tell the world that you may have slipped up.

Credit Lines

Most copyright holders will tell you the credit line they want to see, and they'll tell you that it must go with the material being reproduced. Some publishers like to put all credit lines together, on the copyright page or the page following, and that's usually acceptable. If for some reason credit lines are going to appear in some other location altogether, put a note on the copyright page that says, "Credit information appears on page *x*"—or something similar. Often the literary credits appear in one place, the photo credits in another.

Credit lines are source notes (see Chapter 8), so they should follow the wording requested by the copyright holder. They are no place to get creative with your editing skills. An author requesting permission may suggest the credit line to the copyright holder and ask for approval. In that case the credit lines tend to be more consistent. Remember that credit lines are required for *all material from another source*, no matter how few words it is or whether permission is needed. Credit lines that appear with the material being used take the form of simple footnotes (using the required wording). Credit lines for artwork usually appear at the end of the caption, following the word *Source*, although sometimes the caption appears above the art, the credit line below. Table credits are given in a table footnote following the word *Source;* the source note is the first note after a table. (For more information about table footnotes, see Tables in this chapter.)

If the credit lines are being grouped in the frontmatter, it is customary to include an opening sentence similar to the following: "Grateful acknowledgment is made for use of the following material." The credit lines that follow then use the requested wording.

Changes in Quoted Material

When permission is granted, it is for the exact material; if changes are made in the material, the copyright holder should be notified. When you copyedit, if you see that the author has adapted illustrations or prose in some way, be sure that the permission letter indicates that this is acceptable.

Can you make changes in quoted material? In general, other than correcting obvious typographical errors that crept into the tearsheet during composition, no. Indicate spelling or other errors by *sic* (see Chapter 4). Don't use *sic* for every situation not in accordance with your material's style; it is intended to point out only those passages that might cause the reader some concern. (See Chapter 4, Brackets.)

Typographic changes can be made in quoted material. For example, if the original author set off lists with a's and b's in parentheses and the style in your manuscript is to use 1's and 2's followed by periods, make the change. Another acceptable change is renumbering of illustrations. If your author numbers illustrations consecutively throughout the material and has picked up several readings, each with its own numbering system, change the numbers to follow your style.

ARTWORK

If you copyedit nothing but fiction, you're not likely to see many illustrations. If you work for a magazine, you'll probably find that the art director keys and places the art, although you may be asked to work with the art department in handling it. But copyeditors who work on nonfiction, textbooks, or reports see lots of artwork and should know how to deal with it.

There are four kinds of illustrations:

1. line drawings
2. halftones
3. combinations
4. typeset art

Line drawings consist of lines and type only, with solid black or solid color dots and bars and patches; there are no shades of gray or shades of color anywhere. Cartoons are usually line art, unless they contain gray.

Halftones are what we think of as photographs. They get their name from the halftone process used to reproduce photographs in print. Photographs are continuous in tone. But printed halftones are nothing more than a series of large and small dots. A printing press can either lay down ink or not lay down ink; the appearance of shades of gray or color comes from how big the dots are and how close together. In printing a photograph, a screen is laid over the photo. As the photo is exposed, its light areas are translated into small dots far apart, its dark areas into large dots close together. If you looked at a photograph through a special magnifying glass called a loupe (available for about $10 at all art supply stores), you would see nothing but continuous tone. But if you looked through the glass at a photograph reproduced in a book or newspaper, you would see a series of dots, in different sizes and spaced differently. The whole photo would be nothing more than hundreds of dots.

Combinations consist of line drawings with screened (shaded) areas, or halftones with type or added line art overlays. Screens are made of dots. A 10 percent screen would have smaller dots farther apart than a 90 percent screen would; the farther apart the dots are, the lighter the shading becomes. The use of screens means that the compositor must shoot overlays for the shaded areas with a special camera technique, and that's more difficult than shooting a straight line drawing. *Pocket Pal* and *Production for the Graphic Designer* (see the bibliography) show examples of these camera techniques.

Typeset art, very simply, is art that the compositor can set. Some compositors can handle very complex pieces of art; others can "draw" only what you could do on your own typewriter. The art director or production manager should tell you which material can be typeset (or *compset,* as it is sometimes called).

How to Mark a Manuscript for Art Placement

Regardless of who is doing the art, an artist or the compositor, all illustrations must be called out in the left-hand margin of the manuscript. Can you see why? How else would the makeup person know where to place the art in page makeup?

Some illustrations are easy to place; they have text references, such as "See Figure 6.2." These figures can go wherever there's room for them, because the reader can be directed to them. In the margin, then, you will write and circle "Fig. 6.2." But what about unnumbered figures (often called *cuts*), which have to go exactly where they belong? They, too, must be called out in the margin. I recommend that you give each cut a number, not a letter, so that you don't run out of identification codes after the twenty-sixth item. Decorative halftones—sometimes used for chapter openers or for visual appeal throughout the chapter or article—should be assigned cut numbers, as should small drawings that fall in the middle of a paragraph, cartoons, and every drawing not otherwise identified.

Always be sure that you use the same number in the left-hand margin that you are using on the art and in the caption (and in the art log, described shortly). *Doublecheck!* Does the text say "tree"? Does this figure look like a tree? Does the caption *say* it's a tree? Then you can be fairly sure you have the right figure in the right spot. But I've seen authors supply sixty-five illustrations for which they have sixty-four text references and sixty-seven captions. So you must be very careful and systematic when you copyedit an art program.

Remember, all illustrations, whether typeset or drawn, whether numbered or unnumbered, whether substantive or decorative, must be identified by number on both art and manuscript. Captions, which are supplied as a separate manuscript, should also be keyed by figure number or cut number.

Copyediting Art

Sometimes, if you are a freelancer, you will be given the manuscript without the art, which will have been copyedited already by the publisher. You should still watch for discrepancies, however, and verify all numbering systems (you may be given an earlier rough copy of the art manuscript for reference).

If you are asked to copyedit art, treat it just like text. Be sure the illustration does what the text says it does. If the text says "photo," your graph will not do. If the text mentions a dotted line, check that the line is not in fact dashed. If color is mentioned, ask the editor whether color will be used; if there is to be no color, use the term *shading* or *crosshatching* instead, but be sure to tell the artist what to do. You might also indicate for the artist where darker and lighter shading can be used to correspond to greater and lesser density. Check that art and text use the same terminology and abbreviations. Capitalize or lowercase labels consistently. On graphs, put axis labels in the same position each time, and be sure tick marks (the short lines that stand for positive and negative numbers on each axis) are used consistently; mark whether grids are to be retained or dropped (usually they're to be dropped; the author uses graph paper only for plotting). Mark math the same way you would for a compositor (see Chapter 11). If you can, indicate the approximate finished size the illustration should be (¼ page, ½ page, etc.), and be sure to treat similar figures the same way.

Copyedit all line art together, watching for similarities. This step is especially important when the art comes from a variety of sources. On each figure indicate the figure or cut number and the manuscript page number on which the reference to it appears. Create an art log (to be discussed shortly) with the same information. Be sure you have a separate piece of art for each figure, including typeset ones; if you come across a figure within the manuscript for which you have no art, tell the publisher. Be aware that the art manuscript and text manuscript go to two different places (even if the compositor can set the art, it gets handled separately and at a different time), so there must be two separate manuscripts.

Photographs

You must handle photographs very carefully. Ideally you should work with a copy of the photo, not with the original. If you do receive original photos, follow these instructions:

1. Never glue, staple, or paper-clip photos; these substances make marks that prohibit reuse of the photos.
2. Write all information on self-stick labels or Post-Its to be affixed to the back. (Do not put Post-Its on the face of the photo; they can damage the emulsion.) If you write on the back of the photo, subsequent users will have to get rid of your marks, whereas they can simply peel the labels off. Write the label out first, then stick it on the photo. If you stick the label on first and then write, you will make an impression on the face of the photo that will show up in reproduction.
3. Write any instructions or labeling on overlays attached to the back of the photo with removable tape (Post-It tape is one brand). Do not tape overlays to the face of the photo, even in the white border; when the overlay is removed, it may take part of the photo with it.
4. Do not write in ballpoint pen on overlays; it leaves an impression on the photo. Pencil or felt-tip pen used *lightly* is best. Be careful not to use a leaky pen on lightweight paper, or the ink will mark up the photo.

Mark each photo (on the self-stick label) with the figure or cut number and the number of the manuscript page on which the author refers to it, and include that information in the art log.

If you have access to them, manila envelopes all the same size make neat holders for photos. Use a size large enough to accommodate the largest photo, and put each photo in its own envelope. Label the envelope with the same number as you labeled the photo. A photo manuscript of envelopes of one size is a lot neater than one containing various-size pieces.

Monitor carefully the content of photographs. You should always have model releases on hand for all identifiable persons in the following situations:

> any lone individual
> people in institutions (such as mental hospitals and prisons)
> children in classrooms
> drug users and persons in gambling casinos (U.S.)
> indoor pictures where you may be invading privacy
> outdoor pictures in poor taste

That certainly narrows down the field, doesn't it? Look at it this way. A person attending a basketball game indoors is giving up some privacy, but that same person in the privacy of a doctor's waiting room has the right to believe he or she is safe. If someone takes a picture in that waiting room, there had better be a model release available when that picture is published.

Then, too, be careful what the caption or text surrounding the photo says. A bus line is an outdoor location, and a photograph of one therefore does not violate the privacy rule. But if the caption says, "One out of six people uses drugs," you're not being very fair to the people on the bus line, so you'd better have their permission.

When dealing with photographs, it's a good idea to keep the following thoughts in mind:

1. Be sure the photo is in good taste.
2. Be sure that the surrounding text material does not distort the intention of the photo.
3. Use positive captions.
4. Recommend that the photo be retouched if necessary.

Here's an example of the third suggestion. I once saw a psychology textbook that had a picture of an old woman at a pottery wheel. The caption could have said, "Old people get bored easily because they no longer go to a job every day." Instead this caption said, "In old age people have the time to do the things they never could before." Do you see the difference? In looking at the photo, I was able to see how happy the woman looked, how content; someone looking at the same picture with that first caption might have seen a very sad and lonely person. If the captions are positive, it is less likely that the publisher will be hauled into court for violating someone's privacy.

Any time you say something negative or argumentative, you leave yourself open to a possible problem. Think of the "One out of every six" caption; if my face is in that photo, you can bet I'm saying, "Oh yeah? Which am I, drug user or not?"

Creating an Art Log

Most publishers will provide their own art log forms, which you will fill in as you copyedit (unless the publisher has already copyedited the art). I recommend that you use a different page of the log for each chapter (if you're doing a book) and that you intersperse cuts with numbered figures (i.e., that you deal with all art, whether cuts or numbered figures, in sequence, rather than separating the log into two sections). Most logs begin at the left with a place for the figure number. Subsequent columns ask for the old figure number (if the figure came from an earlier edition from which it may be picked up); the manuscript page number on which the reference appears; the number of parts to the figure (such as *a*, *b*, and *c* or *top* and *bottom*); and the kind of figure (line art, halftone, etc.). Sometimes there is space on the log for the source.

If you do not get a log from the publisher, make your own for the project and include the information just given. As you copyedit, you may find other information that will be useful; sometimes, for instance, it is helpful to have a very brief description of each figure on the art log. Naturally, your choice for the description will depend on the subject. In a math book, it would hardly be effective to say "graph" next to thirty-two figures and "Venn diagram" next to the thirty-third. But to say *"a = b," "x = sin y,"* and other names of graphs can be useful: Even if you can't tell whether the proper figure is there, at least the author will know at a glance.

COPYEDITING TABLES

Like illustrations, tables must have a specific home within the text. Small tables are often unnumbered, meaning that they must appear right in position, wherever they are in manuscript. Lengthy tables should always be numbered so that the compositor or dummier has some leeway in placing them. Normally any table that has a title should be numbered and displayed.

Call out tables in the left-hand margin of the manuscript, as you would illustrations. Whether you work with a separate table manuscript or with tables on the same pages as the manuscript text is of no consequence; all material is being handled by the compositor, so no separate manuscript is needed.

Few authors present tables satisfactorily, but a good copyeditor can help. Tables are intended to display a lot of information graphically, so that it can be assimilated easily; if the table has been laid out poorly, it is not doing its job. Always read tables carefully, and ask yourself, Should these column heads be side heads (row heads) instead? Can column heads be added for clarity? Are the table notes clear and helpful? Does the table title accurately describe the content of the table? Redesign tables if necessary.

Once you have decided on the basic format for a table, key it carefully. How many head levels should there be? Are there any cross heads? Is the material on the left side part of the table or is it a group of side heads? Here is a table showing two levels of column heads, a cross head, and some side heads.

(TN/TT) Table 1.7 Selected Family Characteristics

	(T₁) 1977		1976
	straddle rule		
	(T₂)	Median	Median
(Tᵢ) Characteristics	Number[a]	income	income
(CH) All Races			
ALL FAMILIES (SH)	57,215	$16,009	$14,958
Type of Residence			
Nonfarm	55,042	16,140	15,065
Farm	2,172	12,637	11,663
Inside Metropolitan			
Areas	37,841	17,371	16,001
(TB) 1,000,000 or More	21,572	18,196	16,771
Inside Central Cities	7,993	14,677	13,700
Region			
Northeast	12,936	16,804	15,405
North Central	15,308	16,845	15,942
South	18,724	14,567	13,419
West	10,247	16,512	15,484

(TSN) Source: Adapted from part of a table prepared by the U.S. Department of Commerce, Bureau of the Census (Washington, DC: Government Printing Office).

(TFN) [a] In thousands.

After you have keyed the table, reread it for sense. If it's not set up clearly, rekey it.

Always copyedit all tables together after you have checked them against their text references and copyedited them in context. Be sure you have used abbreviations consistently and have keyed similar tables the same way.

Long Tables

Some tables appear to be vertical, others horizontal. The table you just saw is vertical; it has only three columns of figures. Tables with many columns rarely fit a book page unless they are turned sideways (in which case they are called *turned* or *broadside* tables). If you suspect that a table may have so many column heads that it will not fit if placed in standard position, tell the compositor to turn the table if necessary. That's all you have to say. It will be up to the publisher to be sure the table is turned the correct way in pages. (Turned tables *always* begin at the left side of a page, whether they appear on a right page or a left page; i.e., you have to turn the book 90° clockwise to read all turned tables.)

Instead of turning a table, it may sometimes be desirable to break it across facing pages, with some column heads on the left page and the rest on the right (or, if necessary, still more column heads on the next left page). But always begin on a left page, and tell the compositor that the table must go on facing pages (or facing pages plus the next left).

Sometimes vertical tables—or even turned tables—cannot fit on one page; what do you do then? Normally the table title and column heads should repeat on each page of the table. On turned tables that begin on a left page, however, you needn't repeat the column heads on the right page, because the columns still line up under their heads. If the turned table goes onto a new left page, though, repeat the title and column heads. Direct the compositor to repeat the title and column heads whenever you think it will be necessary. Figure 10.1 shows examples of continued tables. Note that after the table title, the word *Continued* appears within parentheses. There are other systems for "continued" lines than the ones shown in the figure; my choice is an italic word *Continued* (with a capital letter) within roman parentheses. When the reader must turn the page to a new left, a "continued" line is given at the bottom of the right-hand page as well.

Table Rules

Whether a table is to have rules is usually a designer's decision, but certain rules are standard. Most tables have a rule between the title

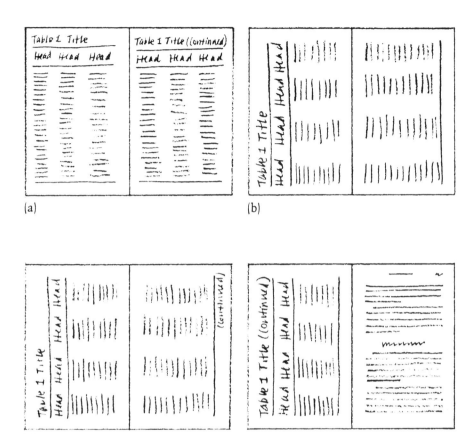

Figure 10.1. Thumbnail sketches of three kinds of continued tables. (a) Wide table on facing pages. Because there are several column heads, some must go on the left page and the rest on the right. The title repeats on the right page. (b) Turned (broadside) table on facing pages. The table is long but not wide. It begins on a left page, turned. The bottom of the table continues on the right page. Both pages turn in the same direction, and the table can be read by turning the book or magazine clockwise by 90°. (c) Turned table of more than two pages. This, too, is a turned table, but it can't finish on just one spread. It begins on a left page and continues to a new spread. Each spread ends with a continued line, and each new spread begins with the repeated title.

and the column heads, below the column heads, and at the bottom of the table, before any footnotes. If there is more than one level of column head, the levels are separated by *straddle rules* (also called *spanner rules*), which extend only over the width of the columns they cover (see the example in the table shown earlier in this section). Straddle rules are used to indicate which lower-level heads are included under the umbrella of a higher-level one.

Table Footnotes

Footnotes to tables go immediately after the end of the table, not at the bottom of the page. The preference is for the source note, if any, to go first, then general table notes, then finally specific footnotes. Footnotes to tables are called out with superscript lowercase letters; you may use either roman or italic (the publisher may have a preference), but be consistent! Numbers are not used for table references because they can be misinterpreted as statistics. Within the table, these references appear in sequence reading *across* the table body, not down the columns.

The source note is introduced by the word *Source*, which can be treated in any fashion the designer chooses (usually by putting it in italic or small caps). If the table has general notes, the word *Note* will be treated the same way. *Note* comes on a new line after the source note. Each specific footnote follows on its own line, introduced by a lowercase letter in the superscript position.

Here is a table showing the placement of notes and their references in the table.

Marriage Prospects of Single Men and Women

| Age | Percent of population single[a] | | Percent who ever marry[b] | |
	Male	Female	Male	Female
15	99.4	97.6	95.8	97.4
16	99.0	94.3	95.9	97.4
17	98.1	87.9	96.0	97.3
18	94.6	75.5	96.0	97.0

Source: U.S. Department of Commerce, Bureau of the Census (Washington, DC: Government Printing Office).
Note: "Single" excludes widowed and divorced.
[a]Percent single within specified year of age in 1960, in 5% sample of population.
[b]Percent of white persons single at beginning of year of age who marry during that year and all later years, based on data for 1958–1960.

Some General Rules for Copyediting Tables

1. Be clear what material should indent and what is merely a continuation.
2. If column numbers are intended to add, then the side head referring to the total or subtotal should be indented from the left. Make the indent consistent, usually 2 or 3 ems.

3. In column heads, use dollar and percent signs consistently.
4. Use parenthetical units of measurement consistently in column heads.
5. Keep column heads short.
6. Align digits on the decimal point.
7. When dashes are used for blank entries in the table body, mark them for 1 em, and center the dash within the column.
8. Do not use ditto marks.
9. Add or delete rules consistently; delete unnecessary rules, such as vertical side rules and rules between columns (unless they're present to separate complicated data).

For more detailed rules on copyediting tables, see *Chicago Manual* and the GPO Style Manual.

FRONTMATTER

If you are given the frontmatter of a book to copyedit, you should be aware of the following pieces you will be seeing. (Magazines have frontmatter that includes their standard masthead plus a table of contents for the particular edition; such frontmatter, however, follows a standard design and contains information that can't be edited.)

The *half-title page* consists of the title only: no subtitle, edition, or author. Sometimes the material to the right of a colon is not a subtitle but rather part of the title; then it does belong on the half-title page. The next page is often blank, but in many trade books it is a *card page*, listing other works by the same author. Sometimes, as in some college textbooks, it will be a *series page*, naming the series and series editor. The third page is the *title page*; it lists the title, subtitle, edition (other than the first), authors' names (and authors' affiliations if the book is a text), and publisher's name and location.

By law, copyright information must appear either on the title page or on the back of the title page, so unless there's a serious space problem in the book, the copyright page is almost always the back of the title page. It contains the copyright line (the year of copyright and the name of the copyright holder), the publisher's copyright notice, any information about where the material was previously published, and a variety of other notices as well. For example, if there are some credit lines for material reprinted from other sources, they may be grouped on the copyright page, or a note may appear there directing the reader to some other page where credit lines are given. Some publishers list on the copyright page all the people who worked on the book. Most trade publishers and many textbook publishers also include the printing code there. A simple printing code looks something like this: 89 90 5 4 3 2 1. The first number on the left is the year of the printing; the number farthest on the right, the number of the printing. With each subsequent printing the code is changed. So if you see "89 90 5 4 3," you know that you're reading the third printing, printed in 1989. Many printing codes are much more complicated, so that only the publisher can interpret them. Some trade publishers just spell out the printing rather than using code; you've probably seen it done both ways.

The fifth page in the frontmatter can be almost anything. If the credit lines are not in the book, not on the copyright page, and not called out somewhere on the copyright page, they must by law begin on this page immediately following the copyright page. If credit lines are not a problem, sometimes the fifth page is a dedication, or sometimes it starts the table of contents or preface. Some books, such as contemporary novels, have no table of contents (called TOC in shorthand). Likewise, there may be no preface. In general, nonfiction and texts will have both a TOC and a preface, and the order will vary from publisher to publisher. The *preface* is written by the author of the book; it sets forth the author's reasons for writing the material. A foreword (*not* "forward"!) is written by someone else—a star in the author's field. That person's name often gives so much credence to the work that people buy it because of the endorsement. An *introduction* often gives some necessary background information; sometimes it is considered frontmatter, sometimes part of the book proper.

Some books have other information in the frontmatter as well: Lists of tables and illustrations, maps, chronologies, and many other items may appear. Common sense—and the author's preference—dictates their sequence.

Frontmatter is not numbered with the book. The half-title is page i, the card page is page ii, the title page is iii, the copyright page is iv. Most other main items begin new right pages, and unless you can figure out exactly how many lines of type they will take up, you probably won't be able to figure out their exact page numbers. So label each one after page iv "New right page" (or "New page," if you and the publisher decide). Then in the upper right-hand corner number all frontmatter from 1.

You should not expect to do heavy copyediting on frontmatter; check the TOC against the titles given in the manuscript, and edit the preface as you would text. Anything that refers to something within the manuscript, such as the titles and numbers in the list of tables, must be checked carefully.

BACKMATTER

Besides an index, which is not normally seen by the copyeditor, some books have glossaries, vocabularies, or other backmatter. Along with your other responsibilities, always double-check the alphabetization of these materials.

► **KEY POINTS IN THIS CHAPTER**

As you work, keep these key points in mind. Then when you finish the first reading, look again at this list to see what items you may have missed. In your second reading, pay particular attention to those items.

Physical Copyediting

- Work in brightly colored pen, if possible.
- Print neatly or use your best handwriting; be sure every mark is clear to the compositor.
- White out your mistakes.
- Double-check that all manuscript pages are in sequence and that none are missing.
- Mark interpolated pages with *a* and *b* numbers, and direct the compositor to each such page. (For more than twenty added or deleted pages, renumber the entire manuscript.)
- If you renumber any pages, be sure to renumber their references as well.
- Cut and paste manuscript to keep it in sequence.
- Be sure that all manuscript pages are the same size.
- Always read a manuscript twice, once for sense and once when you copyedit it.

Queries

- Identify each flag with its manuscript page number.
- Write queries on the inside of the flag so that it can still be read after it is pasted down on the back of the manuscript page.
- Write all author and editor queries on flags or Post-Its, never on the manuscript itself.
- Use one color flag for author queries, another for editor queries; alternatively, put all author queries on the right, all editor queries on the left.
- Be sure that all author queries are tactful and clear.
- Keep author queries to a minimum.

Permissions

- Prepare a permissions chart showing what material requires permission and the status of that permission.
- Identify each permission letter in the upper right-hand corner to show what it covers.
- On each permission letter, circle in red the credit line, fee, and restrictions.
- Flag any instances where you are not sure that the material is original and no credit line is given.
- Flag any instances where you suspect libel or bad taste.
- Do not alter any quoted material (except typographically) without the copyright holder's knowledge.

Illustrations

- Call out all art in the left-hand margin of the manuscript.
- Identify each figure with its number and the manuscript page on which the first reference to it occurs.
- Read art against text and caption to be sure that you have the correct figure.
- Read art carefully, watching, for example, for unnecessary grids, superfluous dots, and discrepancies in labeling.
- Mark all labels consistently for upper- or lowercase.
- Treat similar figures the same way.
- Look for consistency between figures, text, and captions regarding references to color, heaviness of lines and curves, abbreviations, and so on.
- Indicate whether grids are to be retained or dropped.
- Position axis labels consistently; make consistent use of tick marks.
- Mark math the same way you would for a compositor.
- Indicate approximate finished size on each figure.
- Handle photographs with care.
- Flag any photographs that should have model releases and don't.
- Alert the editor to situations where photographs may be in bad taste.
- Prepare an art log.

Tables

- Copyedit all tables together.
- Key similar tables the same way.
- Use abbreviations and symbols consistently.
- Mark indents where necessary.
- Align digits.
- Delete unnecessary rules.
- Call out all numbered tables in the left-hand margin of manuscript.

Specialized Copyediting

The copyediting rules you learned in Chapters 1 through 10 apply to almost all kinds of copyediting. Where exceptions are appropriate, I have already given them. But many kinds of copyediting have additional rules and requirements. In this chapter I describe several specialized areas of copyediting, their needs and prerequisites.

COLLEGE TEXTBOOKS

Most college textbook publishers rely on freelance copyeditors. Occasionally they want freelance copyeditors who know production as well. Such people may be asked to pick out sample page copy for the designer (see Chapter 9), deal directly with the author, or do cleanup work on the manuscript after the author has reviewed the copyediting and answered all queries.

Although you may feel that it would be boring to copyedit textbooks, that is not the case. The subject matter may not interest you particularly, but college books raise many problems that copyeditors thrive on. You will almost certainly have to deal with artwork, tables, permissions, and many design elements. Basically the text itself will be easy to work with; simply follow the rules given throughout this book. (Technical texts are another story; see the technical marking instructions on pages 233–248.)

In copyediting college textbooks, never challenge the author: He or she almost certainly knows the subject better than you. Query, sure, but even if you know better, never suggest that you do (and yes, I've seen copyeditors do that). Eliminate sexism insofar as it's practical to do so; if using "he or she" or some other remedy makes the text awkward, try alternating references in paragraphs. In a child psychology manuscript, for example, call the baby "he" in one paragraph, "she" in another.

Style and flair are not important in college texts; the information and the clarity with which it's presented are the critical points. The more technical the material, the truer that is. Follow all the grammar rules, but don't try to make a textbook into a national bestseller. In styling the manuscript, you should be market-oriented.

When copyediting textbooks, be sure that exercises can be completed according to the directions given. If the question says, "Fill in the blanks," are blanks provided? In a matching exercise, should you go from column A to B or from B to A? Are maps readable? Do they include all the points the reader is asked to locate?

Because their manuscripts are so complicated, college publishers rarely hire freelance copyeditors who have no copyediting experience. Even years as a trade copyeditor do not assure you of a job. College publishers want evidence that you understand permissions, artwork, tables, coding, and production; always point out in your résumé or covering letter (see Chapter 13) those difficult projects you have handled and how that experience qualifies you for college copyediting.

If you have no experience, apply first for proofreading jobs, and be willing to read galleys against manuscript (as opposed to reading galleys "cold," just as you would any new book). Exposure to the marks made on the manuscript by the copyeditor—and to how those marks translate into print—will help once you do begin copyediting. Most college publishers are willing to give a small copyediting job to someone who has proofed successfully for them for some time.

Do you need to be familiar with the subject matter? Not at all, although certainly there are areas where some background is helpful. If you copyedit technical materials, you'll have to know the marking rules (see the technical marking instructions), and if you work with languages, you must have at least *some* background. In college publishing, you don't have to be a native speaker, although it may help; if you work for a foreign publisher, however, you must be native to be an editor.

Copyeditors of college texts are not usually expected to check facts; reviewers of the manuscript in its early stages will normally point out errors, and authors are *always* responsible for content. Naturally, though, if something strikes you as odd, you will want to check it just to satisfy your own curiosity! You *should* check spelling of proper names whenever possible. But remember, if you find a discrepancy, don't gloat: The author may be able to show you an equally respectable source showing the spelling the way she or he used it in the manuscript.

EL-HI TEXTBOOKS

If you are interested in copyediting el-hi books (i.e., books to be used in elementary or high school), you will probably need to take a staff job; little el-hi work is freelanced. Ex-teachers have an excellent chance here; all the high-level jobs require a teaching background. Because el-hi material is so low-level, a background in the subject area is not important, and, in fact, English majors are usually preferred. Style is extremely important in el-hi, so form often takes precedence over content, at least for a copyeditor. Remember: You are already an expert in el-hi subjects!

Copyeditors of el-hi books must of course be very strong in grammar, but they need other skills as well. They must be aware of the reading level; sometimes they may be asked to test out parts of the manuscript against reading level charts to be sure that the material conforms. And they must be sure the writing is clear. After all, if a copyeditor can't understand what the author is intending, or if there are contradictions in the manuscript, how will the student learn the material?

If you work on el-hi books, you must be especially sensitive to racism, sexism, and regional idiosyncrasies. If you have ever heard any of the hoopla over attempts (often successful) to ban or censor el-hi books, you know how important it is to watch for any statements or drawings that might cause the book to be rejected by a state or school district. You must catch any double entendres (such as the word *high*). Normally you should watch for and avoid any trade names.

A job with an el-hi publisher involves more than just copyediting; you may actually do some of the writing, you will probably proofread galleys, and you may check all proof stages. Because pictures are so important in el-hi materials, you may also be asked to help select artwork and to check layout on the complete book to make sure that the juxtaposition of art and text is appropriate.

El-hi publishing is very interesting but difficult. Unless you are willing to get totally involved in the material, you should not try to work in that field; college texts may be better for you.

LEGAL MATERIALS

Legal publishers like staff copyeditors because these people have access to the law books and journals around the office. A legal background is irrelevant; a copyediting background is essential. The acquisitions editors are lawyers, so it is unlikely that you will move up in a legal publishing company unless you have at least some law background.

Don't tamper with style when you work on legal materials; it's *what's* said that's important. You should always be in agreement with the editor on what your responsibilities are regarding style.

If you plan to do any legal copyediting, get yourself a copy of *A Uniform System of Citation*, thirteenth edition, published by Harvard University Press and nicknamed the Harvard Blue Book.

RELIGIOUS AND INSPIRATIONAL BOOKS

Religious publishers do more than publish the Bible; in fact, many don't publish either a Bible or prayer books. They often publish philosophical, inspirational, and poetic materials; thus they often employ "poetic" copyeditors, usually on a freelance basis.

Editors in religious publishing are not always priests, ministers, or rabbis; like other editors, they may have an idea and ask the author to help create the work. Likewise, the copyeditors rarely have a theological background, although sometimes such expertise is helpful. Mostly an interest in religion is a prerequisite. Where Greek or Hebrew appears in print, naturally some knowledge of that language is required.

You should check facts in religious copyediting, just as you would in any trade area. A sense of language is helpful, particularly in work on the more poetic materials, but mostly you should be consistent. In religious publishing, capitalization versus lowercasing is important; always be sure you know what style the publisher prefers, and stick to it. Sometimes you will be dealing with translated material in which special phonetic symbols appear. Learn how to use them properly.

Apprenticeship is the best way to break into religious publishing. You might also try to copyedit some lightly inspirational work first, then get into the theology. And be sure you own the appropriate Bible so that you can check the accuracy of references and quotations (if asked!). In Protestant publishing you will need a Revised Standard Version, with access to the New Jerusalem Bible, New International Bible, and New English Bible (rarely the King James Version); for Roman Catholic work you'll want the Douay Version. If you would like to copyedit Jewish material, refer to the Torah. Always have a good historical atlas handy to check the spelling of place names.

Many religious materials will be for religious instruction. If you have the opportunity, read student and teacher materials together, as if you were preparing to teach the class: Perhaps the student can't do the exercise from the information provided.

The following checklist suggests questions to ask yourself about the material you are copyediting:

1. Are biblical references correct? If asked, use a concordance to find and write in the correct reference.
2. Are scripture quotations complete and accurate? Be sure that the version quoted is the one you use for checking.
3. Are the explanations and paraphrases faithful to the Bible? Sources for checking include the New Oxford Annotated Bible, the Revised Standard Version, and *Eerdmans' Handbook to the Bible.*

TESTS

Test writers are experts in their field, but they're not necessarily writers. The copyeditor must do the styling and make sure the questions are clear and logical; she or he may also have to lower the reading level.

To copyedit test materials, you should be familiar with the terminology but need no formal training in the subject. You are responsible for accuracy and consistency, and you should be able to recognize potential problems. You will probably do heavy editing, but have no fear: The author knows this and probably won't get to review your work anyway. If you're afraid to make a change that the author won't see, flag it for the editor. You probably won't have to check facts, of course; in testing, the questions rarely contain them!

One job you will have is checking numbering; you must check not only the complete numerical sequence (questions 1–500, for example) but the lettered subdivisions of multiple-choice questions, such as questions 1*a–e*. You must also be sure that instructions are worded consistently.

If there is art, you should copyedit it carefully against the text. Watch for what the question asks the reader to do; if the idea is to add labels to art, make sure labels don't already appear, and check that abbreviations are consistent.

As you know from your own experience with tests, clarity and consistency are vital. The student has no time to waste trying to interpret what is being asked. Prepare *detailed* style notes, including every instruction, term, abbreviation, number treatment, and so on, that you come across, and refer back to the style sheet often so that you're sure to treat similar elements in the same way. Take pity on the student who reads what you edit!

MEDICAL BOOKS AND ARTICLES

Medical publishers need freelance copyeditors who will stick with them (few staff copyeditors are used). Copyediting medical manuscripts is not the world's most glamorous job, but if you're willing to do it, you'll be paid quite well and be sure of steady work. Most medical material is published by book publishers, and only a few of those. These publishers work not only with books but also with journals and yearbooks.

Doctors don't try to be writers; they just put all the important information down. You, the medical copyeditor, must be sure it's grammatically correct, consistent, and in accordance with accepted rules for spelling, abbreviations, and units of measure. If you can do technical copyediting, you can do medical copyediting. You don't have to check any facts. You will usually be free to make stylistic changes, such as switching the author's sentences from the passive voice to the active.

Some medical publishers require copyeditors to calculate SI (Système International) units. Later in this chapter is a section on SI units, but you should get the *Handbook of the American Chemical Society* for more information.

Check cross-references to other chapters, and query the author if you cannot tell whether a reference is correct. Make sure that columns of numbers in tables tally, and query discrepancies.

Copyedit art and tables according to the rules in Chapter 10, and in general treat medical material the way you would college texts.

If you do a lot of medical copyediting, invest in a couple of special books. *Webster's Medical Speller* is a very small inexpensive book that is worth having. Pick up last year's *Physicians' Desk Reference* (PDR) in your bookstore's remainder section; it describes (and pictures) all the major drugs—what they do, what they contain, what side effects they produce. It's great for hypochondriacs too! A good dictionary of medical terms is *Dorland's Medical Dictionary*. Also write to the American Medical Association and the American Institute of Biological Sciences for their handbooks (in addition to the chemical handbook mentioned earlier). They're inexpensive and worth owning.

SCIENTIFIC AND MATHEMATICAL WORKS

Whether you copyedit textbooks, scientific articles, or nonfiction materials pertaining to science or mathematics, you will need to know how to typemark. You've seen mathematical material presented many times, but did you ever notice how it was set? Did you notice that many of the letters were set in italic? Did you realize that subscripts were set smaller as well as lower than the rest of the line? Were you aware of how the equations were aligned? In this section extensive rules are provided for marking all kinds of mathematical copy in both math and science materials.

Unless you have a degree in the subject, do not expect to understand the material you are asked to copyedit. Most publishers of such material assume only that you are familiar with the terminology—that you recognize immediately whether a word is misspelled—and that you can typemark the math. Having four years' experience as a nuclear chemist is of little value to a copyeditor who does not know that the valence charge sign should go to the right of the number of atoms or that it makes no sense to align the arrows denoting chemical reactions in an exercise set.

It takes a long time to learn all the rules for typemarking technical material; you're not going to be an expert after two manuscripts. Really good technical copyeditors continue to learn even after many years of work. But the rules are not that difficult, and you should not be afraid to start. Introductory college material is a good place to begin, preferably in a field that is not too mathematical, such as geology. Make copies of pages with typemarked equations and submit them with your application for future, more difficult technical copyediting assignments.

You may get very little reading pleasure out of working on technical manuscripts, but the financial rewards can be high. Good technical copyeditors are in demand because so few people understand technical marking. You are never expected to understand the material, but you must of course be consistent and grammatical and follow all the other rules of copyediting. After several manuscripts you will be able to typemark equations automatically, underlining unknowns and slipping in space marks without thinking.

Read over these technical marking instructions now to see the extent of work involved in technical copyediting, and refer to them constantly as you copyedit. With each manuscript you work on you'll find more areas where rules are needed; amend these instructions as you get experience.

Use of Italic Type

1. Use italic type for (mark with an underscore) all unknowns and variables.

$$\underline{x} + \underline{y} = \underline{z} \qquad \frac{\underline{dx}}{\underline{dy}} = \underline{dz} \qquad \underline{f}(\underline{x}) = 3$$

2. Any term (e.g., an unknown) that is set in italic under normal circumstances should remain in italic within italic passages. However, terms normally set in roman (e.g., numbers and operation signs) *should not* appear in italic when they come within italic passages; that is, they should remain roman.

> Note in this case that $\underline{x} + \underline{y} + \underline{z} = 1$.

(See also point 1 under Use of Roman Type, later in this section.)

3. The style of parentheses is governed by the style of the passage *within which they fall*, not by the style of the material they contain.

> $\underline{L}$ is called $\underline{\text{the limit of } f(x) \text{ as } x \text{ approaches } a_0}$
>
> The limit of $\underline{f(\underline{x})}$ as $\underline{x}$ approaches $\underline{a}$ is $\underline{L}$ and
>
> is written...

4. Use italic for single-letter subscripts or for multiple-letter subscripts if each letter stands for a separate word (e.g., *PV*, which stands for "pressure-volume").

> $\underline{H}_{\underline{a}}$

5. Italicize *d* for derivative, *f* for function, and *e* for exponent (but do not italicize exp; see Exponential Form later in this section).

6. Italicize the following chemical abbreviations when used as prefixes: *cis-*, *trans-*, *para-* (or *p-*), *meta-* (or *m-*), *ortho-* (or *o-*), *tert* (or *t-*), and *sec-* (or *s-*); *e*, *n*, and *p* (for electron, neutron, and proton); the orbitals *s*, *p*, *d*, and *f*, and close them up, as in 6*f* orbital; *M* (molar), *m* (molal), *N* (normal), and *F* (formal), and ask the author whether to close them up, as in 10*M*; and biochemical prefixes such as *N*, *O*, and *S*.

7. In graphs 0 is usually a capital italic oh (for origin). On number lines it is usually a zero. (The author does not always type the correct symbol.)

Use of Roman Type

1. Symbols (as opposed to letters and numbers) are always roman. Numbers are roman unless they are part of an italic passage and are used alone in a nonmathematical or only slightly mathematical sense. Used in a set of coordinate points or a mathematical expression they are roman, even within an italic passage.

> Note that $\underline{x} < 1$.
>
> Note that $(1, 3)$ $\underline{\text{is on the curve}}$.
>
> Note that $\underline{5 \text{ is greater than } 3}$.

2. Use roman type for the temperature scale abbreviations F (Fahrenheit), C (Celsius), and K (Kelvin, or absolute). Do not follow the abbreviation by a period. There is no space between the number and the degree sign: 17°F. Also, no degree sign is used with the Kelvin scale: 17 K.
3. Use roman for all abbreviations of units of measure—for example, g (gram), mL (milliliter), and lb (pound). Always leave space between the digit and the abbreviation: 14 g.
4. Use roman for pH and pK.
5. Set in roman all subscript words or abbreviations of two or more letters that stand for words—for example, init (initial), av (average), and eff (efficiency). If, however, the abbreviation is only one letter standing for one of those same words, set in italic. If the abbreviation consists of more than one letter, *each* standing for a separate word, such as *PV* for "pressure-volume," set it in italic (according to the rule set forth in the preceding sentence).

$$\underline{V}_{\text{acid}} \qquad \underline{V}_{\underline{a}}$$

6. Use roman for the following abbreviations: lim (limit), exp (exponent), log (logarithm), ln (natural logarithm), and all trigonometric functions: sin, cos, tan, sec, csc, cot, and the hyperbolic functions (same abbreviations with an *h* on the end: sinh).
7. Use roman for letters when used as labels, as in Brand X, Farmer A.
8. Use roman for the abbreviations of chemical elements (H_2O) and for R (radical).
9. Use roman for s, l, and g (solid, liquid, and gas) when enclosed within parentheses next to an element in a formula.

$$H_2O(s)$$

10. Use roman for parentheses unless they fall within an italic passage.

Use of Boldface Type

1. Use boldface roman for vectors. Delete the overarrow if one appears. Mark boldface in the usual way.

b

2. Use boldface for center dots and multiplication signs occurring between two vectors.

A · B

3. Use boldface for the special brackets or parentheses in vector discussions.

⟨ A · B ⟩

Use of Small Capitals

1. If the author or publisher requests it, small capitals may be used for the names of programming languages, programs, and programming commands; otherwise use solid capitals.
2. Use small capitals for D (dextrorotatory) and L (levorotatory). However, if the author has typed both capital and lowercase in a section, leave the lowercase *d* and *l* as is and mark for italic; change the capital to small capital.

Spacing*

For purposes of the ensuing discussion, space is considerably less than word space in most cases. The mark is simply a light vertical (with no space mark).

1. There should be space before and after operation and relation signs, unless the operation sign is used to designate a positive or negative quantity.

$$x + y + z = 0 \quad \text{but} \quad +3 \text{ [positive integer three]}$$

2. Set space before and after integral ($\int$), summation (Σ), and product (Π) signs; abbreviations for trigonometric and logarithmic functions; exponential functions and limits; and differentials (dy/dx). Set space before a derivative or differential of any shape (d, Δ, δ).

$$x \int y \, dt \quad \sin^{-1} x \quad \log_{10} x \quad \exp x^2 \, dx \quad 2 \tan x$$

*In subscripts and superscripts, disregard all spacing rules; set tight.

Note that subscripts and superscripts close up to trigonometric and logarithmic functions, but space is set between the function and the next term set on the same baseline. If a parenthesis follows the abbreviation, close up.

$\exp\frown(\underline{a}^2/\underline{b} + \underline{d})$ $\qquad\qquad\qquad$ $\exp(a^2/b + d)$

3. Set a space after a comma.[†]

$(x,/y)$ $\qquad\qquad\qquad$ (x, y)

4. There should be no space between a coefficient and its symbol.

$4x + 3y = 2z$ $\qquad\qquad\qquad$ $2H_2O$

If space has been typed consistently in the manuscript, query the author.

5. Each single equation should be displayed on its own line; intervening words are set flush left on their own lines.

6. Always insert a space before a unit of measure:

15 g (grams)

7. Builtup fractions and radical bars are followed by a thin space.

$$\frac{1}{2} \left(\frac{x + 1}{x + 5} \right)$$

$$\sqrt{x}\, n$$

8. Terms to be multiplied (without the use of a multiplication sign or center dot) should not be separated by space, no matter how many subs and supers are involved.

$a^{xy}b_{qrst}c$ $\qquad$ $(abc)(xyz)$

9. There is no space after a comma in the chemical names of organic compounds.

1,4-dimethylchloride

10. Qualifiers are set 2 ems to the right of an equation except in series, where 1 em is enough.

$$\begin{cases} 0 & \text{if } x > 1 \\ -1 & \text{if } x \le -1 \end{cases}$$

[†]See item 9, however.

11. Occasionally two equations will appear on the same line of display; put a 2-em space between them.

$\underline{x} = 3 \boxed{2} \underline{y} = 4$

If one or more words of text separate two equations on the same line of display, put a 1-em space on either side of the words.

$\underline{x} = 3 \square$ and $\square \underline{y} = 4$

12. There is no space around the elements in subs and supers unless setting tight causes confusion.

Breaking Equations

1. If a chemical reaction cannot fit on one line, break it after the arrow.
2. In running text, an equation should break *before* an operation sign $(+, -, \times,$ etc.$)$ or *after* a relation sign $(=, >, \because, \approx,$ etc.$)$, with the exception that mathematical material within parentheses, brackets, or braces should never be broken. Thus, at the end of a text line the equation $4x + 3y = 17$ should be broken either as $4x \lceil + 3y = 17$ or as $4x + 3y = \lceil 17$. Of course, you don't really know where the break will occur, but you can try to anticipate problems, particularly at the beginning of a paragraph.
3. In a display of two lines, the break precedes an operation sign or a relation sign. The first part of the equation goes flush left (or is indented according to the book design) and the second part flush right. If the overlap is less than 1 inch, more of an indent will be necessary. The equation number, if any, goes flush right on the second line, at least 1 em from the end of the equation.
4. In a display of three or more lines, break before operation and relation signs at convenient points. Do not break material within brackets of any sort. At the break all relation signs align; operation signs align there also, but one character to the right of relation signs.

$$\underline{xyz} + 2\underline{x}^2\underline{y} = 4\underline{x}^3\underline{y}^2\underline{z} + 17\underline{x} = \underline{x}^2\underline{yz} + 2\underline{xz}^2\underline{y} = 17\underline{x}^4\underline{y}$$
$$+ \underline{xz}^2\underline{y} - 1\underline{xy}^2 - 48\underline{z}^2\underline{y}$$
$$- \underline{z}^2\underline{xy} + \underline{xz}^3 + \underline{x}^3\underline{y}^2\underline{z} + 8$$
$$= 19\underline{r}$$

Place the equation number, if any, on the last line of the equation, flush right, at least 1 em from the end of the equation. If the equation ends flush right, move it further left.

5. Center an equation number on a multiple-line equation where appropriate.

$$q = \left(\frac{b}{A} + \frac{c}{D} \right) \tag{1}$$

$$g(r) = \begin{cases} 2r + 3 & \text{if } r < 1 \\ 2 & \text{if } r = 1 \\ 7 - 2r & \text{if } 1 < r \end{cases} \tag{1}$$

Alignment

1. Vertical groups of equations should align on the equals signs, regardless of the length of the various terms preceding those signs.

$$\begin{aligned} a + b + c + d + e &= f \\ x &= 17 + 2y \\ 3z + 5 &= 0 \end{aligned}$$

2. If several short displayed equations are separated by text lines of one or two words, align the equals signs of the equations unless by so doing an unintentional structure would be implied.

If

$$a + b + c = 0$$

then

$$a = 0 - b - c$$

and

$$b = 0 - a - c$$

3. In chemical reactions, align arrows only if there is a relationship between the reactions. Do not align arrows in exercises.

$$\begin{aligned} 2C + O_2 &\rightarrow 2CO \\ 2CO + O_2 &\rightarrow 2CO_2 \\ \hline 2C + 2O_2 &\rightarrow 2CO_2 \end{aligned}$$

but

oxidation: $\overset{0}{Al} \rightarrow \overset{+3}{Al} + 3e^-$

reduction: $\overset{0}{Cl} + 2e^- \rightarrow 2\overset{-1}{Cl}$

Subscripts and Superscripts

1. In mathematics, subs and supers almost always follow the term. In chemistry, the current style is for atomic number and weight to precede the element: $^{238}_{92}\text{U}$

2. Supers are set to the right of subs unless the sub has three or more characters, in which case the sub and super align on the left.[*]

$$x_a^2 \quad x_{aver}^2$$

   Degree signs and primes are considered superscripts and also follow this rule, unless within the same manuscript they appear with subs of both fewer and more than three characters.

   $x'_{aver} \quad x'_2$ when in the same book; otherwise x_2'

3. Fractions within subs and supers are set with a solidus (see Fractions, the next subsection).

4. Valences should be written as 2+ instead of ++ or +2.

$$Ca^{2+} \quad SO_4^{2-}$$

   However, stet $+2$ when it is used to describe an oxidation state and is not attached to a chemical abbreviation.

Fractions

You will need to be aware of the following types of fractions.

1. *Case.* This is the most common type of fraction. It consists solely of numbers (no punctuation, letters, or symbols). The numerator appears directly over the denominator, and the entire fraction is the height of only one text line.

$$\frac{1}{2}$$

   If the manuscript has more than just the very simple fractions, consider them as special elements; most compositors cannot supply all fractions as case.

2. *Solidus* (also called *shilling*). A solidus fraction can contain letters, numbers, or symbols. The numerator and denominator appear on the same line, separated by a slash (a *solidus*).

$$a/b$$

---

[*]If the author consistently has typed subs and supers to align, check with the publisher whether to leave that style. With some compositors, aligning subs and supers may be too expensive.

When using the solidus, it is often necessary to add parentheses around one or both terms to make clear what is being divided by what. If you are dealing with single letters or numbers, no parens are necessary. But whenever you are working with fractions containing operation signs, you will need parens. See the example at the end of this subsection.

3. *Builtup.* A builtup fraction can contain letters, numbers, symbols, or even other fractions. The numerator appears directly over the denominator, and the fraction takes up at least one full line for the numerator and one full line for the denominator.

$$\frac{1}{2}$$

4. *Piece.* Piece fractions are seen mostly in nontechnical materials, whose compositors cannot usually set case fractions. The numerator and denominator are separated by a solidus, but the two are on neither the same vertical nor the same horizontal line.

$$\frac{1}{2}$$

The following are some rules about using fractions.

1. Fractions in subscripts and superscripts are always set with a solidus.
2. If all the fractions in a line of display consist solely of numbers, it is all right to use case fractions; normally, builtup fractions are used in display. Sequences of fractions in display, or fractions in close proximity, are treated the same. However, not all fractions in display need be built up: The size of the fraction is governed by the size of the term immediately following it. In other words, a fraction preceding a full-size integral sign is built up; before *log* it is case.
3. Builtup fractions should not be used within the text line unless the author insists, because this will cause the lines to spread. Either display the fraction or use a solidus. See the example at the end of this subsection.
4. If the author has used builtup fractions in running text, where solidus fractions are preferred, you can't simply mark them all for solidus. To be clear what term is the divisor, you will

normally have to add parentheses to either the numerator or the denominator, or both. You may have to ask the author to double-check you.

The following are examples of how to (1) change a builtup fraction within running text to a displayed fraction; (2) make a displayed solidus fraction into a builtup display; and (3) convert a builtup fraction to a solidus fraction within running text. Note the common abbreviations *bu* and *sol*.

1. From builtup running text to builtup display:

   This then becomes $\dfrac{x - y}{y + 4}$ so...

   This then becomes

   $$\frac{x - y}{y + 4}$$

   so...

2. From displayed solidus to builtup display:

   This then becomes

   $\lfloor x/y \rfloor$ *bu*

   so...

   This then becomes

   $$\frac{x}{y}$$

   so...

3. From builtup running text to solidus running text:

   This then becomes $x - y / (y + 4)$ so... *sol*

   This then becomes $(x - y)/(y + 4)$, so...

Note the addition of parens in the last example. Parens were added to both terms here because if they had been attached to only the denominator, it might have been unclear whether the *x* stood alone or was part of the numerator. Of course, the term $x - y$ by itself needs no parentheses.

When you reposition fractions, be sure you decide what to do with the punctuation that follows them. Normally there is no punctuation following display.

Ellipsis Points

1. Ellipsis points in a series have a comma or operation sign on *both* sides. When commas are used, the points appear on the line.

   $$1, 2, \ldots, n$$

   Ellipsis points between operation signs should be centered on the line.

   $$1 + 2 + \cdots + n$$

   If the operation sign is a centered dot, meaning "times," there will be five dots centered on the line, so you may wish to invite the author to make a different representation.

2. In determinants and matrices, missing material is indicated by a series, either horizontal or vertical, of three dots. The dots are centered on the depth or width of the *major element* (disregarding subs and supers) in the row or column.

   $$\begin{bmatrix} a_{11} & a_{12} & \cdots & a_{1n} \\ a_{21} & a_{22} & \cdots & a_{2n} \\ \cdot & & & \\ \cdot & & & \\ \cdot & & & \\ a_{n1} & a_{n2} & \cdots & a_{nn} \end{bmatrix}$$

3. Points of ellipsis are three *spaced* dots. If ellipsis points end a sentence, add a fourth dot as the period. Follow normal spacing rules for ellipsis points juxtaposed to other punctuation; that is, there is space *after* but not before a comma.

Limits

1. In display, limits follow an integral sign.

2. In display, limits are centered above and below signs of summation, product, union, and lim.

3. In running text, an integral sign is 12 points high and straight up and down; it does not slant the way a large integral sign slants in display. In text, then, the limits to the integral sign will appear

aligned: $\int_b^a$. The subscript to the "lim" symbol appears to the right: $\lim_{x \to 0}$. Note that the limit itself is set in subscript type.

Note: You, as copyeditor, will decide whether to have the element displayed or run in to text.

Exponential Form

Simple exponents (x^2) are no problem to the compositor. Furthermore, an exponent may consist of a fraction (see Fractions, earlier in this section, where the use of a solidus for this purpose is explained). However, there is an exponential form that uses e (i.e., an exponent) with a superscript. If this exponent is lengthy or complex, the e should be changed to "exp" (roman) followed by what was the superscript, now set on the line within parentheses (or brackets, depending on complexity), and closed up to the "exp." Thus

$$e^{a^2/b + cd^2 - xyz}$$

becomes

$$\exp(a^2/b + cd^2 - xyz)$$

Note that space is added around operation signs once the exponent is back on the line.

Brackets and Other Aggregation Symbols

1. The size of an aggregation symbol is determined by the depth of the formula it encloses.
2. The order of aggregation is $\{[(\ )]\}$. However, if the author uses another order, check with her or him before changing.
3. Stet the use of double parens when functions are being discussed; that is, normal function notation is $f(x)$ (read "f of x"), and when it is amplified to "f of g of x," there will be double parens: $f(g(x))$. Do not change to parens within brackets. On the other hand, if the author has used the bracket-paren system, leave as is.

Miscellaneous

1. A script lowercase el (ℓ) is normally just the author's way of writing a plain el (script to differentiate it from a "one"); do query the author, but you will probably find that if it stands alone, the letter is meant to be lowercase italic. Alternatively, when used with a lowercase en, a lowercase el means natural log and is written "ln" in roman.
2. A typed lowercase oh in a subscript or superscript position is usually supposed to be a zero, but query the author if you're

not sure. The first one on every page must be identified for the compositor. A typed lowercase oh centered between two letters (f o g) is a symbol for the composition of two functions (read "the composition of *f* and *g*"). The typeset symbol is a small circle (*f* ∘ *g*).

3. Authors usually type a lowercase ex for a multiplication sign. You must cross through it every time it appears to avoid having to label it "multi" or "times" throughout.

$$a \times b = c$$

4. Handwritten Greek letters should be identified the first time they appear on a page. One unusual one is the cap theta, which authors often write as a cap aitch with a circle around it.

5. Mark subs and supers only when there's doubt. You must, however, mark to have supers go to the right of subs.

6. Identify a degree sign the first time it appears on a page.

7. In mathematical copy it is preferable to use the asterisk system for identifying footnotes. However, the asterisk should not go on a letter or number; rewrite so that a word or phrase takes the asterisk.

8. The current preference is to use the forms α (alpha), σ (sigma), ϕ (phi), and θ (theta). The alternatives are a, ς, φ, and ϑ, respectively.

9. The current preference is to use the forms $\leq$ and $\geq$. Note that there is a single horizontal bar.

10. Use $\neq$ (slanted cancellation) but $\not<$ and $\not>$ (vertical cancellations). In a slanted cancellation the cancellation line always goes from southwest to northeast.

11. Short displayed equations should normally appear on their own lines, except when the author separates two by a short phrase on the same line. Preceding text, however, should go flush left (or paragraphed, according to sense). For alignment of these displayed equations, see Alignment.

Hence,

$$a + b + c = d$$

and if

$$\cdots$$

then

$$\cdots$$

12. Overbars, tildes, and carets on subs and supers normally affect leading within a line. Always ask the author if there is an alternative form.
13. $|\underline{x}|$ means "absolute value of x"; it doesn't mean to straighten the x.

Chemical Marking Instructions

1. The oxidation state of an element is set in parentheses closed up to the element.

    osmium(VIII)

2. Follow the style manual of the American Chemical Society for spelling and abbreviations.
3. Use single-barbed arrows for reversible reactions, with the top arrow pointing to the right: $\rightleftharpoons$. Do not change other kinds of arrows.
4. Use hyphens to join numbers and abbreviations to chemical names.

    trans-2-bromocyclopentanol

5. Identify bonds and all other symbols the first time they appear on a page.
6. On most typewriters there is a distinction between a cap oh and a zero, but typists often use them interchangeably. Always mark the incorrect or unclear ones.
7. Be sure there can be no doubt about the use of Cl (for chloride); it could appear to inexperienced compositors to be a cap cee and a "one," or even a lowercase dee if written in script.
8. Usually use the negative exponent for "per" (except in basic texts or if the manuscript is very simple).

    cm s^{-1} not   cm/s

Follow the author's style, and be consistent!

Abbreviations

1. Abbreviations should be used for units of measure only when accompanied by a number.

   15 mL

   but

   measured in milliliters

2. Only the abbreviations *in.* (inch) and *at.wt* (atomic weight) take periods.
3. Abbreviations are always in the singular (don't use lbs for "pounds," for example). Spelled-out units (if you are not abbreviating for some reason, as in semitechnical material) can take a plural.

   15 lb

   but

   15 pounds

Note: With an abbreviation a singular verb is used; with a spelled-out unit a plural verb is used for more than one unit. Be sure to use a singular verb for fractions of units.

   15 mL is   2 pounds are   0.3 pound is

4. If you are using SI (Système international) units, here are the seven basic abbreviations:

m	meter
kg	kilogram
s	second
A	ampere
K	kelvin
mol	mole
cd	candela

   Other common units are

min	minute
d	day
h	hour
L	liter

The prefixes are

M	mega
k	kilo
h	hecto
da	deca
d	deci
c	centi
m	milli
μ	micro

Thus some examples of derived units are

mL	milliliter
cg	centigram
μm	micrometer

5. In semimedical usage, cubic centimeter is abbreviated cc; in chemical matter use cm^3 as the abbreviation. In medical books, mL is used instead.

WORKS IN FOREIGN LANGUAGES

If you can speak, read, or write a foreign language, even if you are not foreign born, your skills will be welcomed by some publisher. Of course, you must be able to demonstrate that you have the normal copyediting skills outlined throughout this book as well. Copyediting foreign languages requires the same attention to spelling and punctuation that we have been looking at in this book; the only difference is that the language is not English. If you work on foreign language materials, watch out for sexism just as you would in English; handle artwork the same way; use the same keying system.

If you work for a foreign language trade publisher (as opposed to a college or el-hi publisher of foreign language texts), you will probably be native born; foreign language publishers need editors and copyeditors who are familiar with all the idioms, not just the few cute ones you learned in college. Nonnatives may, however, handle ESL (English as a second language) books for these publishers.

Because the most difficult material to copyedit is formal instruction in grammar, you will have to take special care with those beginning-level books. Grammar books attempt to teach a language to someone who doesn't know it; there is no room for error in coding or setting up displays. You should be able to suggest alternative approaches to exercises, or flag trivial dialogue, or recognize words missing from the vocabulary. You must be able to decide whether a chart belongs with the material that precedes it or with the material that follows it, and mark for space accordingly. Being a language teacher may help on grammar books, but being a good English-language copyeditor will help even more.

If you can speak, read, and write any language fairly well, don't overlook magazines and newspapers in that language sector of the United States and Canada. Good in Spanish? Put in an application with *El diario*. A French major? What about writing to some people in Montreal? They have dozens of magazines and newspapers, most published in French. We language people have a special skill; we must sell ourselves!

NONFICTION

Nonfiction books and articles can take two main forms: straight text, such as biography or memoirs, and heavily illustrated material, such as a how-to article or an art book. People who deal with straight text can follow the rules given in this book and will seldom find anything out of the ordinary when they work. But if you are copyediting an art-type project, you will need a lot of production background. I recommend that you read James Craig's book *Production for the Graphic Designer* (see the bibliography), which is an excellent introduction to elements of design, composition, and printing. Then you might try to get a staff job as an editorial assistant for a nonfiction book or magazine publisher; such a job will help you prepare for the production aspects of art copyediting.

Articles, books, or brochures that have a lot of art benefit mainly from how the book is laid out; the words are relatively unimportant. Copyediting skills are of only minimal use in handling such materials. Instead you must have a good eye for design and layout. Art history majors have a better chance than the rest of us at this kind of copyediting. When you copyedit, you'll be asked to do the following things, among others: (1) check the measurements of the work (is it really supposed to be wider than it is long?); (2) be sure the work isn't flopped (i.e., backward); (3) make credits consistent (is the Collection of Mr. & Mrs. John Jones the same as the Collection of John and Rose Jones?); (4) check spelling of all proper names; (5) add metric units if they don't already appear; and (6) make consistent references to sizes (is it 20″ × 30″, 20 × 30 inches, or something else?).

Sound like a lot of work? Well, remember that you have very little text to work with, and you don't usually have to read for content. If you have very little experience, plan to start as a freelance or staff proofreader and work up. Beginning with a small publisher is very helpful because you'll be exposed to all kinds of layouts, from books to brochures to ads to posters, and you'll get valuable design experience there.

Of course, narrative nonfiction has its own set of problems. Some how-to books fit into this category if they're not heavily illustrated. Can you think of an example? What about the book you're now reading? Can you think of some of the problems the copyeditor of this book faced? I sure can! There are all those head levels in Chapter 4, for example, and the typemarking in the technical section of this chapter. If you copyedit sports or crafts books or articles, you should at least have an interest in the subject and be willing to teach yourself from the material; how else can you tell whether it's accurate and complete? Authors of such material are not usually writers, so you're the one who can best test the theories presented. True, it is not your responsibility to test the validity of the material; you should merely take notice of obvious errors and ambiguities. But with some projects you may be asked to involve yourself more deeply than usual.

One of the most difficult kinds of material to copyedit is a recipe. *You must be able to visualize the finished product,* and you have to know enough about cooking to know that when the author says "8 cups of flour," there's probably something wrong! (Of course, recipes do get tested; when that cake comes out of the oven, it will look and taste a little strange.) In copyediting recipes, always check that the ingredients are given in the same order as they're called for and that everything is used (and no uncited ingredients pop up in the recipe). Be careful about style and consistency from one recipe to another, whether in a book or article, and watch out that adverbs are used and positioned correctly. Make sure the reader will understand all the directions; if you're told to halve a cucumber and then cut it into ½-inch slices, does the recipe mean to cut it lengthwise? Not according to the picture that accompanied my recipe with that very instruction! Think of the recipes as experiments and the cookbook as a manual so easy to follow that the experiment will always be successful.

Nonfiction copyeditors of all types should be prepared to check facts. But bear in mind that a history book by a historian is more reliable than one by a layperson. Find out something about the author and about what is expected of you before you decide how to proceed.

When you prepare your résumé (see Chapter 13), think of the areas you can specialize in, and point them out. I'm told that some areas where copyeditors who know something about the topic are needed are metrics (being able to convert), computer languages, and map reading. Can you anticipate future trends? What about accounting and finance? If you're involved in these areas now, you may find yourself in the right place later.

FICTION

Everyone wants to copyedit fiction. There's something thrilling about knowing that you copyedited the book that's now a bestseller. But it's not as easy as it sounds. Your style sheet has to be extremely detailed and include everything from word treatment to the spelling of all characters' names to descriptions of people and places, along with the manuscript page reference of the first citation. You must read the manuscript twice, of course, although some copyeditors read three times. The first time is essentially for pleasure and to find out how the book comes out. During this reading you'll be making spelling, consistency, and grammar and punctuation changes and will begin compiling the style sheet. On the second run-through you can concentrate on discrepancies: The doctor returned home at 5 P.M. and now it is 3 P.M.; the sun is rising in the West; the boy looked out over the Atlantic Ocean from his home in Salt Lake City (yes, I've seen all those errors in manuscripts). Once you know how the book or story or play turns out, you'll be in better shape to absorb the information given throughout. Then you can point out the problem areas.

During the second go-through you are not concentrating on the outcome, so you become aware of certain situations overlooked in your first, quick reading: It rained steadily for three days, or Mary left London to live with her mother in Hastings. Nothing vital, but knowing the outcome helps you justify—or not justify—these situations in your mind. On the third run-through you attempt to reconcile those points. With three days of rain, why is it still so hot? If Mary is with her mother in Hastings, how is it that the mother is in Madrid for the summer?

Really experienced copyeditors can get by with two readings. On the first time through, they make checkmarks in the margin next to such statements as the ones I just described. The act of pointing out something helps them remember it. In addition, they note on the style sheet circumstances such as weather, location, and time. On their careful second reading they can catch the problems. You should work the way you feel most comfortable, but be sure to find all the inconsistencies of plot or you'll soon be out of work.

You must also be prepared to face the fact that you may, after your second or third reading, decide to go back and change something you handled consistently all along. For example, you hyphenated "living-room window" (for some reason; it probably wasn't a good idea, as you'll see) throughout. Now, on manuscript page 443, the southerner drawls, " 'livin' room rug," and all of a sudden you wish you hadn't used that hyphen four times *somewhere* in Chapters 3 and 7. Not to mention "dining-room fireplace" near the bottom of the page around where Nina and Harry were discussing Mama's will (now, where *was* that? . . .). If you think *you* have problems, remember that nothing drives a proofreader mad faster than having to go back over 300 pages looking for hyphens to remove once he or she realizes that there's massive inconsistency.

Fiction copyeditors have to check facts (or at least spot-check them, for instance by looking up ten things that *might* be wrong); watch for anachronisms (were there pay telephones in World War I?); determine appropriateness of dialogue (you want to retain the flavor but still make it clear what the characters are saying and what they mean; this is especially true when dealing with British writers, who use expressions not all American readers will understand); check the internal clock of the material (the chronology of events); and be on guard for questions of libel and taste. Naturally you will be reading for structure, spelling, capitalization, punctuation, accuracy, and the like, but you must always remember that the material is the author's, and you must retain the flavor of the manuscript. If the author doesn't consistently use "that" in restrictive sentences, so what? It's not really wrong to say "which," is it? Follow the author's style for the series comma (unless given other instructions by the publisher), but make sure to pick one style and use it consistently even if the author hasn't. In other words, in fiction copyediting you should keep your hands off the manuscript, without letting it be wrong.

If you are not prepared to take this kind of care with your work, do not become a fiction copyeditor. Consider being an editor instead, simply looking for an interesting story with a pleasing style; or a reader, choosing one manuscript over another for possible publication. But a fiction copyeditor must take extreme care with the material.

Furthermore, you will find as a fiction copyeditor that there are all sorts of new uses for punctuation marks. Remember how swear words are indicated in comic books? With asterisks and "at" signs and other symbols found on the typewriter (*@!&#★!). So punctuation marks have new uses in fiction. The apostrophe is the best example. Grammar books tell you all about the apostrophe to indicate possession, or to represent a missing letter in a contraction, or even to form a plural in some cases. But to a fiction writer the apostrophe can have an even more important function: It can set the tone. Without knowing a thing about the characters, what difference can you spot between someone who says, "Goin' to Chicago on the mornin' train" and one who says, "I'm going to Chicago on the morning train"? At least a difference in education.

As a fiction copyeditor you must put yourself in the character's shoes—read the dialogue as the character would say it. Watch for places the author left *doing* for *doin'*. Be sure the apostrophe is there at all. Check whether the period is in the right place relative to the apostrophe. Check that there's space *after* the apostrophe, not before, or in some cases that there's no space before *or* after (such as quicker'n).

Here are some more expressions used in dialogue; from these you can pattern others you see.

> where're, outa, oughta, a-fixin', wanna, more'n, 'fore, 'cause

What other colloquialisms can you think of, and how would you spell them?

Do not suggest that a character should be more fully developed; that's up to the editor to point out. When you find serious problems with the dialogue, do not attempt to fix it without checking first with the publisher or author. Do not change plot situations because you found errors; simply point them out. Unless the reader would be hopelessly confused by Britishisms, leave them alone, and just make suggestions to the author. And never, never tamper with the author's style.

DRAMA

Drama, of course, is a form of fiction. Most plays have already been done professionally before the script is ready to be published, so the bugs are probably gone. If you want to work with drama, you have two choices: Get a staff job with a play leasing and publishing service (the two largest are Samuel French and Dramatists Play Service, and their copyediting staffs are very small), or sign up for the odd play published by a standard trade publisher, such as Random House, on a freelance basis. There are lots of amateur productions that would welcome editorial assistance too.

Never query language in a play, but do read for accuracy. Check that the play calls for all the props given in the prop list and that no props are called for that aren't on the list. Be sure that the stage directions work—that someone exited the room before reentering it, that the door downstage doesn't open onto a cellar instead of a bedroom, and that all characters are present who are supposed to be. You will also have to make the stage directions and speakers' names conform to the publisher's style. A typical play has all stage directions, including setting, given in italic, and the speakers' names in all caps, followed by space, with the dialogue run in, turnovers flush left. There are, of course, lots of other possibilities. Remember to spell out numbers in dialogue (see Chapter 7) unless they become unwieldy.

Here's a typical example of dialogue from a play.

> DAWN (*Looking at Richard*) I can't take this worry anymore.
> (*Richard moves D.L. toward the bookcase*) It's too hard
> on me.
> RICHARD (*Smirking*) You never were very strong, dear.

Did you notice that there are no periods after the stage directions in this example, even in the complete sentence? Of course, in lengthy stage directions consisting of complete sentences, there will be periods except after the last one.

If you have an interest or background in drama, try to get work in the field. Although reading plays is not for everyone, some of us enjoy it almost as much as going to the theater itself.

POETRY

Poets are gifted people; rarely will one make such a major error in a poem as to render it worthless. You may not like the poem or agree with its sentiment, but you can be fairly sure it says exactly what the poet intended.

Consequently, you may not make any change without querying, except for the obvious typo. Query spelling and meter and punctuation—don't change anything yourself. Unless you see a change in the pattern, you should not change the capitalization at the beginning of the line or the punctuation at the end. Query the author if you feel there has been a mistake. A couple of possibilities are that every line begins with a capital letter, regardless of whether a complete sentence precedes it, or that only a new sentence or thought begins with a capital letter.

Within text, quoted poems take the same capitalization and punctuation as in the poem itself. Lines are separated by a slash with no space on either side.

> "For lo! his passion, but an art of craft,/Even there
> resolv'd my reason into tears;"

When counting lines for a text reference, remember that 101–105 is *not* four lines!

Most poems are copyedited in-house because they're so short and simple; so if poetry is your bag, look for a staff job, and of course be prepared to copyedit other types of material as well. (Also see Religious and Inspirational Books earlier in this chapter.)

JUVENILE PUBLICATIONS

Someone once said to a friend of mine, a well-known children's book author, "Anyone can write children's books; you only have to know 300 words." He was teasing, of course; it is no easy matter to write a book that children can understand. Either the language is too difficult or the subject is. You as a copyeditor must be aware of both.

Most publishers of juvenile materials employ staff copyeditors only, although occasionally books for older children are done by freelancers. Often the copyeditor is the editor, too, and she or he may handle the production of the material as well. Because publishers get *hundreds* of unsolicited manuscripts for children's reading matter, a good place to start in juvenile publishing is as a reader—someone who goes through all these manuscripts and selects some worthy of possible publication. The job is not high-paying, but it is enjoyable and a good entry-level position.

If you do land a job copyediting children's books or articles, read the manuscript for grammar and details, checking facts of all types. If a word sounds too difficult to you, query the author; don't make the change yourself. You may also be asked to check quotations for accuracy.

As with fiction, the author's style must prevail, so be prepared to keep your changes and suggestions to a minimum.

REPRINTS

Almost all publishers—magazine, book, and newspaper—reprint materials from other sources. It is not up to the copyeditor of such materials to make changes; after all, this is not original stuff any longer—it's been published in this form. The copyeditor must assume that the previous copyeditor had a reason for making the changes that now appear. Errors in spelling and consistency should be corrected, but if something was done consistently wrong, leave it alone. Be sure, when dealing with reprinted material, that you check the status of the permissions, even if your job for the publisher does not include that; small publishers, particularly, are not always aware of the legal difficulties involved in reprinting material. One aspect to watch for is internal quotation of other copyrighted material. If you are reprinting an article for which you have permission, you still must get permission separately for anything within that article that was not created by the article's author. (For further information, see Permissions in Chapter 10.)

MAGAZINES

Why a separate section on magazines, when their articles fall into the categories already described? Well, magazine publishing is special. Magazines have tight schedules, of course—looser than newspapers but tighter than books. Because they're small, they employ only one or two copyeditors (staff only). These copyeditors get involved in all aspects of magazine production, checking layouts, helping to choose artwork and photos, and proofreading the final galleys. Sometimes a copyeditor also writes articles and gets a byline.

Magazines differ from college and el-hi books, how-to materials, legal, medical, and similar projects, and certain other areas in that their articles are written by writers—not teachers, baseball players, or lawyers. The copyeditors on a magazine don't have a difficult job. They do some styling and take care of the obvious spelling and grammatical errors, and of course they make the article conform to house style regarding numbers, the serial comma, and so on. They don't normally have to code copy, because there is always an art department to set the design style, but they may call attention to headings, blurbs, and other copy that they feel might not get designed specially without their cue. Some magazines follow a standard format: Every article is designed exactly the same, or at least parts of articles remain the same from issue to issue (e.g., *Consumer Reports* uses a rating system that must be uniform so that readers will get used to the categories it reports on). *TV Guide* is an example of a magazine with the same format every week, from cover to cover. The copyeditor on magazines that have special styles for recurring situations must be especially careful to use consistent terminology, just as copyeditors of college texts have to make sure that drill exercises are introduced in the same way from chapter to chapter.

Although there is virtually no chance that you'll get freelance copyediting from a magazine, there are lots of interesting staff jobs for beginners. Don't be a snob; just because you've never heard of the magazine doesn't mean that you can't learn a lot and enjoy your job.

NEWSPAPERS

I told you in Chapter 1 that copyeditors on newspapers can make a lot of money (at least on the staffs of big-city dailies). That's because they do a lot of work other copyeditors don't; they edit on video display terminals (VDT's), as I've already described, and they have to do some research to make changes in content. They have to verify the spelling of all terms, and they have to put articles into words the reader can grasp quickly. A good copyeditor may be even more important than a good reporter if that reporter can't make herself or himself understood.

Newspaper copyeditors are chosen for their background and interest in an area, even if they don't know the material completely. They should be very sensitive to libel, sexism, racism, ageism, and obscenity, and they should know how to make appropriate changes when those problems arise. They have to be extremely productive;

the deadlines are for hours of the day, not months of the year. They work long hours and usually start with shift work. If you like pressure and feel comfortable working perhaps at 2 A.M., give this field a try.

▶ KEY POINTS IN THIS CHAPTER

In this section you will find rules for the various kinds of copyediting you may do.

College Textbooks

- Query the author; do not presume that you know the subject better than the author does.
- Eliminate sexism wherever practical.
- Check that exercises can be completed according to the instructions.

El-Hi Textbooks

- Be sensitive to racism, sexism, and regional idiosyncrasies.
- Catch double entendres.
- Watch for and query the use of trade names.

Legal Materials

- Don't tamper with style.
- Get a ruling from the publisher on your responsibilities.

Religious and Inspirational Books

- Check facts, biblical references, and quotations.
- Be consistent in your use of capital vs. lowercase letters.
- Be sure paraphrases and explanations are faithful to the Bible.

Tests

- Check all numerical sequences.
- Be sure instructions are worded clearly and consistently.
- Copyedit art carefully against text.
- Ensure that the student will be able to answer the question from the instructions given.

Medical Books and Articles

- Check that manuscript is grammatically correct, consistent, and in accordance with accepted rules for spelling, abbreviations, and units of measure.
- Calculate SI units if requested.

- Check cross-references.
- Query discrepancies in tabular results.

Scientific and Mathematical Works

Italic vs. roman type
- Use italic for unknowns and variables, whether within roman or italic passages.
- The style of parentheses is governed by the style of the passage within which they fall.
- Use italic for single-letter subscripts or for multiple-letter subscripts if each letter represents a separate word.
- Use italic *e* for exponent.
- Use italic for the chemical prefixes *cis-*, *trans-*, *para-*, *meta-*, *ortho-*, *tert-*, *sec-*, *m-*, *o-*, *t-*, and *s-*; for *e*, *n*, *p* (electron, neutron, proton); for the orbitals *s*, *p*, *d*, and *f*; and for *M*, *m*, *N*, and *F* (molar, molal, normal, formal).
- Use roman for numbers and operation signs, whether within roman or italic passages.
- Use roman for temperature scales; for abbreviations of units of measure; for pH and pK; for lim, exp, log, ln, and all trignometric and hyperbolic functions; for s, l, and g (solid, liquid, gas); and for labels.
- Use roman for subscript abbreviations that are or that stand for words, unless the abbreviation is a single letter.
- Use roman for abbreviations of chemical elements and for R (radical).
- Use roman for parentheses unless they fall within an italic passage.

Boldface
- Use boldface for vectors.
- Operation signs appearing between two vectors should be bold, as should special brackets or parentheses in vector discussions.

Small capitals
- If the author has typed capital D and L (dextrorotatory and levorotatory), use small capitals.
- Use small capitals if requested for computer terms.

Spacing
- There is space around operation signs; positive and negative quantities are closed up.

- There is space around integral, summation, and product signs; abbreviations for trignometric and logarithmic functions; exponential functions and limits; and differentials. There is space before but not after those functions when they are followed by parentheses or are subscripts or superscripts.
- There is space after a comma and before a unit of measure.
- There is no space between a coefficient and its symbol.
- There is thin space after a builtup fraction.
- Terms to be multiplied are not separated by space.
- There is no space after a comma in the chemical names of organic compounds.
- Two equations on the same line are separated by 2 ems of space; if a word intervenes, there is 1 em of space on each side. Qualifiers are set 2 ems to the right of an equation or 1 em in series.
- The oxidation state of an element is set in parentheses closed up to the element.

Breaking and aligning equations

- Break a chemical reaction after an arrow. Do not align arrows if no relationship exists.
- In running text, break an equation before an operation sign or after a relation sign; do not break mathematical material within parentheses.
- In display, break before an operation or relation sign. Align on relation signs and indent operation signs on the first character after the relation sign.
- Do not break material within brackets.
- Place an equation number on the last line of the equation, flush right. Center it vertically on a multiline equation.
- Short intervening phrases between equations go flush left on their own lines.

Subscripts and superscripts

- Atomic number and weight precede the chemical element.
- Mark to place supers to the right of subs unless the sub has three or more characters, in which case align sub and super on the left.
- Use a solidus for fractions within subs and supers.
- Write chemical valences with a digit and a + or −.
- Mark subs and supers only when they're unclear.

Fractions

- Use case fractions when only digits are involved; use solidus fractions if there are letters.

- Use builtup fractions in display only.
- The size of the fraction is governed by the size of the term immediately following it.
- When changing builtup and solidus fractions, add or delete parentheses as necessary for clarity.

Ellipsis points

- There is a comma or an operation sign on both sides of ellipsis points.
- Ellipsis points are three spaced dots, with a fourth period at the end of a sentence.
- In determinants and matrices, missing material is indicated by three dots centered on the depth or width of the major element.

Limits and exponents

- In display, limits follow an integral sign and are centered above and below summation, product, and union signs. The limit is centered below lim.
- In running text, an integral is 12 points high and unslanted.
- When e is used for "exponent" and takes two levels of superscript, change to exp, with the rest of the superscript on the line and within parentheses.

Brackets and other aggregation symbols

- The size of an aggregation symbol is determined by the depth of the formula it encloses.
- The order of aggregation is $\{[(|)]\}$; if the author has used some other system, query.
- Stet the use of double parens for functions if the author has used that system, but do not change it.

Abbreviations

- Use abbreviations only with units of measure.
- Do not use periods with abbreviations, except for *at. wt* and *in.*
- Do not make abbreviations for units of measure plural.
- Use a singular verb with an abbreviation.

Miscellaneous

- Determine what symbols the author wants for a script lowercase el, capital and lowercase oh, lowercase ex, and handwritten Greek letters; mark the first time on each page. Identify the first chemical bond and degree sign on each page.

- Use a single horizontal bar for the signs for "greater/less than" or "equal to." Use a vertical cancellation for "not greater/less than," but use a slanted cancellation for "unequal to." Where slanted cancellations appear, they go from southwest to northeast.
- Use a single-barbed arrow for reversible chemical reactions; the top arrow points to the right.
- Use hyphens to join numbers and abbreviations to chemical names.

Works in Foreign Languages

- Treat foreign languages as you would English.
- Suggest alternative approaches to exercises.
- Flag trivial dialogue.
- Watch for words missing from vocabulary.
- Determine how structures should look when printed, and mark accordingly.

Nonfiction

Art books
- Check the measurements of the work.
- Be sure the work is not flopped.
- Make credit lines consistent.
- Check spelling of all proper names.
- Add metric units if requested.
- Make references to sizes consistent.

How-to books
- Try to learn the material from the manuscript.

Cookbooks
- Visualize the finished product.
- Watch style and consistency from one recipe to another.
- Be sure that adverbs are used and positioned correctly.
- Make sure the reader will understand all the directions.

Fiction

- Read the manuscript once for general plot and a second time to be sure that the story can turn out the way it does from the information given.
- Watch for errors in fact and chronology.
- Put yourself in the character's shoes to determine appropriateness of dialogue.
- Do not tamper with the author's style.
- Keep track of the distinguishing features of each character.

- Alert the editor if you feel that the material is in bad taste or may be libelous.

Drama

- Read plays for accuracy but not language.
- Check that the prop list accurately represents the needs of the play.
- Be sure that stage directions work; make them consistent.
- Spell out numbers in dialogue.

Poetry

- Correct typos only. Query all other changes, including spelling and meter.
- Do not change capitalization at the beginning of the line or punctuation at the end, but query the author if it does not follow an established pattern.
- Within text, quoted poems follow the printed poem's capitalization and punctuation; lines are separated by a slash closed up on both sides.

Juvenile publications

- Read the manuscript for grammar and details.
- Check all facts.
- Query the author if a word choice seems inappropriate.
- Check quotations for accuracy if requested.

Reprints

- Correct errors in spelling and consistency, but do not touch anything done consistently, even if it's wrong.
- Check the status of permissions.

Magazines

- Make the article adhere to house style regarding numbers, the series comma, etc.
- Indicate headings and other elements according to house style.

Newspapers

- Verify the spelling of all terms.
- Put articles into words the reader can grasp quickly.
- Be sensitive to sexism, racism, ageism, libel, and obscenity, and make appropriate changes when needed.

C H A P T E R **12**

Proofreading

If you read an article or a book and find an error, you probably blame the compositor. But you should be blaming the proofreader. The proofreader must read every character in the proof, looking for typographical errors, spelling or punctuation errors, errors of fact, inconsistencies, and other discrepancies. In fiction publishing, the final check for plot sense and consistency is left to the proofreader. In more complex fields of publishing, the proofreader may be expected to check facts, the position of artwork relative to the text, numbering of footnotes, and so forth. Of course, if a proofreader is used for a last-minute check of accuracy, the publisher runs the risk of spending a lot of money for corrections that were not caught earlier.

The average company won't take a chance on an untried copyeditor; thank heaven for proofreading. To get started in copyediting, be prepared to spend several months or even a couple of years as a freelance proofreader. Why is proofreading such a good introduction to copyediting? Think again of the production process. The author writes a manuscript, which the copyeditor marks up in pen or pencil. The compositor sets type from that marked-up manuscript, including the errors made by the copyeditor. The proofreader then reads that newly set type against the marked manuscript. If the compositor didn't understand something the copyeditor marked, the proofreader probably won't either. But the compositor is typing along at dozens of words a minute and doesn't have time to figure out what the copyeditor meant; the proofreader can read each word as slowly as necessary. As I like to say, the proofreader gets to see the results of bad copyediting. In reading proof, not for enjoyment but letter by letter, the proofreader can't help but notice all the little problems and inconsistencies that the copyeditor, by getting involved in the whole project, overlooked.

Here's an example of a copyediting problem that the proofreader can learn from. Years ago I was the production editor on a statistics manuscript with at least 25 pieces of art per chapter. The author had typed the manuscript with art references in place, like this:

```
This is the way the manuscript looked with the art refer-

ences in place.
```

Figure 9.3

```
But unfortunately she did not paragraph the succeeding

material, so when the compositor removed the art reference,

the type looked like this:
```

That is not paragraph style. The copyeditor should have marked each sentence following an art reference either to run in (if it continued the thought of a paragraph) or to begin a new paragraph—that is, to indent on a new line (if it began a new thought).

Many copyeditors lead charmed lives. They work on a manuscript and then go away. Maybe they get a call again from the same company they worked for, maybe not. Whichever happens, they often don't know how that company felt about their work. If I use you to copyedit and then don't call you again, maybe it's because I went out of business. Maybe it's because I won't have another project for you until next year. If that's the case, am I likely to remember what I didn't like about your work? The problem is that a copyeditor rarely gets to see the results of poor copyediting. Even if I had told the statistics copyeditor to mark for new paragraphs or for run-in text following an art reference, he may not have been able to visualize why his way was wrong. But the proofreader does and—I hope—learns from the copyeditor's mistakes.

Don't look down your nose at the prospect of proofreading. It makes an excellent introduction to copyediting.

MARKING CORRECTIONS IN PROOF

On the inside front cover are all the copyediting and proofreading symbols. Those symbols used only in proofreading are indicated by an open circle; they're the ones that have to do with things that can go wrong at the compositor: wrong font (incorrect typeface or size), broken type, incorrect alignment, crooked type, unequal spacing, an inverted letter (almost impossible to do nowadays; in the old Linotype machines, sometimes the letter dropped into its chamber upside down).

Proofreading involves making two marks for every correction (plus a third signal, to be discussed later): one in text and one in the margin. (Recall that the compositor is looking at the margin to see which lines require resetting; the mark within the line indicates where the correction goes.) Use a slash to separate each correction in the line. If the same correction occurs twice in a row, with no other correction in between, write the correction and follow it by two slashes (that's instead of writing the correction twice). If the correction appears more than two times in sequence, then write the correction, follow it with a slash, and then add (circled) "3x," "4x," or however many times it occurs.

Figure 12.1 shows a marked-up sample galley. Not all the possible symbols appear in this sample, but you can see the others on the inside front cover.

In marking corrections, do not rewrite the word, phrase, or sentence in addition to calling it out with symbols. Occasionally, however, a single word will require several changes, and in that case it will be neater to simply rewrite the word properly.

Keep marks as simple and clear as possible, and do not mark twice for one correction. For example, if you delete a word, do not mark to close up the space left by the deletion; close up only within a word. The compositor will know that you don't want space left where the word was! Similarly, to change one character to another, don't use both a delete sign (to get rid of one character) and a caret (to insert a new one); instead use the mark ⟨ , which means "delete and insert." You learned about this symbol in Chapter 2, and you can see the symbol in action in Figure 12.1.

Any time you use a term consisting of letters (instead of a symbol) that you do not want set, circle it. Some examples in Figure 12.1 are *tr, sp,* and *lc.* Also circle any explanatory notes to the compositor; for example, in chemical materials you may want to identify a horizontal bar as a bond, and whenever you want a slash to appear, you'll probably write "set" next to it. Those identifications should appear in a circle.

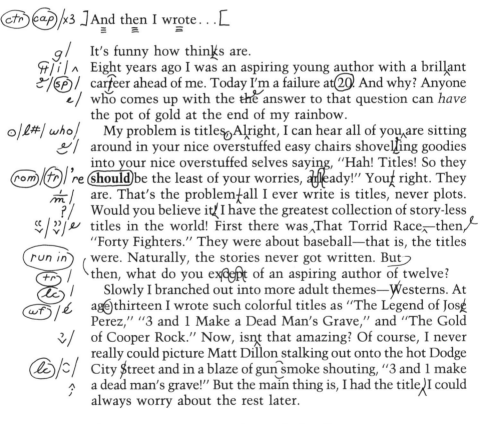

Figure 12.1. A portion of a marked galley.

THE PROOFREADER'S RESPONSIBILITIES

Most people agree that the proofreader is expected to do at least the following tasks:

- Catch typographical errors.
- Query inconsistencies.
- Correct errors.
- Check numerical sequences and alphabetical order.
- Check all formats.
- Check end-of-line syllabication.
- Indicate to whom charges should accrue.

Let's look at each of these areas now.

Typographical Errors

Proofreading is a lot tougher than it sounds. Basically, the trick is to "photograph" in your mind a small section (say, a few words) of the manuscript, then compare it with the same words on the proof. What makes the task harder than it should be is that the manuscript is typed (or tearsheet) and the proof is typeset. That means that the characters you're reading are not the same shape in both places. If they were, you could superimpose the mental picture you've taken of the manuscript onto proof and compare them for rough edges; instead you have to translate each character as it comes up.

Always remember that you're reading proof against manuscript, not manuscript against proof; it really doesn't matter whether the manuscript is correct—only that the proof is. If the manuscript reads "the idae is to," it's fine (better, in fact) if the proof correctly shows "the idea is to." (On the other hand, it is never the compositor's responsibility to correct errors, only to set what appears in manuscript. Many compositors do, of course, fix the obvious typo.)

When you proofread, hold the proof in front of you, with your pencil ready. Hold the manuscript off to one side (which side will depend on what's comfortable to you). Look first at the manuscript, registering a small amount of copy in your mind. With the picture still in your mind, look at the proof in front of you (keep your pencil on the proof to hold your place) and "spit out" each character of the picture in your mind in sequence. Are the characters on the proof the same and in the same order? If they are, return to the manuscript for another batch of characters.

Be sure to sound out, whether silently or aloud, what you are seeing on proof. Let's say you've taken a mental picture of the phrase "a psychological advantage." As you compare that with what you see in proof, you should be grouping syllables or other letter combinations small enough to deal with at a time; after all, it doesn't matter what the manuscript had (you know what it's supposed to say even if it contains typos), but the proof must be perfect. Therefore, you should be looking for the following letter groups: a psy-cho-logi-cal. Notice how none of the groups is more than four characters. Except in rare instances, four is about all you'll be able to manage. Notice also that the groups are roughly the same as syllables. There's a reason for that: Reading in syllables allows you to watch for odd or symmetric letter groups. Do you remember back in Chapter 2 my example of the letter combination *identy*? At the time I pointed out that you need to be careful when you insert the missing letters. That's because one of the missing letters is a *t*, but there's already a *t* there; thus, there's symmetry around the other missing letter, the *i*. Certain letter combinations are simply harder to work with than others. Here's another example: *sociology*. Now that may not seem so bad, but think about the characteristics of that word. First, there's symmetry around the *l*. Second, the *o* and the *c* are similarly shaped. Finally, the very narrow *i* is surrounded by a bunch of fat characters and may get lost. Still not convinced, huh? You think you can proofread that word as a whole word? What about now?

SOCIOLOGY

Now you really have to look for that *i*, don't you? In fact, reading something in all capital letters is harder than reading upper- and lowercase. Whether it's in Avant Garde, as this one is, or normal reading type, the only correct way to read *sociology* is to read so-ci-ol-o-gy. Yep, that's right—by syllables. Why do you have to read every single syllable when you got by on *psychological* with combining logi-? Because of symmetry. There's nothing in *logi* to confuse you into thinking you've already accounted for that *i*.

Sounds hard, right? Don't worry; you do get used to it. But you're right, it is hard. And it gets harder when you read words you're not familiar with. I work in foreign language publishing, and most of our freelancers are native English speakers; they don't notice typos in French the same way they do in English. All the more reason to read by the syllable. Fortunately, the foreign languages we deal with have very easy rules for syllabication: A syllable ends with a vowel. (Yes, that is an oversimplification, but it's pretty close.) So our proofreaders can read *j'ai é-tu-dié la le-çon* as easily as others read psy-cho-logi-cal. But what about people who read calculus? Anything written in symbols (including languages in other alphabets) involves that picture-taking method I mentioned earlier, but instead of comparing it syllable by syllable, you need to compare the shapes of the manuscript and the proof. Someone I worked with years ago on engineering magazines said that she read along normally until she came to a formula, then "pronounced" the formula in her head as "bpdiuft," (that may not have been her exact pronunciation). In other words, when she said "bpdiuft," she was registering the formula in her brain just long enough to compare it with what she saw on proof. If necessary, she'd go back and take another picture. In fact, that's what I do too. True, calculus formulas are technically English. I can read "summation-b-over-c-space-italic-f-paren-italic-x-paren-space-italic-dx," but I can also just take a picture of what all that looks like and see if that's what the compositor set. But don't try this at home until you get good at it. If you proofread math, start slowly, maybe by photographing the numerator and denominator separately or by reading up to the first space.

Inconsistencies

If you're lucky, you'll be given the copyeditor's style sheet. Read it over carefully before you begin. No, you won't remember everything that's on it, but you may remember while you're proofreading that something you've just come across *is* on that style sheet, and you can check it out. At the very least, commit to memory the styles for numbers, abbreviations, and the like, and refer to the style sheet for bibliographic styles as you proofread those entries.

How do you find inconsistencies? Well, that's part of what proofreading is all about. Keep reminding yourself that you're not reading for pleasure. Watch for the same kinds of things you learned to watch for in the early chapters of this book. Was *decision-making* hyphenated on galley 3, and now on galley 17 it's two words? Did one galley say *World War I* and another say *Second World War*? It's your job to watch for such inconsistencies. What happens if you find an inconsistency and nothing appears on the style sheet? First be sure you're correct. Could there be a reason for the two styles? Perhaps the war references appeared in direct quotations. Maybe one *decision-making* was a preceding adjective and the other a predicate adjective or a noun. If you can't make a case for having similar terms treated two (or more!) different ways, then one is wrong. Sometimes, however, you'll need to check with the publisher before making global changes. Remember in the example in Chapter 3 how you saw Dory and Dorie? Neither is wrong, but they can't both be there. Which is it? Ask. Until you get a ruling, you can put a light checkmark in the margin of the proof each time the word appears.

Errors

If you find an out-and-out error, of course—something that was incorrect in manuscript too—change it. Among the most obvious errors you will encounter are punctuation errors (a comma preceding an open paren, for example), spelling errors, and incorrect capitalization. With the use of this book and others in the bibliography, you'll be well armed to make corrections that will enhance the value of the material you're reading. But you must always be sure that you're changing a real error, not merely a preference. Remember that I said that the first choice in *Webster's* is the preferred spelling? Well, that means that the second choice isn't wrong! Some companies, of course, have preferred house styles, and in such cases you should freely mark to adhere to house style. But even that won't always work; trade publishers, for example, almost always follow the author's preference (but if the author doesn't seem to be following a preference, go to it!). One of my staff production editors had an author who wanted to spell *earth* with a capital *E*. The editor prepared a style sheet showing the word with a lowercase letter. The author, in approving the style sheet, indicated that she wanted the capital letter. Now, our house style, as well as the style of most style guides, was to use a lowercase letter, and the editor so informed the author. He got a reply that she wanted *Earth*, and by golly, that's what she got. She obviously had given the issue a good deal of thought, and she felt more strongly about it than he did.

Proofreaders, whether they read expensive proof or easy-to-correct printout, must be sensitive to the author's style. They cannot be minicopyeditors, making changes *they* think improve the material. Their job is to correct proof where it differs from manuscript and to make minor changes that the copyeditor and author have overlooked. Their suggestions are often welcome, but no production editor wants to have to pore over the proof trying to separate the actual corrections from the grandiose ideas and mounds of queries.

Numerical and Alphabetical Order

If you read textbooks or tests, you'll need to check the numerical order of questions. Watch the subentries too (a, b, etc.). Yes, I know that's the copyeditor's job, but who's to say that the copyeditor did it? Besides, the compositor could have left out an entire question. You may think that can't happen very often, but it does, especially when the questions in one exercise are similar to those in another; just as you lose your place sometimes when reading, so does the person sitting at the computer typing question after question that looks pretty much the same as the previous one.

Numbers also occur in lists and, heaven help us, in bibliographies. Do you remember in Chapter 8, when you were wearing your copyeditor hat, that I said to turn a numerical referencing system into a name-date system if possible? Now that you're proofreading you know why! Yes, a proofreader should check that all bracketed numbers—references to an end-of-chapter or end-of-book reference list—are correct and sequential.

Sometimes you'll get page proof to read—galleys made up into pages just like the ones in the printed piece, with artwork and tables and footnotes in place. In such a case you'll need to check the following numerical sequences:

- *Folios (page numbers).* On facing pages the left page will always have an even number.
- *Footnotes.* If a numbering system has been used, each chapter should begin again with 1. If symbols appear instead of numbers, the first footnote on each page begins with an asterisk, the next with a dagger, and the third with a double dagger (see Chapter 8). If, however, some other system occurs, do not change the system just to agree with my book (and everyone else's)! Call the publisher immediately for a ruling. Chances are you'll be told to leave the notes alone as long as they are consistent with each other. (For example, if in Chapter 2 the footnotes don't begin with an asterisk on each page but rather run through the whole chapter, you'll be asked to be sure that other chapters follow the same pattern.) Why not change the whole system of notes? Well, it's not really wrong, just poor style, and it's very expensive to correct all those characters (both in the footnotes and in the in-text references).
- *Captions and references to figures and tables.* In some material the art will be numbered consecutively throughout. In most textbooks, a double-numbering system is used (or even a triple one): Figure 3.7 is the seventh figure in Chapter 3; Figure 4.2.1 is the first figure in Section 4.2 (which is the second section in Chapter 4). Above all, of course, be sure that the caption and in-text reference carry the same number!

You may have to check alphabetical order. In my current position, I often try out new proofreaders on our most unglamorous job: reading end-of-book vocabularies in a foreign language. Before you tackle an index, glossary, vocabulary, or other alphabetized list, reread Chapter 3's section on alphabetizing. If you do work with foreign languages, be sure you know its special rules (such as that in Spanish, *ch* comes between *c* and *d*). When reading anything with subentries, remember to alphabetize them too. Usually articles and conjunctions are ignored in the alphabetizing process, but if that hasn't been done by your copyeditor (or if it's been done inconsistently), check the magnitude of the problem before suggesting one method over the other; most publishers will choose the cheaper solution.

Format

Regardless of what material you are proofreading—a book, an article, a report, or something else—some plan was made for the appearance of the material. As you learned in Chapter 9, every element has design specifications, or specs, associated with it. Depending on the material you are proofreading, you may be given sample pages or specs showing what the final page is supposed to look like. Even if you have no such cheat-sheet, you can determine at least whether the material looks reasonably well ordered. Is there no clear relationship between head levels? If not, maybe the compositor did not use the proper point size for one. Do the heads clash with the body of the material? If so, maybe the wrong font has been used for one or the other. Do similar items have the same indent? When heads or captions or footnotes or other items turn over to a second or third line, do the turnovers position the same way in all cases? Is there the same amount of space above and below the same element each time it occurs? You can answer all these questions, and many similar ones, without knowing anything about the specs. My proofreading test has specs to check, and sometimes people tell me they can't read them. That's fine, because I can teach them to do that. But do they notice when things *appear* different every time they come up?

Syllabication

When you come to a hyphenated word at the end of the line, don't just assume that the compositor's modern technological equipment has inserted the hyphen correctly. Yes, the compositor's proofreader is checking too, but you must sound out every word yourself and check the ones you're not sure of.

Rules for syllabication in English are quite complicated; you may remember that from third grade. You may even remember some of the rules. But don't trust your memory. For one thing, times—and hyphenations—change; for another, the third grade is too long ago to swear you're right. I'm not suggesting that you look up every single end-of-line hyphen, but you must look up at least the ones that don't end in vowels or between two consonants (those are the simplest rules we have in English). Don't be ashamed when you have to look up the same word several times in an article or book; it happens to me all the time. (It's just like spelling; look up every word you can't swear to.)

It's fine to check syllabication as you proofread, but it's good to make a separate pass after you're finished as well. Bear in mind that you're doing a lot while you're reading, not the least of which is reading both manuscript and proof at the same time. Taking a few extra minutes at the end of a chapter or article just to check the hyphens will produce the best results.

Identifying Changes

A few pages back, I referred to a third mark for each change. If the publisher asks you to (many will not), you should identify each change as either PE (printer's error) or EA (editorial alteration). (No, a typo is not really a printer's error, but the term has remained from the days when printers typeset the material, then hand-printed it.) PE's include typos of all sorts (provided the manuscript was legible) and errors in format. (If you don't have specs to check, you won't know which format inconsistencies are PE's and which aren't. Just alert the publisher to the problem.)

Anything that the copyeditor could reasonably have been expected to catch but didn't is an EA. All inconsistencies, spelling and hyphenation errors, punctuation problems, and the like, are the copyeditor's responsibility; when they are wrong, they are EA's. Also considered EA's are typos made because of bad handwriting or other unclear manuscript.

Above each change you mark in the margin, write EA or PE and circle it. These marks can be very light; they're not for posterity but rather for billing information only. (Of course, if several changes in a row are EA, it's neater just to write EA once. Each time an error accrues to a new source, write the EA or PE, but then not again until it changes.)

COMPUTER SPELL-CHECK PROGRAMS

If you're proofreading your own computer-generated work, watch for computer errors. Spelling programs tell you only whether such a word exists, not whether it's correct in the context. And it says nothing about missing words. Missing verbs are easily spotted, but what about "do" versus "do not"?

The hardest errors to catch are missing words, words that transfer or change a letter but still make a real word (*calvary, cavalry; of, if; abode, adobe*), words that mean different things according to how they're spelled (*discrete, discreet*), words with repeating letter combinations (*milliliter*), and numbers. The easiest errors to catch are garbage in the middle of a word—but if they're so easy, the compositor's proofreader has probably already caught them. Recall from Chapter 1 that the compositor outputs type, which is then read by the compositor's own proofreader; then the errors are fixed and new type is output. That's what you see. I frequently tell people who write to me asking for advice on getting a job to try to get a job proofreading for a compositor. Such people learn to spot minute problems, such as hyphens for en dashes and 9-point type when 10 was requested.

PROOFREADING IN PAIRS

My very first job interview after college was for a proofreading job at a law firm. There, two people read all materials aloud to each other. I've done the same even in nonlegal situations. Proofreading pairs develop their own signals, such as reading boldface in a deep voice and italic in a high voice. They also use abbreviations, such as "point" for a period, "hy" for a hyphen, and "com" for a comma.

Here's a passage that appears in print.

> A **proofreader,** unlike a **copyeditor,** makes all marks in the margin. He (she, often!) watches for errors in fact, grammar and punctuation errors, and—*especially*—typos. Proofreading is not a high-paying job, but there's a lot of work available.

Now here's how that passage might be read out loud.

> A proofreader com [last two words in deep voice] unlike a copyeditor com [last two words in deep voice] makes all marks in the margin point. He paren she com often slam close paren watches for errors in fact com grammar and punctuation errors com and em especially [last word in high voice] em typos point. Proofreading is not a high hy paying job com but there poz ess a lot of work available point.

Some proofreading pairs indicate ends of sentences in ways other than by saying "point," and some use other terms, such as "bar" instead of "em." Here are some popular proofreading expressions. They're not the only ones proofreaders use, and you may even develop your own.

Abbreviated Term	*What It Stands For*
point	period
com	comma
colon	colon
sem	semicolon
query	question mark
slam	exclamation point
hy	hyphen
poz	apostrophe
em	em dash

en	en dash
paren	opening paren
close paren	closing paren
quote	opening quotation mark
close quote	closing quotation mark
three up	each of the next three words begins with a capital

Don't feel you have to read in pairs to do a good job; it's not that much easier than reading alone. In fact, it requires additional skills that we haven't discussed; for example, the partner holding the proof has to be trained in listening. And you won't get paid more by reading with a partner, nor does the task go more quickly. Paired reading is normally something that occurs in-house, not freelance, especially on statistical or legal data, when a mistake is costly indeed.

That's proofreading in a nutshell. What follows is a list of rules to keep in mind while proofreading. Not all of these points were discussed in the chapter, but they are your responsibility as a proofreader, and together they make up a checklist of things to watch for.

► RULES FOR PROOFREADING

- Use acceptable proofreading symbols.
- Do not rewrite the word, phrase, or sentence in addition to calling it out with symbols; do, however, write out any words that would be too complicated to correct with symbols.
- Every change except broken type needs three marks; a caret in text, an explanatory symbol in the margin, and an indication of PE or EA. (You can combine corrections with just a single EA or PE indication where appropriate.)
- Mark as PE's errors already noted on proof by the compositor, but do not mark as PE's questions the compositor has merely raised. Do not mark broken type as a PE. (Don't mark broken type at all until pages.)
- Marks for PE and EA should be small and circled. Keep them out of the line of actual corrections. A single designation can cover several corrections.
- Keep marks minimal and clear, and do not mark twice for one correction. If you delete a word, do not mark to close up the space left by the deletion. Close up only within a word (wheel-chair → wheelchair). Similarly, to change one character to another, just use the mark ⋏ ("delete and insert"): sy⋏bol.   *m/*
- Mark corrections in order, from left to right, regardless of which margin you use.

- Follow each correction symbol with a slash. If the *exact same* correction appears twice in a row, with no other corrections in between, write the correction and follow it by two slashes (i.e., do not write the correction twice). If the correction appears more than two times in sequence, indicate 3x, 4x, or whatever, after the correction and slash.
- Write corrections firmly in lead pencil only.
- If you wish to raise a question, use a Post-It with a faint arrow to the word being queried. Never write a caret in place, because the compositor often assumes that a comma is wanted.
- Mark corrections for boldface or italic, as appropriate. That is, if the word or letter being replaced is italic, mark the new word or letter for italic as well.
- Watch for missing and incorrect punctuation at the end of a sentence. A statement must end with a period, a question with a question mark. The font of punctuation should usually be the same as the font of the character immediately preceding it.
- Be sure that the paren adequately clears italic words within parentheses, especially where ascenders are involved.
- Watch that *en* dashes are used to indicate ranges (page numbers, years, etc.) and that *em* dashes are used to indicate parenthetical material.
- A footnote reference or symbol should normally follow any mark of punctuation except a dash or a parenthesis.
- Watch that boldface, italic, and roman are used consistently.
- Watch for correctness of paragraph indents and indents on heads and lists; consistency of capitalization in heads; presence or absence of punctuation after table titles; and so forth. Check all elements against specs if requested.
- Check that periods align in numbered lists; lettered lists normally align on the left.
- Check numerical and alphabetical sequences of all kinds.
- Indicate missing boxes, rules, art, braces, and so on, to be done in page makeup.
- Key art by transferring coded numbers from the manuscript to galleys.
- Correct accented letters by replacing the entire letter with the correct one: $\acute{e} \rightarrow é$; $\acute{a} \rightarrow$ a. Do not correct the accent alone.
- Question terms that can be spelled (or accented) in more than one way (*septiembre, setiembre; oir, oir*) unless there is clearly a preference in manuscript (in which case the aberrations are EA's).
- Verify end-of-line hyphenation.

Additional Things to Check in Pages

- Check that running heads, folios, and drop folios are consistent; read running head copy.
- Check the sequence of folios.
- Check placement of art and tables relative to text mention or logical position.
- Mark broken letters. Should they occur frequently, do not mark every time, but alert the publisher in a covering note. Do not mark poor inking.
- Read captions carefully. Be sure that the text discussion of the figure agrees with the caption, and that both agree with the art.
- Flag missing cross-references that you cannot fill in.
- Be sure that there are at least two lines of text below a head at the bottom of a page.
- Mark widows (less than three-quarters of a line before a new paragraph at the top of a page) and orphans (three or fewer characters on the last line of a page).
- Check that footnotes are positioned at the foot of the page on which their text reference appears.

Getting Work

If you can copyedit, you can earn a decent living your whole life. Even after you retire from a full-time staff job, publishers will still hire you to work freelance. And if you want to make some extra money while you work at another job, freelance copyediting is a good way to do it. Most of this chapter refers to freelance copyediting, either full-time or part-time, although wherever appropriate I've included information about entry-level staff positions.

You probably won't be able to start your publishing career as a full-time freelancer. You have to get some staff experience under your belt. Admit that you may need to begin as an editorial assistant, something of a glorified secretary. But many publishers, especially book publishers, let the editorial assistant, or EA, write her or his own job description up to a point. Yes, there'll be typing and filing, but you'll also be learning the terms and making the contacts that you'll need throughout your career. Maybe you'd prefer to work for a magazine, doing proofreading or fact checking, or for a newspaper, as a copy-person. But do get that experience.

Many copyeditors join professional organizations, such as Editorial Freelancers Association in New York or editcetera in the San

Francisco Bay Area. Many of these groups test you; they have stringent requirements, and belonging to that group is an honor and is well respected by potential employers. Even if you don't join the organization, take advantage of its courses or other resources.

YOUR RÉSUMÉ

To get your name into a publisher's file, you must start with a good résumé. Don't try to get by with the same one you used for your last teaching job. Publishers want to believe that you have the experience they're looking for, so you have to adjust your résumé to reflect that experience.

Your having worked on a college yearbook will mean very little to publishers; *everybody* did that. And have you looked at that yearbook recently? It's probably filled with copyediting errors you wouldn't want anyone to notice and that *you* never noticed until you read this book! The best related experience, if you haven't actually done any copyediting, is proofreading. A good proofreader has the qualities publishers want to find in copyeditors: an eye for consistency and detail, great care, adherence to schedules. In fact, if you can't find work as a copyeditor, try to get work proofreading, which publishers often give out more readily. Then you can use that experience to get copyediting assignments.

Lots of places need proofreaders; use your imagination, and don't be afraid to ask. Try your local newspaper (particularly the kind that is given away because neighborhood merchants support it with their advertising), or offer to proofread the Christmas catalog for the department store in town. And do a thorough and careful job! Even if you lose money on your first couple of jobs, you'll get a good reputation, and that's priceless.

Even when you start to look for copyediting jobs, play up on your résumé any proofreading experience you've had. Don't overstate writing and research. Remember, writing is not copyediting, and frequently publishers have had trouble with writers who annoy authors, miss deadlines, or overcharge, so they couldn't be less impressed with a writing background. You need to show practical experience in the areas publishers *want*.

A good résumé for a copyeditor is divided into four parts. At the top of the page give your name, address, phone number (be sure to include area code), and business address and phone number. If you're interested in freelance work and don't want your employer to know it, include a note on the résumé that all phone calls made to your business should be treated as personal calls and that all mail should be marked "personal."

It is illegal to discriminate against an employee because of age, sex, or marital status. Therefore you needn't include your birthdate and family situation; some people do, merely because the information is interesting.

On the second part of the résumé include your employment history, beginning with the most recent job. Give the name of the company, approximate dates of employment, your title, and your job responsibilities. You don't have to supply addresses or supervisors' names, but be prepared to provide them if asked. Be careful that all years are covered; if you combed beaches in Hawaii for a year, say so; don't make the person reading your résumé wonder where you were—and suspect the worst. Leave out the short, less relevant jobs; it's better to appear that you spent the time hunting for the right job than to appear willing to take anything at all.

After employment history goes educational history. Give the names of any colleges you attended, even if you don't have a degree. Don't include high schools unless they were specialized and pertinent (such as Brooklyn Technical High School or High School for the Performing Arts). If you did well in college, give a grade point average. State not only your major and minor but also other subjects you think would interest a potential employer. Remember: You are trying to show how well rounded you are. If you have taken appropriate continuing education courses or studied at a publishing institute, be sure to include those items. Include any foreign study and knowledge of foreign languages as well.

At the end of the résumé list your special accomplishments and interests. If you have received any professional honors or are a member of a special organization, say so. Can you type 80 words a minute? Do you belong to MENSA? Are you listed in *Who's Who*? Are you a semiprofessional or even a professional musician? Don't hide it! Make a particular point of any skills you think the employer can use. Play up your organizational skills, your varied interests. If you've edited anything before, by all means include a list. You can even put down things you've written (after all, they *are* special accomplishments); just don't overemphasize your writing experience in the main part of the résumé. Feel free to include photocopies of letters from satisfied authors or pages from published works where your name is mentioned.

A few words about minorities: If you are a minority member, yes, some companies will hire you on that fact alone; employers are very sensitive to the Equal Employment Opportunity Commission (EEOC). However, do not point directly to your minority status; hide the information under background or special interests, for instance by saying, "Member, black caucus. . ." or "Studied Hispanic literature and culture at. . ."' I once received a résumé from a man who pointed out that his objective was to eliminate discrimination against a particular religion and that he was somehow planning to use my company (I don't remember how!) as a forum for that goal. Needless to say, that résumé went into the wastebasket without further thought.

Keep the résumé to one or two pages. It should look attractive, but you needn't have it designed and printed professionally. Employers are not the slightest bit impressed with fancy résumés; you're not looking for a design job, after all. If you do have your résumé printed, keep it simple. Don't go in for fancy-colored paper; white, cream, tan, and gray are the best colors. If you type it yourself, be sure to use a clean ribbon that makes a sharp impression; a carbon ribbon is ideal. If you can produce your résumé on a computer, so much the better; then you can tailor it to the particular job you're seeking at any time. Furthermore, you can easily correct those typos that invariably sneak in. Laser printing gives your résumé a professional look at a reasonable price. Your town probably has a copy center that provides laser printing services, or maybe your friend works in an office that has a laser printer. Whether your résumé has been designed professionally or simply typed, you can take it to a duplicating house—you don't need a real printer—and get the job done for about 10 cents a page. If the résumé is two pages, staple it in the upper left; it may look terrible, but why run the risk of a paper clip coming off and page 2 being lost?

No matter how professionally you prepare your résumé, the most important thing you can do is *proofread it carefully* before running it off. If necessary, have someone else check it for you (and perhaps even critique it). Do not allow *any* copyediting or proofreading errors to creep in. When I find a poorly written résumé, I dump it in the wastebasket. Anyone who can't take the time to sell herself or himself properly won't make much of a copyeditor.

Don't worry if your current résumé doesn't fit this pattern; if you're merely looking for entry-level staff work, the résumé is not as important as the personal impression you make. But once you get that experience we've been talking about, redo your résumé to play it up. The stronger your desire for freelance work, the more your résumé should reflect your experience. But avoid listing too many academic qualifications: You may appear unable to do anything but go to school.

One last word about résumés. If you have not attended college and do not have work experience relevant to copyediting, do not prepare a résumé. Instead write (type) a letter explaining your experience, background, and appropriate coursework. Your wording is particularly important. Stress your organizational skills, how fast you can work (and how well you meet deadlines), your neatness—anything you can think of that transfers well to copyediting. It may not work, but it's better than putting down on a résumé your lack of educational experience.

THE COVERING LETTER

A good covering letter can mean the difference between whether you get work or not. Sound hard to believe? Well, it's true. I can think of a few letters I've received that have made me want to go out and *find* work for the writer!

Maybe I'm getting ahead of myself. The first thing to keep in mind is never—I say it again—never go into a publishing company unannounced and ask to see the managing editor. If you're in the neighborhood and want to drop off a résumé, fine, but always include a handwritten note to that effect: "I was in the neighborhood and didn't want to disturb you, so I'm leaving my résumé with you. I'll call you in a few days and ask for an appointment." Here is the simple truth of the matter: Even if the managing editor is not busy and *could* see you, she or he will never want to admit that. Let's face it: Everyone wants to feel important, and if you come in unannounced and assume that someone can see you, you're assuming that that person isn't important enough to have other plans. Not an auspicious beginning. I *never* see people unannounced, even if I'm sitting there twiddling my thumbs in boredom, and I never give them work when they try again. Just a matter of principle. And don't call regarding openings either. With the proper letter, the company may want to create an opening for you where one does not now exist.

If you don't know to whom to write, call the company and ask the switchboard operator; be sure to get the spelling of the person's name right. Avoid writing the personnel department, and never address your letter to "Editor." At least look as if you're truly interested in the job!

Now, back to the letter. Your letter shows that you have respect for the managing editor (or whomever it's addressed to), and that's what you want to show. If appropriate, make some personal mention of the editor: "I heard you speak at the Book Show last month and I was so impressed that I . . ." Whenever you can, refer to the kind of books the company publishes: "Even as a child I remember reading your 'We Can Play' books, and now . . ." Give a brief summary of your experience and qualifications in the letter: "Although I have not copyedited since college, I have done some proofreading (see my résumé) and consider myself extremely conscientious and observant." At the end of the letter, mention that you will be calling in a few days to request an appointment. An appointment is usually not required for freelance copyediting; I have never met at least half of the people whose names are in my file. But it never hurts to make yourself known; managing editors take kindly to people they've met. And more than anything, what you're doing by asking to set up an appointment is showing how important you assume the managing editor is! Yes, it may seem frivolous, but you have to play the game. If you have a copy of a test you've taken elsewhere, by all means include it. Samples of your work may help too.

I've received excellent letters informing me that I'd be getting a phone call in a week—and it doesn't happen. When you say you'll call Tuesday, call Tuesday. Otherwise your letter (which is sitting in the managing editor's Hold box) will go unceremoniously into the trash. Even if you have a job offer in the meantime, follow up and explain your new situation. Who knows? Maybe your impressive letter can land you an even better job if you make that Tuesday phone call. Be sure you know the phone number. Some companies may have moved since the time you wrote to them; my own company had an unlisted number (it's a long story). When you say you're going to call, you'll want to be sure it's possible.

If you're looking for a staff job, it's not usually a good idea to say so in your letter! Chances are, the managing editor has no openings right now and won't hesitate to tell you so when you call. The real trick is to get a foot in the door; say instead that you're interested in hearing about the company or about publishing opportunities in the area. The managing editor will be flattered that you came to him or her! Then during your interview you have the opportunity to make such a good impression that the managing editor will think of you as soon as an opening does occur.

TAKING A TEST

People with a lot of copyediting experience come to publishers by word-of-mouth recommendation or on the basis of their reputation. In my file, I have many names of people whom I've never tested; I hear they're good, and that's enough for me. Many publishers who responded to my questionnaire said the same thing: They go by reputation, not a test. If you're experienced and want to work for a particular publisher, a letter and résumé listing other publishers as references are often enough.

If you don't have any copyediting experience, however, you will almost certainly be asked to take a test. Do not feel insulted; how else is the publisher supposed to know what you can do? Copyediting tests are not usually like tests you took in school. For copyediting tests, cheating is required! You're sent five or six manuscript pages, and you have at least a couple of weeks to copyedit them. Use all the reference books you can find. Just don't ask a friend to do the test for you. That may work once, but you'll never get away with it in the long run. Some companies probably still use on-the-spot tests, where you're given only a dictionary and 2 hours. In that case read the test through once to see the magnitude of the problem. Then begin work, never spending too much time on any one point. Use the dictionary for all questions of spelling (and sometimes even of style), and try to remember the points in this book!

Never miss a deadline for a copyediting test. After all, if you can't do six pages in 2 weeks, how reliable will you be on a real manuscript? If you're in the process of moving or studying for the Bar, for heaven's sake don't ask to take a test! Wait until you can spend the time, then request one. The sooner you send it in, the better; you don't *really* need 2 weeks, do you? And the publisher will believe you have a real interest in the company, a real commitment to a career in publishing.

If something comes up that makes you miss a deadline, drop a note explaining the delay. *Do not call.* A large department may get five letters a day and have ten or fifteen tests outstanding at one time. Your name by itself means nothing. But a little note can be attached to your original letter and résumé so that when you do return the test, the connection can be made.

Be extremely conscientious on the test, more so even than on the manuscripts you get as a result of your successful test. Like your résumé, your test must sell your abilities. Plan to average nearly an hour per page overall. Reread your work at least four times, going over every mark to be sure it's in the right place. The test I took for one staff job took me 5 hours for six pages. It's the same test I gave out for the next 12 years, after I became managing editor. But even after seeing hundreds of versions of that test come back and thousands of different ways of changing things in the test, I found only one thing I would do differently now if I were taking that test again myself.

Before you take a copyediting test, read over the key points at the ends of Chapters 2 through 10, and after you've completed the test, double-check that you've done the following:

1. Key all elements (e.g., footnotes) that aren't running text.
2. Check footnotes and bibliographies for consistency.
3. Write queries on flags attached to the manuscript.
4. Do not rewrite, but make those few suggestions for rewriting that will really improve the material.
5. Retype passages only if absolutely necessary. If you must retype, always include the original manuscript as well so that the

publisher can see how you marked the changes.

6. Watch for missing words when you've made changes or insertions. Is everything in the right place?
7. Reread all marks as if you were the compositor. Is everything clear?
8. Write neatly.
9. Follow a style manual.
10. Follow directions.
11. Look it up!
12. Do not call the publisher immediately after you send in a test. The person who corrects the tests may have other things to do and will resent being pestered. You will hear one way or the other once your test has been corrected.

Many people attach a note to their test saying, "I didn't know what style you wanted me to follow, so I used *Chicago Manual*." Although such a disclaimer is not necessary, I don't take off for it either. Bear in mind, we *know* you don't know what style we want you to follow (unless we tell you.) What we want to see is whether you can pick a legitimate style and follow it consistently. If you can, there's a good chance that you'll be able to follow *our* style too.

When you take the test, keep in mind one final rule about tests: They are a brief representation of a real manuscript; do no more and no less than you would on an actual manuscript. Your test is the only example the publisher has of how you will work out; deal with it accordingly.

There are really no right and wrong answers to the copyediting test that follows or to any copyediting test. But there are some elements that can be right or wrong. One applicant's completed test appears after the blank test; check her answers and changes against your own. Can you see why she made those changes? Do you agree with everything she did? Do you have any suggestions for points that she missed?

```
Chapter 1. The Disappearing Daily
```

```
New York Looses a Newspaper
This October's demise of the New York Mirror was perhaps the
climax to the long line of daily papers which met their ends
after the 1920's. With its average daily circulation of
```

851,929(1), the Mirror was the second best selling paper of New York City, being topped only by the Daily News, to whom many of its columns now go.

Some people believe that many of the casualities are appropriate. One of them was the New York Graphic, which specialized in pictures of corpses, call-girls, and blood-ridden accidents. According to Bernard A. Weisberger, ''when the Graphic could not get pictures of what the tabloids called 'slayings', it faked them.''

When you look at the many papers now gone, such as the New York Sun and the Philadelphia Public Ledger and the Boston Transcript you must be wondering, Are newspapers gradually disappearing, or is there an up and down trend? In its Spring, 1962 issue, the Columbia Journalistic Review attempted to answer this question, at least partially in the minds of its readers, by presenting both sides to the argument. Basil L. Walters, head of the Newspaper Research Associates, pointed out that nobody things that automobiles are going out of style merely because some of the models are dying out. He goes on to say that newspapers are alos springing up. Los Angeles for example is served by a locally-printed Wall Street Journal along with the National Obersver and the New York Times western edition.

Along with this theory on newspaper expansion was another article in the Review: ''How Lima Became a Two-newspaper Town.'' When a small city has a monopoly on the news, it often happens that another paper will spring up as competition. Or, when towns are growing, as nearly all towns are, there is a need for a second, third, or maybe

even fourth newspaper to cover all the people. In other
words, newspapers are not dying out everywhere. According
to Walters, ''Newspapers 'ain't' fading. Those which do not
deserve to live will not only fade, they'll die and make way
for brash youngsters with fire and zeal. That's as it should
be if we are to avoid a static society.(2)

Footnotes

(1) As quoted in the 1963 Information Please Almanac.

(2) Weisberger, Bernard A., The American Newspaperman,
University of Chicago Press, 1961, p. 188.

(3) Walters, Basil L., from The Columbia Journalism Review,
Spring 1962, p. 57.

Chapter 1. The Disappearing Daily) — *cN/cT*

(1) New York Losses a Newspaper

This October's demise of the New York Mirror was perhaps ~~the~~ *a*
climax ~~to~~ *in* the long line of daily *news? that* ^papers ~~which~~ met their ends
after the 1920's. With its average daily circulation of
851,929(1), the Mirror was the second best-selling paper ~~of~~ *in*
New York City, ~~being~~ topped only by the *New York* ^Daily News, ~~to whom~~ *(which picked up*
many of its columns ~~now go~~.

To ~~Some~~ people ~~believe that~~ many of the casualties are
~~appropriate~~ *warranted* ~~such victim~~. One ~~of them~~ was the New York Graphic, which
specialized in pictures of corpses, call girls, and blood-
ridden accidents. According to Bernard A. Weisberger, *(au: identify)*
''when the Graphic could not get pictures of what the

tabloids called 'slayings', it faked them.''

When you ~~look at the~~ many papers now gone, such as the New York Sun, and the Philadelphia Public Ledger, and the Boston Transcript, you must be wondering, Are newspapers gradually disappearing, or is there an up=and=down trend? In its spring 1962 issue, the Columbia Journalistic Review attempted to answer this question, at least partially in the minds of its readers, by presenting both sides ~~to~~ the argument. Basil L. Walters, head of the Newspaper Research Associates, pointed out that nobody things that automobiles are going out of style merely because some of the models are dying out. He goes on to say that newspapers are ~~alos~~ springing up. Los Angeles, for example, is served by a locally printed Wall Street Journal along with the National Observer and the New York Times, western edition. of the ~~Along with~~ this theory on newspaper expansion was another article, ~~in the Review~~ ''How Lima Became a Two-newspaper Town.'' When a small city has a monopoly on the news, it often happens that another paper will spring up as competition. Or, when towns are growing, as nearly all towns are, there ~~is~~ a need for a second, third, or ~~maybe~~ even fourth newspaper to cover all the ~~people~~. In other words, newspapers are not dying out everywhere. According to Walters, ''Newspapers 'ain't' fading. Those which do not deserve to live will not only fade, they'll die and make way for brash youngsters with fire and zeal. That's as it should be if we are to avoid a static society.(2)³

(2) ~~Foot~~notes

(1) As quoted in the 1963 Information Please Almanac.

(2) Weisberger, Bernard A., The American Newspaperman, University of Chicago Press, 1961, p. 188.   *chicago?*

(3) Walters, Basil L., *in* ~~from~~ The Columbia Journalism Review, Spring 1962, p. 57.

ABOUT THE MONEY

If you take an entry-level job in a publishing company, you can expect to earn less than $18,000 the first year (and sometimes a *lot* less). But you will probably receive company benefits (a health plan, paid vacation, plenty of holidays, and other things that sometimes make up for low salary). Most of all you'll gain terrific experience. If you ever decide to do full-time freelance work, your first publishing employer may want to help you out with lots of work. At the very least you will have picked up names of other people to contact. And you will have avoided the catch-22—that you need experience before you can get experience.

For some reason I cannot understand, most publishers still pay free-lancers by the hour. Hourly rates vary from $10 to $20. Now before you think about ruling out those $10 publishers, remember that there are all kinds of copyediting. Some is very simple and will take you no time at all; that might be a very fast $10. Others involve rewriting, research, or other tasks that are worth more money. Ask what the job pays, and see if it's worth it to you.

Personally, I prefer a per-page or per-job rate. Paying by the hour penalizes copyeditors who work quickly. If I pay $14 an hour to a copyeditor who handles 7 pages an hour, he or she is getting $2 per page. But the copyeditor who does 10 pages an hour is getting only $1.40 per page. I believe that rates for straight copyediting of college texts should run from $2 to $2.50 per page, for fiction and nonfiction about $1.75, and for el-hi materials perhaps $2. Rewrite, technical, and foreign language copyediting could go to $3 or even higher. On the same per-page rates, the fast copyeditor does extremely well, getting as much as $30 an hour. And of course hourly earnings can go even higher.

OK, those are 1989 figures. How often do rates go up? I believe the publisher should raise the hourly rate by at least 50 cents a year, depending on inflation. You have the right to request more money as you get experience. Believe it or not, publishers frequently let their copyeditors set the pay scale. I could go along for years paying Sue $10 an hour unless she asks for more. Meanwhile, aggressive Sally has been getting $12. Why shouldn't copyediting be like any other job? If your boss says, "I'm getting my money's worth," then he or she is willing to pay for you. But if you think you're worth only $10 an hour, who am I to disagree? Yes, it is true that some publishers simply will not be able to afford you after a certain point—but other publishers will. Find out what the going rate is, and determine how you fit into it. Are you better than those people? If you have reason to believe you are, ask for more money. If the publisher finds out that you really are, you'll be in demand. And don't let publishers take you for granted. If you're working steadily for a publisher who isn't paying well and you have a good reputation, lay down the law: More money or you walk.

I know a copyeditor who had a staff job with a major publisher and now works exclusively for them on a freelance basis. They have a good thing going: I'd pay at least $3 more an hour than they're paying. If I were this copyeditor, I'd say: "Never mind my attachment to the publisher. I have a great reputation—other publishers beg me to work for them but I'm always tied up with someone who's underpaying me." Very little can be more important than having steady work, and if you can work out a relationship with a company that will keep you busy all the time, you may be willing to work for a lower rate. There are extenuating circumstances, of course. Not having to handle art, permissions, messy manuscripts, and the like may be worth more than the extra money to some copyeditors. Each person must decide that issue for himself or herself.

One good way to keep in touch with freelance rates is to join a professional group, such as the two I mentioned earlier. *Literary Market Place* (LMP) lists many editorial groups throughout the country. Some have a small membership fee, for which your name may be added to the list they send to clients, and they often have meetings to discuss health plans and other group benefits. If you don't know where else to begin, check at your local college; most offer journalism courses of some kind, and the department may have received flyers from these freelance organizations. Or contact the major publishing courses—the ones at Denver, Howard, Stanford, or Radcliffe, for example—to see what information they have. If nothing is available in your area, why not start something yourself?

RELATING TO THE PUBLISHER

Staff copyeditors have to handle whatever projects they're assigned (at least until they can claim seniority), but freelancers can't be too fussy or they won't get called often. You may be stuck with a lot of messy, incomplete jobs. If you've had your fill, ask the publisher to give you a break next time. Of course, people who can handle the most complicated, sloppy, boring projects will be in demand for that talent.

Even if you do have to take an occasional job that's missing some art or a bibliography or Chapters 1, 5, and 6, get complete information from the publisher. What is expected of you? Are you supposed to do just the normal number of things, or does the publisher think you're going to be retyping but you don't know it? Get in writing what the publisher wants, even if you work for this publisher frequently. Or even better, *you* tell the publisher what you intend to do on the project.

Also ask the publisher something about the manuscript's background—how did the project come about, what else has the author written, how likely is it that the author will accept your changes? Keep this information in mind with every change you make.

A good relationship with the editor, production editor, or other in-house contact is essential. The production editor will help you get another job from that publisher or will keep you unofficially black-listed from just about every other publisher in the area. Word travels fast in the publishing industry! Even if your work isn't top-notch on a particular project, being on good terms with the production editor may earn you another chance. Keep in contact, but not so often as to be annoying. And do remember that you are performing a service: The publisher is your customer, and the customer is always right.

KEEPING YOUR NAME ON FILE

There are a lot of good freelance copyeditors around, but some get used frequently and others hardly at all. To make sure *you* are in the former group, you have to do something extra. Here are a couple of ideas about what makes a special copyeditor.

1. Provide covering notes for the author, compositor, and editor. The note to the author may have a list of pages on which there were queries—something easy to refer to. For the compositor a list of special symbols or notes on how you've marked something may help. Remember that the editor would have to prepare this note anyway, and if you've saved the editor some work, well, isn't that a good idea? List for the editor pages on which you have editor queries, or things you think a proofreader should watch for.

2. If you were asked to handle permissions or artwork, then do a special job—something that will make the publisher say: "I have another book with similar problems. I think I'll give so-and-so a call again."

3. Don't do just what you're asked to; do a little something extra. Retype the figure captions if they need it; draw up a list of tables if you think it would be helpful, even if the publisher may not

end up using it; provide an extra copy of the style sheet for the proofreader; offer to prepare a list of art callouts for the artist; ask if you should prepare copy for running heads. Always be thinking, How can I make the publisher's job easier so that they'll want to use me again?

4. Prepare a professional-looking bill. No, you don't need a special letterhead, and for heaven's sake don't supply an invoice with a note saying "Net terms: 10 Days." That's not professional—merely threatening. But type your bill neatly and include the date and year, your name, address, and social security number (the publisher may not require it, but why make them come after you if they do?), the author's name and book title (including edition, if any)—and get these right—and the work done. Always tell the number of manuscript pages and anything special you did. And of course give the rate and total. To show that you accept responsibility for your work, *always sign the bill.*

Here's the way your bill may look:

```
                        INVOICE
July 10, 1988


To: Candace Robbins
    Pleasure Press
    P.O. Box 14
    Boulder, CO 80300


From: James R. Franklin
      10 Locust St.
      New York, NY 10000


For copyediting Lorne Smith, MOLECULES AND MICROBES, Second
Edition, and for preparing revised table of contents.


              mspp. 1-171 at $2.25 per page: $384.75
                                   postage:    9.35
                              TOTAL DUE: $394.10
```

James R. Franklin

Check with the publisher about postal and telephone charges; most allow them. (Reimbursable expenses are nontaxable.)

5. Feel free to drop a line to the managing editor every so often to say you're free now and looking for work. Don't call unless you're personal friends or have worked together frequently.

And, of course, never limit yourself to one publisher. A publisher may never be able to use you again, not because you were no good but for any one of a dozen reasons. And if you've cut off everyone else, you may have no one to turn to for work when your old employer can no longer use you. The more publishers—and kinds of publishers—you can work for, the better off you'll be keeping a steady flow of work.

AND A FEW OTHER POINTS

Don't overextend yourself. It's a temptation to accept every job that comes your way, but you'll never be able to do a good job on all of them and keep them all on schedule. Believe me, publishers respect copyeditors who turn down work. They believe that the copyeditor is in demand, and isn't that reassuring? Maybe you can handle two manuscripts at once, but how many more than that can you do? If a publisher calls you when you already have another commitment, ask for complete details: How many manuscript pages, how complicated, what else is needed besides copyediting, what is the schedule? Tell the publisher you'll look at your schedule and call back. Then do so. Review your current workload and determine where a new project could fit in. Are you going away for a week? Do you have evening plans so that you couldn't work then? Call the publisher back within a couple of hours with your decision. Your professionalism will impress them.

Freelancers always complain about how long it takes to get checks. I'm sorry for you, but I think you're foolish if you stop working for certain publishers because of it. Smaller publishers sometimes issue checks in-house and pay within a week; they ruin things for larger publishers, which have to work through their accounting departments. And bureaucracy being what it is, there's often a 6-week lag. My advice is to never expect a check in anything less than 6 weeks, and plan accordingly. If you get it in 3 days, hey, terrific; but be fair and give the accounting department a chance to do its thing. In an emergency ask the editor to put a rush on the check, but use that tactic only when necessary or you'll get a reputation for crying wolf.

Most publishers will accept partial bills if you want to work that way, particularly on a project that takes several weeks. Usually only two billings are reasonable, and once again I caution you not to ask for partial payments every time; it can be a real annoyance to publishers. (And just think how nice it will be to get that one huge check!)

Finally a word about taxes. Do not assume that because you are not on a payroll you are not on the tax rolls. *Report all freelance income.* I advise you to get an accountant at tax time; she or he will tell you how much you can deduct for pencils, phone, bus fare, and all those other expenses you never realized could be taken off your taxes. Save your receipts, and note on each one what it was for. All those tax deduction stories you've heard are true, and now they're working for *you.* I know someone who made over $30,000 one year and paid under $200 in taxes—doing just the kind of work you want to do. May all your deductions be enormous!

▶ KEY POINTS IN THIS CHAPTER

The Résumé

- Downplay writing experience and academic qualifications.
- Don't emphasize minority status with the hope of bullying the managing editor into hiring you because of it, but do not hesitate to include subtle references to it.
- Cover all years, even if you had no relevant work experience during the time; if you worked very briefly at an unrelated job, leave it out. You can explain in person that you were looking for appropriate work during that time.
- Include all relevant courses of study, including continuing education classes.
- If you have special skills, such as reading knowledge of a foreign language or familiarity with computers, mention them.
- List materials you've edited.
- Keep the résumé to two pages, neatly typed (on a computer if possible, and laser printed) and on paper of a neutral color.
- Proofread your résumé carefully.

The Covering Letter

- Do not expect to see the managing editor when you drop off your résumé; instead say that you'll call in a week or two for an appointment, then do so.
- Take the opportunity in your letter to refer to the kind of material the company publishes.
- Do not hesitate to contact managing editors for information only.

Taking a Test

- If you're invited to do a take-home test, use all resources available to you other than having someone take the test for you.

- Never miss the deadline for a test. If you will be unable to meet the deadline, notify the managing editor promptly, by mail.
- Reread your work at least four times, watching especially for missing words, for letters inserted in the wrong place, and for legibility.
- Key all elements.
- Check footnotes and bibliographies for consistency.
- Write queries on flags attached to the manuscript.
- Do not rewrite; suggestions, however, are always welcome.
- If your changes necessitate partial retype, attach the marked pages along with the retyped ones.
- Follow directions.
- Do not call the publisher immediately for the test results.
- Remember that the test is the only evidence the publisher has that you will do acceptable work on an actual manuscript.

Money

- Do not be afraid to ask for a raise from a publisher for whom you have worked steadily for some time.
- Allow 6 weeks for the check to come before you contact the publisher to complain.

Working with the Publisher on an Actual Project

- If you don't get in writing a list of the publisher's expectations, provide your own list of what tasks you will perform.
- Ask about the history of the project, and keep the history in mind as you copyedit.
- Provide covering notes for the author, compositor, and editor.
- Provide extra services where possible.
- Prepare a professional-looking bill.
- Do not call the managing editor to ask for work; drop a line instead, saying that you're free.
- Do not limit yourself to one publisher.
- Don't accept more work than you can handle.

No Copyeditor Should
Be Without...

Copyeditors buy reference books the way some people buy clothes or record albums. Although you needn't rival your local library branch with your collection, certain reference books are absolutely indispensable, and others, according to the kind of copyediting you do, may be desirable or have specific uses. I have listed on the following pages those books that I have found especially useful over the years and in writing this book. After you read my comments about each book, you will be able to decide whether you should add the book to your own collection. Become thoroughly familiar with the contents of the books you choose so that you will be able to turn to the proper book when you need it.

Whenever possible, I copied the bibliographic information off the title page of my own copy of these books. If a newer edition is available, I took the information from the 1987–1988 *Books in Print.*

DICTIONARIES

A good dictionary, it goes without saying, is indispensable to anyone, not just copyeditors. Most publishers have a preference, so before you invest in anything really fancy, check around to see what the publishers in your area are using. A standard desk dictionary is not expensive, so you may want to purchase a couple to cover yourself. The following dictionaries are, for the most part, my own favorites and in any case the ones I've found most popular with publishers and copyeditors alike.

Webster's Third New International Dictionary. Unabridged. Springfield, MA: Merriam, 1981.

No doubt about it: This is the granddaddy of them all. It has its critics, those perfectionists who feel it can't hold a candle to the *Second*, but with the *Second* now considered a collector's item, the *Third* is winner and still champ. As books go, it is one of the best buys on the market, and I highly recommend that you buy it. If you feel you can't afford that expense right now (it's about $75), then buy *Webster's New Collegiate Dictionary*, ninth edition. Almost every U.S. publisher recommends *Webster's*; you really can't go wrong. But beware: Buy only a Merriam-Webster dictionary. Companies sometimes say they publish a Webster dictionary; that's because they're *based* on Noah Webster's work.

The Random House Dictionary of the English Language. Second Edition Unabridged. New York: Random House, 1987.

The second edition of *The Random House Dictionary* has been widely reviewed and almost uniformly praised. A new feature is notes on pronunciation—that is, stories about why something is pronounced the way it is. If you like to read dictionaries, you won't want to be without this one (and it's more attractive than *Webster's*).

The American Heritage Dictionary of the English Language. Boston: Houghton Mifflin, 1981.

This upstart dictionary was first published in 1969 and created an immediate stir. For current American usage it's well worth owning, but few companies ask you to follow it in copyediting.

The Second Barnhart Dictionary of New English. New York: Harper & Row, 1980.

This is one of the finest specialty dictionaries to be published in recent years. To write the book the authors combed the newsweeklies and other current periodicals for coined terms. In the book the editors give the term, part of speech, definition, and at least one example of usage from a newspaper or magazine. Where necessary, the book also provides pronunciation, but many of the listings are simply new usages of familiar words, such as *grab*, as in "How does that grab you?"

Oxford English Dictionary. Compact Edition, 2 vols. New York: Oxford University Press, 1971. Supplement 1987.

Anything this large (it was originally published in thirteen volumes) and known chiefly by its initials, OED, has to be treated with respect. I wonder whether this was a good idea gone bad. I happened to be at the printer when this book was being readied for shipping, and at that time I thought, "How often would I use a dictionary that I needed a magnifying glass to read?" (If you're not familiar with the book, I should explain that it comes in two enormous volumes, and each page is a reduced version of four pages. The two volumes are packed in a slipcase with a drawer containing a powerful magnifying glass.) Personally, as I realized all along, I would rather have the thirteen-volume original set and simply make room on my bookshelves (and in my budget). Because of its incredible unwieldiness, I have used the compact OED only once, to look up "copyediting." It wasn't there. Or if it was, I didn't see it. I found the edition so difficult to read with the magnifying glass that I decided to take my chances without it. The good news is that every once in a while the Book-of-the-Month Club offers the compact OED very inexpensively if you join the club. And if you've ever wanted to know every dirty word in the English language, then the OED is for you. (Of course, the OED is unsurpassed as a source of historical examples.)

STYLE

Style can be almost anything, but I'm using it here to mean choice—choice of capital versus lowercase, hyphen or no, dash or colon. Style can also mean usage, so if your favorite book is missing from this list, look under Usage.

The Chicago Manual of Style. Thirteenth Edition. Chicago: University of Chicago Press, 1982.
> If you can afford only one book besides a dictionary, this is the one to buy. It is the handbook of the book and magazine publishing industry (newspapers, oddly enough, rarely use it). Read it cover to cover and use it often. The best section, and the one most worth committing to memory, is the "Names and Terms" chapter, which tells you (for instance) not to capitalize french fries.

Skillin, Marjorie E., and Robert M. Gay. *Words into Type.* Third Edition. Englewood Cliffs, NJ: Prentice-Hall, 1974.
> Most copyeditors really like this book, although I find it difficult to read; it's too chatty for the kind of book it is. It contains a lot of good information, however, especially the excellent sections on typography and production that every copyeditor should learn well. A new edition is long overdue.

Webster's Standard American Style Manual. Springfield, MA: Merriam, 1985.
> I find this book an excellent combination of *Chicago Manual* and *Words into Type,* and I highly recommend it.

U.S. Government Printing Office Style Manual, 1984. Washington, D.C.: Government Printing Office, 1984.
> This has to be one of the best buys of the century. If your town has a federal center with a bookstore, you'll be able to pick up this book there. If not, write to the USGPO in Washington. The book has the best list of government abbreviations that you'll find anywhere, along with all sorts of information that you can hardly ever find, such as plant and insect names and how to hyphenate Norwegian proper names. I was surprised at how many respondents to my questionnaire recommended this book; I thought I was one of the few people to know about it!

Jordan, Lewis. *The New York Times Manual of Style and Usage.* New York: Times Books, 1976.
> This book, too, got its fair share of recommendations, and, not surprisingly, the *New York Times* thought it stood alone. If you ever wondered why the *Times* calls a convicted male felon "Mr.," this book tells you. Arranged alphabetically by term, much of it is nothing more than the proper spelling of place names or people's names, but it's a useful and interesting guide.

Webb, Robert A., ed. *The Washington Post Deskbook on Style.* New York: McGraw-Hill, 1978.

> This book is a style manual for the newspaper; it covers punctuation, typography, and usage, among other points. It has a chapter on ethics, written by Benjamin Bradlee, setting forth the *Post's* policies. My favorite section is the discussion of sexism, which is placed in a chapter called "Taste and Sensibilities." Nice touch.

French, Christopher W., ed. *Associated Press Stylebook and Libel Manual.* Revised Edition. Reading, MA: Addison-Wesley, 1987.

> This book was among those recommended by the people who responded to my questionnaire. Personally, I'm not very familiar with it. My own favorites are the ones already listed and discussed.

GRAMMAR

There's really only one book here. It's used in almost every college in the country and even in many high schools. Harcourt Brace Jovanovich tells me that it has sold over 10 million copies since first publication, more than any other college textbook.

Hodges, John C., and Mary E. Whitten, with Suzanne S. Webb. *Harbrace College Handbook.* Tenth Edition. San Diego, CA: Harcourt Brace Jovanovich, 1986.

> This book is in its tenth edition, so by now the publisher must be convinced that its format is appropriate, but I never could understand why it breaks everything down into numbers, letters, and symbols (such as "ap" for apostrophe). Nevertheless, if you can overlook its format and get right down to the nitty gritty, you'll find here the most concise grammar rules anywhere. The examples, many taken from literature, are superb. If you can't find the book in your local bookstore (either trade or college campus) or remaindered in an earlier edition (just as good) in the Barnes & Noble catalog, write to Harcourt. Every copyeditor should have it and refer to it often.

Sabin, William A. *The Gregg Reference Manual.* Sixth Edition. New York: McGraw-Hill, 1984.

> Having said that there's only one really good grammar book, now permit me to suggest another entry, recommended to me by a student. The grammar rules in this book are excellent, and I use it frequently. It has a rather silly section on how to type papers (it tells you to put two spaces after a period), but the rest is worth perusing.

USAGE

For the purpose of this bibliography, I have chosen to treat usage differently from style or writing, but in fact many of the books in these areas overlap. As I use "usage" here I mean "word choice."

Fowler, Henry W. *Dictionary of Modern English Usage.* Second Edition revised and edited by Sir Ernest Gowers. New York: Oxford University Press, 1965.

Why this book, by a British author and publisher, should be the king (or, more appropriately, the queen) has always been a mystery to me. Far more of the respondents to my questionnaire recommended it than its counterpart, *Modern American Usage,* discussed next. By no means complete, Fowler's (as it is commonly called) nonetheless provides extensive discussion of some tricky constructions and explains what preposition to use in what construction (*oblivious to* or *oblivious of*?). Some of the passages are so long that you'll be sorry you asked, so this book is not for the faint-hearted. But if you want the definitive statement about the appropriateness of *as to* or whether to use *which* in a restrictive clause, you'll buy this book.

Follett, Wilson. *Modern American Usage: A Guide.* Jacques Barzun, ed. New York: Hill & Wang, 1966.

Far less popular than *Modern English Usage,* this book nonetheless has the advantage of belonging exclusively to us in the Colonies, so from a purely nationalistic point of view, we tend to regard it highly. I suggest that you buy the Warner paperback edition and read the articles that interest you most.

Copperud, Roy H. *American Usage and Style: The Consensus.* New York: Van Nostrand Reinhold, 1980.

I have to admit that I know very little about this book. The person who copyedited the first edition of my book quoted it to me every time he disliked something I wrote. Copperud compares nine usage guides and gives the majority opinion, citing where the discrepancies are. It's a useful book when you don't want to rely on one single authority.

Bernstein, Theodore M. *The Careful Writer: A Modern Guide to English Usage.* New York: Atheneum, 1979.

Much more accessible than *Fowler's,* this book does for American English what Follett should have. It is simply an alphabetical list of words often misused with discussions of why they're wrong or how they can be made better. It is easy and enjoyable to read and refer to.

————— . *Watch Your Language.* New York: Atheneum, 1965.

This book is similar to *The Careful Writer* but goes into style as well. Bernstein was for many years a columnist and managing editor for the *New York Times;* his column "Winners and Sinners" pointed out examples of bad and good usage as they appeared in *Times* stories. *Watch Your Language* gives some of the examples from those columns and further describes proper comma use, headline writing, and other points. Its one drawback is that while it tells you what is *incorrect,* it sometimes doesn't tell you how to *correct* it. Unfortunately, those of us who have used the wrong term often don't know the correct one. It's also a rather ancient book, and some things that Bernstein holds to are no longer considered correct. But he does make many interesting points.

Safire, William. *What's the Good Word?* New York: Times Books, 1982.

This author may be most familiar to you through his syndicated column. He writes with wit and immediacy; his favorite targets are the government, politicians, newspapers, and himself as he corrects errors in usage or explains regionalisms. This book is a compilation of items from his columns.

_____ . *Take My Word for It.* New York: Times Books, 1986.
More columns. Enjoy!

Morris, William, and Mary Morris. *Harper Dictionary of Contemporary Usage.* Second Edition. New York: Harper & Row, 1985.
This book has only limited appeal, but I include it here for its many examples of how once-inappropriate constructions make it into the language. The authors chose a panel of 166 authors and editors and polled them on word usage. Arranged like the Follett and Fowler and Bernstein books, this book contains comments from the panel on many entries and occasionally the results of a poll of the panelists—for example, only 30 percent would use *host* as a verb, but 35 percent would use *cohost* (hmmm). This book is useful in that it's very current and contains colloquialisms, such as "She will go to Boston Monday week."

Success with Words: A Guide to the American Language. Pleasantville, NY: Reader's Digest, 1983.
This terrific book has hundreds of short and medium-length entries that describe the difference between cocoa and cacao or give the various forms of difficult words, such as *to wake.* Its best feature is the recommendations it gives when appropriate.

WRITING

Granted, I've told you several times in this book that copyeditors are not supposed to rewrite. I nevertheless feel that they must be able to recognize good writing when they see it and to make or suggest appropriate changes in a pleasing style when needed. There is one good book on writing:

Strunk, William S., Jr., and E. B. White. *The Elements of Style.* Third Edition. New York: Macmillan, 1979.
Yes, he *is* the author of *Charlotte's Web.* In just 85 pages this book lays out all the rules of composition (in the sense of writing, not typesetting) and provides good usage rules as well. Its brevity no doubt accounts for the fact that it may be the biggest seller of any reference book.

EDITING

Cook, Claire Kehrwald. *The MLA's Line by Line: How to Edit Your Own Writing.* Boston: Houghton Mifflin, 1985.
Confused by the title? This book is copyrighted by the Modern Language Association, and typographically it appears to be entitled *Line by Line*, but the copyright page shows it the way I have it. More than anything, this book is an old-fashioned grammar book, albeit a bit too chatty for me.

Plotnik, Arthur. *The Elements of Editing.* New York: Macmillan, 1982.
If the title sounds familiar, wait until you see the cover. It's clearly meant to be a companion piece to that other Macmillan book, *The Elements of Style.* The book contains information not readily found elsewhere: copyright law simplified, photography for editors, and how to do research.

MISCELLANEOUS

This category is my favorite. There are lots of good books that copyeditors should own that don't fall into one of the earlier categories. Some of these books, as I've indicated, are indispensable; others are merely fun and useful.

Roget, Peter M. *Roget's International Thesaurus.* Fourth Edition revised by Robert L. Chapman. New York: Harper & Row, 1977.

Although you can get by with a good dictionary, no self-respecting copyeditor would be without this book. If you do any writing at all, you must have one. In case you've never used a thesaurus, I'll tell you that it's an alphabetical listing of words, with each word "defined" by several synonyms. When you need a synonym, consulting a thesaurus is a lot easier than hunting through a dictionary.

McCormick, Mona. *The New York Times Guide to Reference Materials.* Revised Edition. New York: Times Books, 1985. Originally published as *Who-What-When-Where-How-Why-MADE EASY.*

What a great idea! A guide to reference books, this small book is divided into topics, such as politics, history, literature, and dictionaries. If you want to check a fact about music, for example, this guide will tell you that there's a biographical dictionary of musicians, a concise music dictionary, a jazz encyclopedia, and so on, with short descriptions that help you choose which book will answer your questions.

Literary Market Place. New York: Bowker, published annually.

Anyone interested in doing freelance work needs *LMP*, if only every other year. It lists thousands of U.S. publishers, giving contact names as well; many Canadian publishers are also listed. There's a geographical index, so you can pick the publishers in your own area to contact for full-time staff jobs. But that's only the beginning. *LMP* also lists book manufacturers, literary agents, copyeditors, photo researchers, and others connected with publishing.

Craig, James. *Production for the Graphic Designer.* New York: Watson-Guptill, 1974.

Buy this book! It is the best overview of production and typography I've seen. Even though you may have no interest in or skill at design, you should be aware of production techniques if you want to be a good copyeditor. The book is well written and well illustrated. It needs a new edition badly.

Miller, Casey, and Kate Swift. *The Handbook of Nonsexist Writing.* New York: Lippincott & Crowell, 1980.

Are you having trouble finding ways to change *he* to something else? Get this book! It probably could be a little shorter (after all, how much can you say about *he?*), but it gives lots of suggestions for avoiding sexism in language.

The Harper Dictionary of Foreign Terms. Third Edition revised by Eugene Ehrlich. New York: Harper & Row, 1987.

If your author thinks it *de rigeur* to use foreign terms throughout the manuscript, you'll want to check their spelling in this book. The meanings are given, too, of course, so you can pick up some pointers on being *au courant.*

Harris, William H., and Judith S. Levey. *The New Columbia Encyclopedia.* Fourth Edition. New York: Columbia University Press, 1975.

OK, for sheer beauty, nothing beats the *The Random House Encyclopedia.* But don't fall for a book that reduces all the world's knowledge to facing-page spreads. This is the book you want (if you can't afford a full-fledged, multivolume encyclopedia). You can pick it up at big discounts in many bookstores or through book clubs.

Bartlett, John. Emily Morison Beck, ed. *Bartlett's Familiar Quotations.* Fifteenth Edition. Boston: Little, Brown, 1980.

You really don't need this book, because correct use of quotations is the author's responsibility. But you can please your publisher by verifying many quotations you come across, and besides, *Bartlett's* is *fun.* Use it by looking up a key word in the index, from which you'll be directed to the precise quotation and the speaker.

Highlights of the New Copyright Law. Library of Congress Circular R99. Washington, DC: Government Printing Office, 1976.

This pamphlet, available from the Copyright Office, Library of Congress, Washington, DC 20559, outlines the 1976 revision of U.S. copyright law. You need to understand at least this much about the law so that you'll know whether the material you're copyediting is protected.

Pocket Pal. Thirteenth Edition. New York: International Paper Company, 1983.

There's a lot of excellent information about printing, color separation, and page makeup in this very inexpensive little book, but it's poorly arranged and written. If you're good at muddling through things, perhaps you can make some sense of the prose. The pictures are good, though, and for its price the book is certainly worth having.

Books in Print. New York: Bowker, published annually.

Don't buy this book! I mention it strictly for reference. It comes in three formats—by author, title, and subject—and lists all general-interest books (including texts) currently in print; that's why it's published annually. Caution: Do not use this book as a precise title or spelling guide; I've seen the same book treated *three different ways* in the three *Books in Print* volumes. You can find *Books in Print* in all bookstores and libraries.

Publishers Weekly. Published fifty-one times a year by Bowker.

This is a great magazine to subscribe to, and if you want it, that's the best way to buy it. It's sold off very few newsstands, and if your company subscribes, it'll be weeks before you get to see it. It's also available at most public libraries. It's intended for booksellers to see what's coming in trade, but it has far more appeal than that. There's a section on job promotions and appointments, so you can see who's doing better in publishing than you are; there are interesting articles about technological advances and book sales and books in China and just about anything else you can think of that has to do with publishing. The rights column is especially interesting to trade copyeditors. There's a listing of job openings, both staff and freelance, around the country and sometimes the world. (It's for this last feature, no doubt, that the magazine disappears so quickly at your company.) The magazine is useful to authors, too, for the trends it describes and for its periodic discussions of libel, author unions, copyright protection, and other relevant advice.

Grammar Hotline Directory. Published by Tidewater Community College. The directory lists U.S. and Canadian schools that staff grammar hotlines. (What a good idea!) Send a self-addressed, stamped, legal-size envelope to Grammar Hotline Directory, Tidewater Community College, 1700 College Crescent, Virginia Beach, VA 23456.

The Editorial Eye. Published once a month by Editorial Experts. This monthly newsletter contains many useful features: a lead story on everything from how fast you should edit to getting along with a designer to desktop publishing; book reviews, including books and pamphlets peculiar to specific corporations; helpful editing rules; and "black eyes"— amusing mistakes published in newspapers and brochures. A subscription is not cheap—several dollars for each eight-page issue. For more information, contact Editorial Experts, 85 S. Bragg Street, Alexandria, VA 22312.

Lots of copyeditors have reference books pouring off their shelves; which books depends on their field. *The Merck Index, Physicians' Desk Reference,* and *Lange's Handbook,* for example, are indispensable to medical and chemical copyeditors. Most copyeditors have at least one new almanac around. If you copyedit a foreign language, naturally you'll need an accepted dictionary in that language. There are even spellers for legal and medical copyeditors. College textbook copyeditors rely on technical manuals, such as *Mathematics into Type* and the *Handbook of the American Chemical Society.* Look into your local bookstore, especially at the hardcover reference section, where you'll find dozens of books you'll want to have, then pick two or three of the best. Maybe it'll be a biographical dictionary or a dictionary of abbreviations—whatever you think you'll use or enjoy most. And check with your employers about their recommendations.

In writing the first edition of this book, I used as references three works not described above. I would like to credit them here.

Butcher, Judith M. *Copy-editing: The Cambridge Handbook.* Cambridge, England. Cambridge University Press, 1975.

McNaughton, Harry H. *Proofreading and Copyediting: A Practical Guide to Style for the 1970's.* New York: Hastings House, 1973.

O'Neill, Carol L., and Avima Ruder. *The Complete Guide to Editorial Freelancing.* New York: Barnes & Noble, 1979.

Swanson, Ellen. <u>Mathematics into Type</u>. Providence, Rhode Island. American Mathematical Society, 1971. (ISBN 0-8218-0053-1; Library of Congress Card Number 72-170708)

Index

COPYEDITING AND PROOFREADING SYMBOLS

Those symbols used only in proofreading are indicated by a circle in the margin.

℘ delete; take ~~something~~ out

⌣ close up with‿in the line

℘ delete and close up

∧ insert with‸caret

spacemark

▢ em space

⍁ en space

¶ Start a new paragraph

(break) start a⌐new line (start a

                  new line)

⌐ flush left

¬ flush right

(run in) run in⌐

   ⌊with previous line

(stet) let it stand

(tr) transpose

(sp) spell out (abbrev.)

(cap) set in capital letters

(lc) set in ⟋OWERCASE letters

(sm cap) set in SMALL capital letters (LIKE THIS)

(ital) set in italic (*like this*)

(rom) set in (roman) (like this)

(bf) set in boldface (**like this**)

⊙ period

⸴ comma